ETHICS IN PUBLIC ADMINISTRATION

ETHICS IN PUBLIC ADMINISTRATION

UNDERSTANDING ETHICS, CORRUPTION, AND PUBLIC POLICY

Edited by

Meriem Doucette

California State University—Fullerton

David Adams

California State University—Fullerton

Bassim Hamadeh, CEO and Publisher
Janny Li, Acquisitions Editor
Kaela Martin, Project Editor
Christian Berk, Production Editor
Jackie Bignotti, Production Artist
Michael Skinner, Senior Licensing Associate
Natalie Piccotti, Director of Marketing
Kassie Graves, Vice President of Editorial
Jamie Giganti, Director of Academic Publishing

Printed in the United States of America.

CONTENTS

FOREWORD V

PART I FOUNDATIONS OF ETHICS 1

CHAPTER 1 FOUNDATIONS OF ETHICS IN PUBLIC ADMINISTRATION 2

PART II WHAT IS ETHICS? 11

CHAPTER 2 WHAT IS ETHICS? 12

See Where You Stand: 60 Second Ethical Dilemma 12

Introduction to Chapter 12

Reading 1 What is Ethics? 15
By Joseph Gilbert

Case Study 34

CHAPTER 3 APPROACHES TO ETHICS 35

See Where You Stand: 60 Second Ethical Dilemma 35

Introduction to Chapter 35

Reading 2 Approaches to Ethics: The Study of Ethics 37
By Lynn Sharp Paine

Case Study 47

CHAPTER 4 TOWARD AN ETHICS 48

See Where You Stand: 60 Second Ethical Dilemma 48

Introduction to Chapter 48

Reading 3 Toward an Ethics 50
By Thomas Oles

Case Study 66

PART III ETHICS AND THE LAW 67

CHAPTER 5 WHEN THE UMPIRE THROWS THE PITCHES 68

See Where You Stand: 60 Second Ethical Dilemma 68

Introduction to Chapter 68

Reading 4 When the Umpire Throws the Pitches 70
By Pamela S. Karlan

Case Study 73

CHAPTER 6 GIDEON'S MUTED TRUMPET 74

See Where You Stand: 60 Second Ethical Dilemma 74

Introduction to Chapter 74

Reading 5 Gideon's Muted Trumpet 76
By Pamela S. Karlan

Case Study 78

PART IV ETHICS IN PUBLIC ADMINISTRATION 81

CHAPTER 7 BIG QUESTIONS FROM COOPER AND ROHR 82

See Where You Stand: 60 Second Ethical Dilemma 82

Introduction to Chapter 82

Reading 6 Big Questions in Administrative Ethics: A Need for Focused, Collaborative Effort 84
By Terry L. Cooper

Reading 7 On Cooper's "Big Questions" 105
By John A. Rohr

Case Study 108

CHAPTER 8 PUBLIC SERVICE, ETHICS, AND CONSTITUTIONAL PRACTICE 109

See Where You Stand: 60 Second Ethical Dilemma 109

Introduction to Chapter 109

Reading 8 Ethics for Bureaucrats 111
By John A. Rohr

Reading 9 The Problem of Professional Ethics 117
By John A. Rohr

Case Study 124

CHAPTER 9 ETHICAL PROBLEMS IN PUBLIC CAREERS: LYING 125

See Where You Stand: 60 Second Ethical Dilemma 125

Introduction to Chapter 126

Reading 10 Ethical Problems in Public Careers: Lying 127
By Allison Graham and Lance M. Liebman

Case Study 137

PART V CORRUPTION IN GOVERNMENT: WHAT'S GOING ON HERE? 139

CHAPTER 10 CORRUPTION OF ETHICS: DOMESTIC BRIBERY OF PUBLIC OFFICIALS: HONEST SERVICES FRAUD 140

See Where You Stand: 60 Second Ethical Dilemma 140

Introduction to Chapter 140

Reading 11 Corruption of Ethics: Domestic Bribery of Public Officials: Honest Services Fraud 142
By Orrin K. Ames III

Case Study 157

CHAPTER 11 THE DIRTY-HANDS THEORY OF COMMAND 158

See Where You Stand: 60 Second Ethical Dilemma 158

Introduction to Chapter 158

Reading 12 The Dirty-Hands Theory of Command 160
By Sidney Axinn

Case Study 173

PART VI ETHICS AND PUBLIC POLICY: UNDERSTANDING THE ETHICAL DIMENSIONS OF DECISION MAKING 175

CHAPTER 12 ETHICS FOR POLICY ANALYSTS 176

See Where You Stand: 60 Second Ethical Dilemma 176

Introduction to Chapter 176

Reading 13 Ethics for Policy Analysts 178
By William K. Bellinger

Case Study 204

CHAPTER 13 PUBLIC REPORTING OF SCHOOL PERFORMANCE: ETHICAL ISSUES 205

See Where You Stand: 60 Second Ethical Dilemma 205

Introduction to Chapter 205

Reading 14 Public Reporting of School Performance: Ethical Issues 207
By Peter Godard

Case Study 224

EXTENDED CASE STUDIES 225

Ethics of U.S. Government Action and Inaction: Is Louisiana Being Treated Like a Colony of the United States? 226
By John T. Lambert Jr.

Fire or Be Fired 236
By John L. Pape and James M. Banovetz

FOREWORD

I am honored that the coeditors, Drs. Meriem Doucette and David Adams, asked me to write the foreword for this important book. As a Virginia Tech alumni and a disciple of Dr. John Rohr, as well as a university professor who has taught both undergraduate and graduate public administration ethics, I recognize the relative dearth in the field of collections of ethics readings such as this and the consequent need to help fill this gap for students and civil servant practitioners.

This work is value-added, since it is one of only a handful that assembles several substantive public administration ethics selections in one volume, in addition to original case studies, which will provoke critical analysis of ethical dilemmas. The readings are logically presented, with attention to Socrates's admonition for avoidance of generally applicable definitions by removing ambiguity of the key term, *ethics*, by providing a description, rather than an operational definition as might be expected in an authored, rather than edited, book. Appropriately, the editors do not delve into the realm of meta-ethics (i.e., what morality itself is), as a pure philosopher might, but do follow the description of ethics with writings on the normative level of ethics, including Utilitarian, Deontological, and Aristotelian Virtue ethics.

The editors proceed by clarifying the essential distinction between the proverbial ceiling (i.e., the moral ideal[s]) and the law (i.e., the moral minimum), which is the proverbial floor in ethics. This distinction reminds us that just because something is legal doesn't mean it's necessarily ethical (e.g., Nazi antisemitic legislation from 1933 to 1939 and the institution of slavery in US history). As Justice Oliver Wendell Holmes, Jr., stated, "This is a court of law, young man, not a court of justice." Ideally, the laws will also be just or ensure justice, but merely keeping the law (i.e., as a "value-neutral" administrator) is not enough to be an ethical civil servant (i.e., as a "value-based" administrator).

The editors transition in Part 3 from normative-level ethical considerations to the applied level of ethics for bureaucrats. The dialectic between Cooper's (2004) "Big Questions" and Rohr's (2004) brief response to those "Big Questions" is a critical starting point for any student or practitioner of public administration ethics. Where Cooper (2004) identifies five useful normative foundations for public administration ethics (i.e., [1] Regime Values, Constitutional Theory, and Founding Thought, [2] Citizenship Theory, [3] Social Equity, [4] Virtue, and [5] The Public Interest), Rohr (2004) extends the conversation, arguing that Cooper's "five approaches to ethics are empirical rather than normative" (Rohr 2004, 125), giving attention to legal aspects of ethics, such as conflict-of-interest and financial disclosure laws.

Doucette and Adams endeavor to rectify the scarcity of articles Rohr (2004) highlights by including writings that argue that public administrators are morally obligated actors via their oath to the Constitution, with their administrative discretion (i.e., their most powerful tool) allowing for and demanding ethical decision making, as well as exploring issues such as lying, bribery, and the problem of "dirty hands." The book concludes with a focus on ethical decision making by policy analysts. Importantly, Doucette and Adams draw on more established scholars in the field, such as Cooper and Rohr, but also allow discursive space for newer voices in the discipline.

I am privileged to have studied under Dr. John Rohr and fortunate to have been teaching public administration ethics at the undergraduate and graduate level for 13 years and counting. I am delighted to have this new resource Doucette and Adams provide.

—Shawn Erik Schooley, PhD
Associate Professor, St. Cloud State University

PART I

FOUNDATIONS OF ETHICS

CHAPTER 1

Foundations of Ethics in Public Administration

As individuals, we often seek to find easy answers to complex problems, but as students and practitioners of public administration, we recognize that those easy answers are few and far between when conducting the public's business in the public interest. Empirical evidence, values, norms, principles, and cultural mores often serve as tools or "instruments" for solving problems (Waldo 1980). But which instrument do we use? How do we decide? This is the fundamental difficulty faced by public administrators nearly every day. More importantly, these are ethical questions at the heart of nearly every decision made by a public administrator. As Svara (2014) notes, "Ethics are integral to public administration." In the American context, ethics are necessary to ensure that the public sector upholds the values and rights articulated and codified in the law.

Public administrators face ethical questions concerning our values when practicing **administrative discretion**. When a police offer decides to give a warning instead of issuing a traffic ticket, when a high school principal decides to suspend one student and expel another, when a case worker decides to cancel a welfare benefit, they are using administrative discretion. "The proper exercise of administrative discretion authoritatively allocates values, determines who gets what, promotes the common good, etc. Persons performing these functions govern and should therefore somehow respond to the values of the people" (Rohr 1998, 19). These values are eloquently expressed in founding documents such as the Declaration of Independence. They are the declared rights of all Americans: life, liberty, and the pursuit of happiness.

To Aristotle and the ancient Greeks, the goal of human life is happiness. This is achieved only when one provides a *good* contribution to a meaningful human community over a lifetime: self-fulfillment comes from service to community (Aristotle 1999). This is the spirit that many public servants bring with them to work every day. But what makes one's contribution good, and who or what helps us to become good contributors to our community? Indeed, what is good? Answers to these questions come from ethical principles, from societal norms, and from the values of the people and their government. The difficulty lies in determining what is right, what is wrong, and ultimately, what is good for the public. This book offers a selection of readings about ethics in the public service for those wanting to participate in this noble enterprise.

Public servants are endowed with a moral obligation to defend the values of the American regime—the founding values—on behalf of the body politic. To understand and embrace this obligation, public administrators must realize the conflict between bureaucratic values and democratic values (Raadschelders and Stillman 2017, 14). Indeed, in a country of federalism, the challenge is to "square Jefferson's decentralized sense of democracy with Hamilton's stress on national unity and still preserve ... democracy" (Raadschelders and Stillman 2017, 14). According to Gawthrop (2017, 334), democracy seeks the "good," but governance—or the system—can get messy when it is turned over to the people. This is the challenge of (self-)government that those engaged in the public's business have faced for millennia.

An understanding of ethics does not provide those in public service with concrete answers to moral dilemmas, but it does provide guidance when we must ask critical questions about morality, and it helps us to systematically seek answers supported by good reasons. Public administrators use **normative ethics** to guide decision making. The focus of normative ethics is on how one acts in a given situation, how one decides something. However, there are so many competing normative ethical principles. Ultimately, no principle is absolute in its ability to deal with every moral dilemma and choice. The challenge for those who do make decisions—those who exercise administrative discretion—is to choose an ethical framework and stick with it or to apply different ethical approaches in different situations. This is the purpose of this book.

Developing, honing, and practicing an ethical principle is fundamental to public administration. Gawthrop (2017, 333) writes, "The linkage between ethics and democracy is, to a significant extent, forged by the caliber and character of how the public service is advanced in the name of democracy." This is even more the case when much of the public's business—and public administration itself—is organized by the values of bureaucracy; those principles of hierarchy, specialization, rules, rigid division of labor, and formal lines of authority that prize facts and efficiency above all else.

The foundations of public administration were built on the idea that politics and administration were separate entities—a dichotomy between facts and values. Woodrow Wilson and early public administration theorists (e.g., Goodnow 2009 [1914]) embraced this politics-administration dichotomy, arguing that the separation would allow administration to be a "value-free endeavor and thus the legitimate subject of scientific analysis" (Fry and Raadschelders 2014, 121). Administration theories subsequently came to reject the idea that the two can be separated, because exercising administrative discretion, scientifically or otherwise, is a value-laden endeavor.

Luther Gulick (1937) sought a science of administration and embraced the scientific method. His vision of public service values was limited to efficiency, but claiming efficiency as the ultimate value for administration is a political claim. Gulick realized that efficiency for efficiency's sake was insufficient in a democracy, writing that "we are in the end compelled to mitigate the pure concept of efficiency in the light of the value scale of politics and the social order" (Gulick 1937, 193). While efficiency is still a fundamentally important value in pursuit of the public good, we must recognize complementary and competing values as well. This is the reason public administrators must have an understanding of ethics and should strive for ethical competency. Choosing between values, even in the face of facts, is a quotidian administrative function.

So how do we choose among values? How do we balance "value-free" objective science with other values held by the public? In a postpositivist world, do we even view science as objective? We live in a time of chaotic clashes of human interpretations about what is true and what is fake, what is right and what is wrong. Which decision is the right one? Which decision is morally defensible? Whose facts and judgments are viewed as right? Is it the scientist, the bureaucrat, the expert, the loudest speaker, the most powerful, or the most affluent? Nietzsche (1966 [1886]) answered this long ago, saying the only moral principle passed down through the ages is that the strong can dominate the weak. The Founders acknowledged this in 1787 when drafting the new Constitution for the United States. Checks and balances, separation of powers, and the system of federalism were all designed to "render an unjust combination of a majority of the whole very improbable, if not impracticable," as Madison wrote in *The Federalist Papers* no. 51 (Rossiter, 1999, 321).

The Founders were heavily influenced by the Enlightenment thinkers, such as Thomas Hobbes, John Locke, and Adam Smith, among others. This influence led to the creation of a government that values basic rights, freedom, neutrality, equality, and justice. Distributive justice and redistributive justice claims are normative claims: they determine who gets what reward and who gets what punishment. The values enshrined in basic rights, freedom, and equality often hinge on the limits of human conduct: what is harm, when is it allowed and disallowed, and who decides? John Locke and the Founders influenced by him are considered classical liberals who believed that no one should be allowed to harm themselves or others and that freedom has limits, which is ultimately a normative claim.

The authors throughout this book deal with the basics of ethics and ethical reasoning in the American context from numerous perspectives relevant to public administration, including law, corruption, and public policy. They discuss the basics of ethics and different types of ethical questions so that public administrators can address ethical dilemmas while keeping the public interest in mind.

This raises the question of how one should act in the public's interest when conducting the public's business. The articles in this book suggest that we can act efficiently, we can do what is legally right, we can do what is politically right, or we can do what makes us feel good. For some of us, the act that brings about the greatest good for the greatest number is the ethical principle that guides one's action. As Mr. Spock said at the end of *Star Trek II: The Wrath of Kahn*, "The needs of the many outweigh the needs of the few." This concept is known as **utilitarianism**, and it is most associated with the English philosopher and jurist Jeremy Bentham. He argued that an act is morally right if, and only if, it brings about the greatest happiness for the greatest number of people, or the greatest good for the greatest number.

Utilitarianism embraces a consequentialist theory of utility because what is best depends on the situation. In some situations, people may be sacrificed or used as a means to an end. The institution of slavery is a horrific but apt example of utilitarianism (and it was opposed by Bentham). It is also consequentialist because the notions of "good" and "happiness" are ambiguous and situation-specific (i.e., what may be good for one person is not necessarily good for another). Utilitarianism comes in two forms. **Rule utilitarianism** argues that we should follow rules that are designed to achieve the greatest good even if it requires personal sacrifice. **Act utilitarianism** argues that we should always act in a way that maximizes the greatest good. In the end, the general problem with this ethical line of reasoning is that utilitarians are willing to sacrifice the rights of the few to achieve the happiness of the many. This is why the Founders sought to check, balance, and separate power and authority, to ensure that no individual person's or group's rights would be sacrificed. Over time, the notion that what is good for the greatest number may not be good for the fewest number began to challenge utilitarian approaches to government actions and distributive justice. In 1971, John Rawls (1971) introduced his *Theory of Justice*, arguing that all inequalities resulting from utilitarian distributions should be made to benefit those who are worst off.

Deontology is another classical ethical perspective, and it is most closely associated with Immanuel Kant. It is a nonconsequentialist, duty-based ethic. From this perspective, one's intent matters: an action is right as long as it is done from a sense of duty. In other words, an action is worthy or unworthy depending on one's reason for doing it, not because of the consequences of the action. Kant maintained that all actions done with a sense of duty should be done by contemplating whether our actions will be done in such a way that they can become a universal principle—a rule or maxim, as he called it, by which we wish everyone to operate. Actions are guided by these maxims without regard for the consequences of the action. In contrast to utilitarianism, people are to be treated as ends not as means, because it recognizes the intrinsic worth of all humans. For Kant and deontologists, this sense of duty must be trained and developed through education and thoughtful contemplations for it to become morally sound and justifiable.

Aristotle articulated a third classical perspective, **Virtue Ethics**. Like Kant, Aristotle felt that doing proper actions—acting virtuously—is something that must be developed and trained over time. Virtue, to Aristotle, is a means between extremes in specific situations, and morality is essentially bound up with bringing about the ultimate human good. Embracing this perspective, the public administrator can recognize and balance the values inherent in both utilitarianism and deontology and determine which may be more appropriate in a given situation (Tong 1986). Aristotle's goal was to create a virtuous citizenry, one with a happy and well-ordered community because those in power create morally sound decisions (Aristotle 1999). Beyond the great debates between the Federalists and Anti-Federalists at the American nation's founding, they all also had the desire for a virtue-centered citizenry (Richardson and Nigro 1987).

These ethical basics—the classical perspectives—and their related normative claims are addressed in the next three chapters of this book. They provide a plain-language review of many of the basic concepts and principles discussed elsewhere throughout the book, highlighting how to make ethical decisions and behave in ethical ways. The focus isn't entirely on public administration, but the situations discussed are those faced by public decision makers every day. A general understanding of ethical principles and where they come from is important for those engaged in the public's business. We have to ask questions about whether decisions are made based on epistemological considerations or facts, public values or political commitments. Unless public servants "confront the moral dimensions of their occupation squarely, they cannot act in the public's best interest" (Tong 1986, 8). When it comes to decision making, public administrators often face and attempt to accommodate both political and ethical values, making hard choices between them (Tong 1986, 44). In the remainder of the book, parts 2 through 6, the authors expand on these fundamentals with a focus from a legal perspective, a general public administration perspective, a view of ethics and corruption, and ethics in public policy.

The law gives public administrators guiding principles for ethical decision making and actions. Much of this comes from the founding documents, such as the Declaration of Independence, the Constitution, and *The Federalist Papers*, as well as from cases argued in front of the Supreme Court and lower courts at all levels of jurisdiction. Chapters 5 and 6 discuss the explicit role of the Supreme Court in determining how we interpret and apply the values inherent in the American people. These values include freedom, equality, and property, as well as diversity, rule of law, community, and the distrust of government that have been present since the founding of the republic. But no matter how we may turn to the Court for guidance in interpreting and applying these values in an ethical way, its opinions still generate varying interpretations. By reading and understanding these opinions (and dissents), a public administrator can interpret and apply ethical and political values in whatever situation they face.

Part four of the book expands this discussion by further elaborating on American values and ethical decision making for public administrators. In chapter seven, Terry Cooper discusses citizenship theory and Aristotelian virtue ethics and how they assist in conducting the public's business, especially when balancing competing demands. He posits that the public interest can serve as a moral guiding compass because it is both an obligation and a reminder about how to act on behalf of the public. Public organizations are important as well for the ethical development (or deficiency) of public administrators. Indeed, there is a link between strong ethical culture and organizational performance. Ethical leadership and competency among members of an organization are believed to lead to better results in the outputs and outcomes it generates (Menzel 2015). Cooper's (2004) view reflects Madison's in *The Federalist Papers* no. 51, making it clear that organizations can and ought to be used to channel one's self-interests for the public good.

Building on Cooper's arguments, in chapter 8 John Rohr discusses how public administration provides stability as politicians and political appointees come and go. This fact highlights the importance and necessity of the neutrality of the civil service. Of course, there is occasionally the problem of the technocratic elite and a bureaucracy that is malicious or otherwise nonresponsive to political directives. And on occasion, those civil servants are upholding ethical values in the face of political challenges. Whistle-blowers are a good example of this (O'Leary 2006).

Nevertheless, the importance of bureaucratic discretion and the influence of politics in administrative decision making heightens the need for ethical competency among bureaucrats and all of those engaged in public administration. With the demise of the politics/administration dichotomy and the rise of a civil service, empowered with administrative discretion, Rohr's greatest contribution to our understanding of public service ethics comes from a career seeking the answer to a simple question: "How can a democratic regime justify substantial political power in the hands of people who are exempt by law from the discipline of the ballot box?" (Rohr 1998, 6). Rohr makes an important point about the moral exigencies public administrators face: particular principles and ethical values held by an individual may be challenged by what is an appropriate course of action for a professional civil servant. One may have to sacrifice one's personal interest for the interest of the public.

Rohr spent much of his career looking at how the Constitution and the legal system can give ethical guidance. Rohr (1998, 1) identifies "the ethical problem that is peculiar to the career civil servant: the responsible exercise of administrative discretion." In Rohr's opinion, public administrators should accept the moral obligation to put themselves in touch with the values of the American people through the values of the American regime—the values, principles, passions, and beliefs that have guided the majority of Americans for generations. These are found in the Constitution and in Supreme Court decisions. Rohr's argument is rooted in the obligation of bureaucrats in a democracy to use their discretionary (i.e., governing) power in a manner that is consistent with the values of the people in whose name they govern (Rohr 1998). Indeed, public administrators explicitly or implicitly take an oath to uphold the Constitution and the values it represents.

Elsewhere, Rohr has written about the role of the Supreme Court as an ethical guide for public administrators (Rohr 1989). He suggests that studying salient Court cases involving the regime values of freedom, property, and equality, among others, can lead to a greater understanding of the values of the American people. Reflection on these cases provides the public administrator legitimacy in his or her actions, especially as his or her administrative discretion increases over time. Rohr identifies four characteristics of the Court that make it suitable for ethical reflection on the values of the American people, guiding one's action in the public interest. The first is that it is "institutional," in that it provides historical continuity. Its opinions reflect American values at a particular time and, more importantly, the longevity of the institution allows these values to evolve over time, reflecting the mores of new generations of justices and Americans, while looking to the past for guidance (Rohr 1989).

The second characteristic of the Court is its "dialectical" nature, which is found in the justices' concurring and dissenting opinions. These offer public administrators alternative ways of looking at the same problem. This back-and-forth process helps one to understand the conflicts inherent in the interpretation of regime values. Third, the opinions of the Court are "concrete," whereas philosophical principles and values are often abstractions (e.g., "good" and "happiness"). It is imperative to make discretionary judgments based on concrete values and principles to provide legitimacy to one's decisions. Finally, the Court answers "pertinent" questions. As discussed in chapters 5and 6 of this book, the Court answers pertinent questions of the day and sometimes hot-button issues that are being debated around the country. Values and decisions relating to equality, freedom, and property are pertinent to every public administrator. By understanding the Court's reflections on regime values, public administrators can make bureaucratic judgments in the best public interest, giving credence and legitimacy to administrative discretion (Rohr 1989).

To challenge the reader's understanding of the material presented in this introduction and the first eight chapters, chapter 9 provides several short vignettes, or hypothetical cases, upon which to reflect and apply the various concepts. Chapters 10 and 11 take a different approach by focusing the discussion on corruption. Chapter 10 introduces several court cases that deal with the bribery of elected officials and quid pro quo circumstances. The chapter highlights how the values of free speech (i.e., freedom) and distrust of government are interpreted by the courts. Even though the focus is on elected officials, the principles apply to public administrators and civil servants of all stripes. As well, it should remind the reader of George W. Plunkitt of Tammany Hall (Riordon 1963). The focus is on the institutional nature of the Court and how values are interpreted differently over time.

Chapter 11 introduces an important concept in public service ethics: the dirty hands theory. It is a consequentialist theory that describes how those in power (and those empowered by administrative discretion) may use immoral or unethical means to achieve a desired goal or end. The notion comes from Sartre's play with the same name, as well as from Machiavelli, who wrote that the appearance of ethical rightness is more important that employing such ethics. Anyone who is familiar with Cesare Borgia—Machiavelli's (1992 [1513]) Prince or Nietzshe's (1966 [1886]) ideal ubermensch—will understand this concept, which is that the goals of glory, survival, and expression can justify immoral actions. While the chapter focuses on extremely hierarchical bureaucratic organizations, such as the military and police forces, with clear chains of command and designees of ultimate responsibility, it highlights the concept that is applicable to any public administrator.

With this concept in mind, readers should challenge themselves to think of the prevalence of the problem of "many hands" in public administration (Rohr 2004). Regarding policymaking, Tong (1986) writes,

> What is frightening about contemporary policymaking is the feeling that the decisions most likely to affect society for better or worse are made not by identifiable persons but by an amorphous collectivity whose willy-nilly processes cannot be stopped once they are started. (p. 68)

The business of the public is regularly conducted without clear chains of command, and new theories of public organization seek to flatten bureaucracy and hierarchy; there may potentially be many dirty hands and the concomitant difficulty of assigning blame for unethical actions.

Regardless, from a legal perspective and from the point of view of public scrutiny, a public administrator should never justify unethical or immoral means to achieve a desirable end. Whatever the justification, it won't stand up to public scrutiny, and, in many instances, just means don't achieve the desired goal (e.g., Matthews 2008).

The last two chapters of the book focus on ethics and public policy, as well as the ethical dimensions of decision making. Chapter 12 focuses directly on policy analysis and the decisions made by policy analysts. After reviewing regime values and the values inherent in utilitarianism, the notion of distributive justice is structured through the lens of classical liberalism found in the writings of John Locke, reform liberalism found in the theories of John Rawls, and neoclassical liberalism found in the theories of Robert Nozick. Using the economic theories of utility and social welfare, the author describes how each approach to distributive justice impacts the most well-off and least well-off in society, challenging policy makers and policy analysts to explore the diversity of ethical theory.

The final chapter of the book also focuses on decision making, but from the lens of reporting educational performance. Throughout the book, the focus has been on different ethical frameworks. In this chapter, the author applies two of the dominant frameworks (deontology and consequentialism) to consider how to most ethically report performance data. The author recognizes that the process of interpreting and presenting data is fraught with conflicting views from various stakeholders and that it is important for anyone to think carefully about what values are guiding their decision-making process (though arguably even more so for public-sector employees, who have greater demands for transparency and accountability). Decisions have consequences, and it is critical for the decision maker to also view their decisions from an ethical lens.

This book on ethics for graduate students and practitioners of public administration provides a clear view of different ethical perspectives and applies them to different situations. However, we do not always respond to ethical dilemmas in practice the way we think we would, so you will be challenged at the beginning of each chapter to apply your developing ethical frameworks to an ethical dilemma. Many of the ethical dilemmas that public administrators face in practice do not have the luxury of lengthy decision making, so this will challenge you to make a relatively quick decision in each chapter's "See Where You Stand: A 60 Second Ethical Dilemma." A longer case study is provided at the end of each chapter to encourage further critical thinking. Other than chapter 10's case study, which is based on real events, the rest of the case studies are fictional (though highly plausible), so any similarity to a person or real event is coincidental. It is our goal to encourage ethical development and to promote ethical competency among students and practitioners engaged in public service. There are no easy answers or perfect solutions to the dilemmas and decisions facing public administrators, but we hope this book will give you a better roadmap to fully consider the ethical implications of your decisions in public service.

REFERENCES

Aristotle. *Nicomachean Ethics*. Translated by Martin Ostwald. Upper Saddle River, NJ: Prentice Hall, 1999.

Cooper, Terry L. "Big Questions in Administrative Ethics: A Need for Focused, Collaborative Effort." *Public Administration Review* 64, no. 4 (July/August 2004): 395–407.

Fry, Bryan, R. and Jos. C. N. Raadschelders. *Mastering Public Administration: From Max Weber to Dwight Waldo*, 3rd ed. Los Angeles: CQ Press, 2014.

Gawthrop, Lewis C. "Ethics in the Public Service." In *Foundations of Public Administration*, edited by Jos C. N. Raadschelders and Richard J. Stillman II, 333–50. Irvine, CA: Melvin & Leigh, 2017.

Goodnow, Frank. *Politics and Administration*. 1914. Reprint, New Brunswick, NJ: Transaction Publishers, 2009.

Gulick, Luther. "Science, Values, and Public Administration." In *Papers on the Science of Administration*, edited by Luther Gulick and Lyndall Urwick, 3–45. New York: Institute of Public Administration, 1937.

Machiavelli, Niccolo. *The Prince*. 1513. Translated by W. K. Marriott. New York: Alfred A. Knopf, 1992.

Matthews, Richard. *The Absolute Violation: Why Torture Must Be Prohibited*. Quebec: McGill-Queen's University Press, 2008.

Menzel, Donald C. "Research on Ethics and Integrity in Public Administration: Moving Forward, Looking Back." *Public Integrity* 17, no. 4 (2015): 343–70.

Nietzsche, Friedrich. *Beyond Good and Evil: Prelude to a Philosophy of the Future*. 1886. Translated by Walter Kaufmann. New York: Random House, 1966.

O'Leary, Rosemary. *The Ethics of Dissent: Managing Guerrilla Government*. Washington DC: CQ Press, 2006.

Raadschelders, Jos C. N. and Richard Stillman II. "Introduction: The Future of the Study of Public Administration." In *Foundations of Public Administration*, edited by Jos C. N. Raadschelders and Richard Stillman II, 1–19. Irvine, CA: Melvin & Leigh, 2017.

Rawls, John. *A Theory of Justice*. Cambridge, MA: Harvard, 1971.

Richardson, William D. and Loyd G. Nigro. "Administrative Ethics and Founding Thought: Constitutional Correctives, Honor, and Education." *Public Administration Review* 47, no. 5 (September/October 1987): 367–76.

Riordon, William L. *Plunkett of Tammany Hall*. New York: E. P. Dutton, 1963.

Rohr, John A. *Ethics for Bureaucrats: An Essay on Laws and Values*, 2nd ed. New York: Marcel Dekker, 1989.

Rohr, John A. *Public Service, Ethics, and Constitutional Practice*. Lawrence, KS: University Press of Kansas, 1998.

Rohr, John A. "On Cooper's 'Big Questions.'" *Public Administration Review* 64, no. 4 (July/August 2004): 408–09.

Rossiter, Clinton, ed. *The Federalist Papers*. New York: Penguin Group, 1999.

Svara, James H. "Who Are the Keepers of the Code? Articulating and Upholding Ethical Standards in the Field of Public Administration." *Public Administration Review* 74, no. 5 (July/August 2014): 561–69.

Tong, Rosemarie. *Ethics in Policy Analysis*. Englewood Cliffs, NJ: Prentice-Hall, 1986.

Waldo, Dwight. *The Enterprise of Public Administration*. Chandler and Sharp Publishers: Novato, CA, 1980.

PART II

WHAT IS ETHICS?

CHAPTER 2

What is Ethics?

SEE WHERE YOU STAND: 60 SECOND ETHICAL DILEMMA

Imagine that you are in the following situation and have one minute to make a decision about the most ethical course of action:

You work at a large federal agency for a newly appointed secretary who shares a very close relationship with the president. She walks into your office one day and says, "This is Dominick. He is the son of a close personal friend, and now I would like him to be an intern." The agency's internship program is highly competitive and this personal favor violates the rules, but you know how much positive political support can do for your agency. What do you do?

INTRODUCTION TO CHAPTER

There is no singular definition for what ethics is, which at times can frustrate students looking for more structure and clear boundaries. The lack of a universal definition mirrors the foggy nature of the field itself. There is no mathematical formula for determining what is ethical, and what may be ethical to an individual or a particular society may be considered unethical elsewhere. For example, followers of Hinduism consider cows to be sacred, and therefore eating beef would be considered unethical, but followers of other religions or no religion at all would have no such ethical objection to eating beef (assuming they are not vegetarian!). **Ethics** will challenge you to think differently, to focus more on the why than on the what. Why, for example, are you pursuing a graduate degree? Why is more education considered desirable? These value questions are normative, not descriptive, and they are at the core of ethics.

Although there are many models used to determine what is "good," the two most commonly discussed approaches are **utilitarianism** and deontology. There are variations for each of these approaches (the author in this chapter specifically discusses three variants of utilitarianism), but the key is to comprehend the underlying logic between these two approaches. Recall from the introductory chapter that utilitarianism is focused on doing the "greatest good for the greatest number of people," regardless of whether or not the action itself would be normally considered "good." For example, consider Immanuel Kant's famous ethical dilemma. Someone runs by you with a weapon, asking if you saw someone else run by and in what direction they were headed. You ultimately decide not to inform him where the person was headed to prevent potential harm. The utilitarian approach would consider this ethical because you are protecting someone's life, even though lying is normally considered wrong. Conversely, as previously discussed, deontology focuses on the act itself, instead of the outcome, so rules are absolute, such as "always tell the truth." In this example, the focus would be on what you did—lie—and since that is generally considered unethical, your action would then be unethical regardless of the outcome. While in this case most people would likely choose the utilitarian approach, neither of these approaches is perfect and both can be quite problematic in application. They are, however, useful for helping us to understand how we make (and should make) decisions. While that example may not seem particularly problematic (telling a small lie to potentially save a person's life), most ethical dilemmas are challenging because there is not a clear, obvious choice.

As this chapter's author notes, there are other ways to measure what is right, such as what is most efficient or what is legal. Both efficiency and legality are highly relevant to public administrators, but the obligations of a public servant go beyond this. You can perform your job legally and efficiently but still fail to live up to an ethical standard. For example, imagine you work at the US Social Security Administration, processing disputed claims. You follow the rules, and in an effort to be as efficient as possible, you process all the easily resolved claims first (meaning that people with more complicated claims will have to wait longer). While the public sector values efficiency and legality, it also values other qualities, such as fairness and equity, and it is not hard to argue that this approach is not equitable to every individual filing a claim. There is not one set of rules that will produce the most optimal solution; you will still have to consider what is "best." This book will help you create a framework to improve your capacity to make decisions. This is administrative responsibility.

It is also important to consider how we generate an understanding about what is good or desirable. Ultimately, our environment, both personal and professional, plays a crucial role in this determination. What may be considered "good" in a profit-maximizing company like Enron is going to be quite different than what an employee in a social services agency who deals with vulnerable populations thinks is "good." However, regardless of the environment, people still make choices and must be held accountable for their actions.

We are also influenced by stated values such as codes of conduct. How, for example, do the codes of conduct in your organization influence what behavior is and is not considered desirable? Many of you are probably in graduate school because you have managerial aspirations, so understanding the way your employees' ethics have developed will be important for dealing with the ethical dimensions of your leadership role.

This chapter also makes a clear distinction between legality and morality. As the author notes, politicians who make laws are not always holding the moral high ground, so just because something is legal does not mean it is moral. We can agree as a general rule that society works best if we follow the rules, but there is still room for an ethical debate with regard to the law. For example, a police officer is required to arrest anyone who steals because they have broken the law, but is it ethical for him to arrest a struggling single mother who has stolen diapers for her baby because she cannot afford them? Why or why not?

At the end of the chapter, the author discusses the ways in which the groups to whom we are responsible play a role in our decision making about what is right. In the private sector, managers are responsible to their shareholders above all else. Contrast that with the wide range of stakeholders public administrators must consider: the public at large, specific constituencies, politicians, and others. We hope to make it clear that understanding the role of ethics in the public sector is vital, but it is also a lot more challenging than in the private sector.

READING 1

What is Ethics?

By Joseph Gilbert

[...]

In this chapter, we will explore the sources of ethics, similarities and differences between ethics and religion-based morality, and the rather complex relations between ethics and law. [...]

There is no clear, agreed-upon definition of ethics, so description will be attempted rather than definition. Ethics is a branch of philosophy. In its most general sense, it deals with the question of how humans should live. Socrates was quoted by Plato as saying that the unexamined life is not worth living.[1] Ethics is about that examination. Aristotle asked, "What is the good for humans?"[2] Ethics is generally considered to deal with relations of humans to each other. Some mostly contemporary philosophers also see ethics as concerned with how humans deal with other living things and with their environment in general.

One way to describe the field of ethics is that it deals with those actions affecting other people that make us feel good or bad about ourselves. While this description points to important elements of ethics, most philosophers agree that ethics is not just, or not even primarily, about how we feel. Ethics is part of philosophy, and philosophy is a rational discipline. Ethics, then, is also a rational approach to human interactions. Feelings of guilt or pride or shame might well be an indicator that we are dealing in the area of ethics, but almost all philosophers would agree that there is more to ethics than a simple formula stating that human interactions that make us feel good are ethical and those that make us feel bad are not.[3]

Ethics is the study of interpersonal or social values and the rules of conduct that derive from these values. It is about right and wrong actions or intentions in our

Joseph Gilbert, "What Is Ethics?," *Ethics for Managers: Philosophical Foundations & Business Realities*, pp. 24-40, 227-231.

dealings with others. However, there are other ways to judge actions or intentions as right or wrong that are quite distinct from ethics or morality. We can act in ways that are right in terms of efficiency. This means that we act in ways that will produce the most output for the least input. We can act in ways that are legally right, meaning that we have conformed to existing law. As we will see later in this chapter, law and ethics often agree, but also sometimes disagree. We can act in ways that are politically right, meaning that most voters agree with our actions. We can act in ways that make us feel good, even though a rational analysis might decide that our actions were ethically wrong.

Ethics, then, is one way among many to make judgments about our actions and intentions. [...][4] The first of these is that the moral act is the act which provides the greatest good for the greatest number of people. This approach is called utilitarianism. The second approach says that the moral act is the act which recognizes the rights of others and observes the duties that these rights impose on the actor. This approach is named variously by different authors: we shall simply call it rights and duties. The third approach says that the moral act is the act which treats similarly situated people in similar ways with regard to both process and outcome, and maintains a sense of proportion in results. We will call this approach fairness and justice.

There is a fourth approach to ethics which is cited fairly widely in current writings on the subject. It says that the moral act is the one which a virtuous person would perform in a given circumstance. This approach, which has its origins in the writings of Aristotle, is usually called virtue ethics.[5] We will not consider this approach extensively because of some major problems with applying it to real-life situations. Even the proponents of this approach recognize the difficulty of translating it from a theory of moral behavior to a practical means of judging individual actions.

The field of ethics is usually divided into descriptive and **normative ethics.**[6] **Descriptive ethics** simply describes what people say and do. It considers what actions people take that have ethical implications and what they say about these actions. Normative ethics prescribes what people should do. Various lists of "thou shalts" and "thou shalt nots" come within the area of normative ethics. Something as simple as the Golden Rule (do unto others as you would have them do unto you) can also be considered as normative ethics. Many books on business ethics take as their main goal normative ethics. Many managers do not like to be told what to do, particularly in the realm of moral right and wrong. The primary aim [...] is not to tell managers what to do, but to help them recognize when their actions will have ethical implications, and to provide tools for thinking through difficult ethical situations that arise in the course of their work as managers.

Sources of Ethics

All humans have a basic sense of right and wrong, which develops quite early in life and is often modified with maturity and experience. The only exception to this statement seems to be a rather small number of individuals who appear to be without concern for the impact of their actions on other humans. Psychologists label such people as sociopaths. James Q. Wilson has written an interesting and wide-ranging book titled *The Moral Sense.*[7] In it, he argues from a wide array of data and conclusions that humans do have a moral sense, that it shares common elements but shows wide divergence in terms of applications, and that some elements of it seem to be independent of upbringing or schooling. Wilson cites results from several different disciplines, including psychology, criminology, sociology and educational theory, to support his conclusions.

Wilson's discussion in his book summarizes some of the arguments that have gone on for generations as to whether babies are born with some knowledge or inclinations, or whether a newborn baby is a blank slate, with all knowledge and inclinations provided by experience. This is a complex issue, sometimes referred to as the "nature vs. nurture" debate, and has been the subject of a great deal of study and experimentation. The present evidence seems to suggest that, in some ways, newborns are not all alike.[8] In layman's terms, infants are born with personalities or pre-dispositions. All share certain physical instincts, but such traits as excitability or placidity seem to be present in varying degrees from birth. However, a baby's upbringing from its earliest days also has significant influence on how it reacts to the world around it. There is enough evidence to conclude, at least tentatively, that children brought up in secure and nurturing environments show a strong tendency to view the world differently than children raised in less secure and more hostile environments.

David Brooks, in his book *The Social Animal*, summarizes a good deal of research into the ways that infants learn and how early life experiences shape individuals.[9] In his book titled *Moral Minds: The Nature of Right and Wrong*,[10] Marc Hauser reviews available information from several scientific fields and finds evidence for a universal moral sense or instinct in humans. He proposes an evolutionary explanation for this instinct. While all of this research establishes how patterns of decision-making and concepts of right and wrong emerge from early life experiences, it is important to note that influence is not the same as determination. Unless individuals, in at least some instances, make truly free choices, the concept of ethics makes no sense. It is a principle of both philosophy and law that no one is obliged to do what they cannot do.

Such discussion may seem far removed from the topic of managerial ethics, but the sources of an individual manager's sense of moral right and wrong lie to some extent in their personality, and this is impacted by early childhood experience.[11] Parents are clearly one major influence on the sense of ethics that adults bring to their work. Consider the statement, "She has a good work ethic." It is a common way of saying that someone has certain beliefs and attitudes that influence their performance at work. If this can be said of someone in her first job, then the good work ethic must have been formed before they became an employee. For most people, this means that it was formed at home as they were growing up. Here the parents are one obvious influence. Even adults who no longer agree intellectually with their parents' teaching about right and wrong behavior often acknowledge that teaching as influencing their thoughts and actions. Hence parents are one source of the sense of ethics that managers bring to their work.[12]

Other widely acknowledged sources of an individual's sense of morality include peers, teachers, culture and religion. It is important to recognize the reasons why we think and judge as we do, and why others might think and judge quite differently about matters of morality. Most of our ethical judgments are instinctive. That is to say that we do not stop and reason things through, but instead we apply rules and decision-making models that we have come to accept in the past and that seem to fit the present situation. We may not know just why we accept or apply the rule that we do, but our decisions are shaped by the sense of ethics that we bring to a particular situation. Usually, it is only when someone questions our judgment or when results that we find unacceptable cause us to question our own judgment that we engage in conscious review of the sources of our decision-making.

Peers can be siblings, schoolmates, college roommates, fellow workers or members of a club, team or social group to which an individual belongs. One example of the influence of peers on an individual's sense of ethics is the often-noted tendency of teenagers to define themselves by their group of friends. Adults also have their views shaped, at least to some degree, by their peers. It is said that police officers often have a more negative view of humanity than those in some other professions because they spend so much of their time dealing with criminals. Two books about the internal operations at Enron in the last years before its bankruptcy make it clear that employees who went along with the questionable financial dealings were made to feel like successful performers and members of the team, while those who questioned some of the transactions were made to feel like outsiders.[13] In his detailed study of the U.S. government's decision-making before and during the Vietnam War, David Halberstam provides example after example of the powerful influence of peers in various parts of government on individual thinking and decision-making.[14] Several books about the recent financial crisis make it clear that peer influence played a major role at mortgage lenders, investment banks and other institutions involved in the reckless securitization and sale of subprime mortgages.[15] The influence of organizational peers is examined more closely in the last chapter of this book.

Peers can also be members of the same profession. Accountants, attorneys, medical doctors and members of other professions undergo extensive schooling. They learn not only how to minimize taxes or diagnose diabetes, but also how members of their profession act and think. Professional education involves socialization as well as information transmission. As more and more students obtain MBA degrees, this socialization also becomes more common for managers. Obviously, not all accountants or attorneys think alike. However, an argument can be made that members of a given profession think more alike than non-members of that profession. Another factor involving peer influence in the professions is the existence of professional codes of conduct. These are not perfect, and they do not influence all members of a profession equally. However, they do provide a starting point for making some kinds of ethical judgments, and they are more or less widely known within a profession.[16]

Teachers are another source of an individual's sense of morality. Whether it is the simple but often-repeated rules of grammar school or the more involved exposition that occurs in college classes, teachers as authority figures do communicate in ways that influence the reasoning and judgment of at least some of their students.[17] For a case in point, almost all teachers communicate, subtly or overtly, that cheating is wrong. They say this, they write this in syllabi and on exam instructions, and they act on this when they detect cheating. While most schools do not go this far, the U.S. military academies and a few other schools have honor codes that require the expulsion not only of cheaters but of those who know of cheating and fail to report it. Teachers also often communicate the value of doing assignments, or thinking clearly, or doing one's part in group projects. The cumulative impact of teachers does have an influence on the formation of an individual's sense of ethics.

Culture also influences an individual's moral sense. Culture can be defined as the unspoken rules and assumptions about how we do things around here.[18] When considered in this way, culture is subtle because it is unspoken.[19] Most organizations do not have explicit rules that dictate who shall be called by their first name and who shall be addressed more formally. They do not have explicit rules about the use of profanity at work, or the degree to which client information is kept confidential, or the kind of jokes that are acceptable or unacceptable in the workplace. Although none of these things is formalized, there often are unspoken rules. An observer of the behavior of workers at a construction site and at a law firm would notice immediate and profound differences in individual behavior and methods of conducting business. The two have different cultures.

The history of racial discrimination or of sexual harassment in some industries makes it clear that a behavior which is in accord with existing cultural norms is not necessarily morally acceptable.[20] However, an individual's sense of ethics is shaped by the culture or cultures in which he operates. One of the goals of this book is to help the reader to be aware of the ethical implications of managerial actions. Sometimes this awareness requires an examination of accepted cultural norms. Countries have cultures as well as companies. In fact, one of the more interesting issues in managerial ethics concerns the degree to which behavior such as bribery, which is accepted and commonplace in one culture, can or should be accepted in a different culture or by members of a different culture.[21] Another interesting issue concerning culture and ethics is the personal integration of ethical standards in an individual's different roles. Can a person follow one set of standards with her family, a second set with coworkers and a third set with customers or regulators? We will address such issues in subsequent chapters.

Still another significant influence on an individual's sense of ethics, and for some people by far the most important, is religion. People who were raised in a religion, even if they no longer believe or practice it, often have the teachings of that religion as part of their sense of ethics. People who do believe in and practice religion typically find the moral rules or dictates of their religion the most meaningful way to answer questions about right and wrong behavior. What does philosophy have to say about that? As we noted in the last chapter, philosophy does not accept religious teachings, either from sacred books or from individuals with religious authority, as the basis of answers when doing philosophy. Some noted philosophers have been deeply religious people. Obviously, then, the two can co-exist.

Another point worth noting is that truly awful things have sometimes been done in the name of religion. Most religious people would agree that it is not a good thing to tie someone to a stake, surround them with wood and set them on fire in order to encourage them to share one's religious beliefs. Nor is it a good thing to commandeer passenger airplanes and fly them and their passengers into buildings in order to avenge one's god or to send a religious message. Most religious people would agree that doing such things in the name of religion is to misunderstand or misinterpret religion. If religion and philosophy can be compatible, then perhaps in extreme kinds of behavior, philosophy can provide one tool for thinking about when actions are not compatible with a religion.

It is also worth considering that many of the finest things done by humans have been done in the name of religion. Artists and artisans have created cathedrals, statues, paintings and music that are widely acclaimed, and done so in the name of religion. People have taught students, cared for the sick and provided for the homeless with almost no personal financial reward, and done so in the name of religion. When we think about morally good and bad acts by individuals, we cannot do otherwise than acknowledge the impact of religion in shaping many people's sense of ethics.[22]

The forces discussed above are not the only ones that shape an individual's sense of ethics, but they are among the most common and most important. Because each individual brings his or her sense of ethics to the start of any discussion of this topic, it is important to know what has shaped that sense. Often an individual's intuitive sense of ethics is based on past experiences or reflections on those experiences. Unless we are consciously aware of why we accept the assumptions and rules that we do in the area of morality, it is not really possible to reflect on them and decide whether they are appropriate to situations that arise from the task of management. It is often uncomfortable to question our own assumptions, particularly in areas that matter to us. Yet, without knowing what our own individual assumptions are on which we base our own sense of morality, analysis of managerial ethics is reduced to criticism of any theory different from our own, and we do not really have a thoughtful base from which to conduct such criticism.

Since each individual brings his or her own sense of morality to the discussion, and since this individual sense is based to varying degrees on parental and peer influence, past and present religious beliefs and various cultural assumptions, is there any hope of a rational, thoughtful discussion of normative ethics—what a person should or should not do in a given situation? In fact, there is. Take, for example, the issue of rights and duties. Individuals have a sense of their own rights. National cultures vary considerably in their assumptions about rights, but these cultures do shape individual assumptions.[23] On the question of individual rights versus group rights, a person who has grown up in the United States will most probably put more emphasis on individual rights, while a person who has grown up in Japan will probably put more emphasis on group rights. When we translate this general question to the specific application of a manager's right to monitor an employee's email, the first instinctive response of the American will probably differ from the first instinctive response of the Japanese.

As we will examine in more detail later in the book, the issue of privacy in the workplace does have moral implications for managers and for employees. Once this fact is established, we can begin to discuss what rights an employee has to privacy in workplace email communication and what duties, if any, those rights impose on managers. While it is unlikely that such discussion will result in universal rules that all managers everywhere are morally obliged to do or not to do something in this area, our understanding of the issues and awareness of what others think about these same issues can go a long way in determining what constitutes a moral action in a given circumstance.

Ethics and the Law

One other influence that shapes many people's sense of morality is the law. In fact, business people often seem to equate the two. It is remarkable how many of the comments made in their own defense by executives at Enron, Arthur Andersen, Countrywide and other companies involved in scandals said, in effect, "What we did was not wrong because it complied with the law, or with Generally Accepted Accounting Principles." In other words, many people, at least some of the time, do not make a distinction between what is legal and what is moral.

Ethics, as we have seen, is a branch of philosophy. Law is seen as a quite distinct field.[24] Legal systems, or groups of laws, have existed for thousands of years.[25] Law is a function of government, in that laws are made, changed and enforced by governments. Laws apply in specific places and have their standing from the government of countries, states or other political entities or groups of entities (there is some international law). In the case of monarchies, the monarch makes, interprets and enforces the law. There may be elaborate governmental structures for carrying out these tasks, but the ultimate authority rests with the monarch. In the case of democracies, government officials chosen by the people (or, in rare cases, the people meeting as a whole) make, interpret and enforce laws. There are several ways in which legislators and those who enforce the laws are chosen, but the source of authority in legal matters comes from the people and not from a single individual, such as in a monarchy. Typically in a democracy, the Constitution or other foundational document provides rules for how laws are to be made and changed.[26] In the United States, laws can be passed by federal legislators for the entire country. In matters over which the national Constitution does not specify federal control, laws can be made by elected officials at the levels of state, county and municipality. The laws of a given jurisdiction can be changed by legislators of that jurisdiction, according to rules specified in the jurisdiction's Constitution or charter.

Regulations have the force of law, but are generally more specific and are written and approved by regulatory agencies within the framework of the elected government. Regulators are generally appointed rather than elected. Regulations are intended to provide detail specifying how broader laws apply to specific cases and examples. Most businesses are subject to several regulatory agencies and must comply with detailed regulations in such matters as taxation, financial disclosure and product safety. All businesses are also subject to a variety of laws and regulations in matters relating to employment.

In law, unlike philosophy, all in a jurisdiction are subject to the same laws. Two people can disagree about many things in philosophy, and there may be absolutely no practical consequences. If the laws of my state provide for residents to pay income taxes to the state, and the laws in your state do not, you and I can agree or disagree philosophically about the value or appropriateness of state income taxes. However, whatever my philosophical position, I am legally bound to pay income taxes to my state as provided by its laws and will be subject to legal consequences if I fail to do so. You can rejoice in your state's wisdom in not having an income tax, but you still must pay federal income tax if you are a citizen of the United States.

A variety of criminal and civil laws and regulations apply to managers in their role as managers. While it is rare in the United States for managers to be charged or tried for criminal violations, it does happen. Recent changes in federal law, most prominently in the Sarbanes–Oxley Act passed in 2002, make it likely that such criminal charges will become somewhat more common in the future. Involvement in civil litigation is a common fact of life for companies and managers in many industries. Managers are not personally charged nearly as often as companies are, but in many industries most companies have a variety of civil legal proceedings under way at any given point in time. Companies are more often defendants than plaintiffs in such cases, but in some industries, companies regularly pursue legal charges against others to protect patents or licenses or to recover loans or other damages under various contracts.

One consequence of the frequency of business litigation in the United States is that some actions that might be seen as ethical are discouraged because of their possible legal consequences. If a company does something that it later considers wrong, the CEO or other spokesperson might feel that he or she is morally obliged to accept responsibility, and say what was wrong and what the company plans to do about it. If there is a chance that the company or the executive will be sued for the actions in question, the legal advice will almost certainly be to avoid any statement which could subsequently be used as evidence in litigation. Thus, accountability is sometimes in conflict with the prevention of adverse legal consequences.

Ethics and Law Not the Same

While ethics and law deal with many of the same issues, and often come to the same conclusions, there are several reasons why it is not valid to equate one with the other. One consideration is this: law-makers are often not noted for their refined moral sensibility. In fact, in a number of classes when I have asked students whether they would be satisfied to have either national or local legislators make up their moral code, the response has been a rather spirited negative. This should not be surprising, for in a democracy, candidates for office generally do not claim to be the most virtuous or the most morally sensitive individuals in the country. If they did make such claims, one suspects that they would be met with no little skepticism. It seems to be a general rule that saints do not make good politicians, and vice versa. In addition to legislation, much of the legal burden imposed in a democracy is designed by regulators. These are typically non-elected bureaucrats and, like legislators, are not selected for high ethical sensitivity. This is not to say that most politicians and regulators are liars and thieves. It is merely to say that they are not chosen and kept in office because of their moral sensitivity.

Another reason why it is dangerous to equate the legal with the moral is that laws change, while many people expect at least the basics of morality to be unchanging.[27] In the State of

Nevada, prostitution is legal in all but two counties. While the legal status of the act can change from county to county, it is difficult to argue that prostitution is moral in one county and immoral in the next. Early in the twentieth century, the eighteenth amendment to the United States Constitution made production and sale of alcoholic beverages illegal. The twenty-first amendment reversed this position. Morality should stand on firmer ground.

Some actions, such as adultery, are considered by many people to be immoral, yet in many parts of the United States there is no legal prohibition against adultery. Many parents teach their children that it is immoral for the children to lie to their parents, yet there is no legal prohibition against such lies. The absence of a law against an action does not necessarily constitute grounds for deciding that the action is ethical. Is the opposite true?

General Premise: It is Ethical to Follow the Law

All of the major systems of ethics include an assumption in favor of obeying the law.[28] Note that this is an assumption, not an absolute mandate. Each of the major systems of ethics at some point critiques laws and provides a basis for analyzing whether or not a given law is ethical. However, this is different from an approach that makes no presumption either in favor of or against observing the law. Since we must live and work in the real world, it does not make sense to start from an assumption that it is unethical to follow the law. The remaining two possibilities are an assumption that it is ethical to follow the law or a neutral stance that assumes that each individual law or even each individual circumstance must be analyzed to determine whether it is ethical to follow the law. Notice that we have proceeded so far simply by applying logic (that is, by doing philosophy!). It is both impractical and unreasonable to analyze each law or each application of the law, so we will start with the assumption that it is ethical to follow the law.

There is another way of reaching this same conclusion. Laws are made to reflect and protect the values of a society, at least in a democracy. If they do not reflect society's values, new law-makers are elected by the people. While this view is somewhat oversimplified, it is basically descriptive of what happens in democracies over a period of time. Ethics is also about values. If a society values the individual's right to speak his or her mind, its laws will tend to protect free speech, and most censorship will be considered illegal. If a society values the common good above individual rights, it might reflect these values in its tax laws and welfare structure. Wealthy people will also be seen as having a moral duty to contribute in some way to the support of the poor. Thus the values expressed in a democratic society's laws will also be reflected in its sense of morality. Not every law will be considered moral by every citizen, but an assumption that it is ethical to follow the law will fit comfortably in the large scheme of things within that society. In the United States at the present time, it is neither illegal nor generally thought to be immoral for an executive to make a good deal of money.[29] However, it is illegal, and is generally considered to be immoral, for that same executive to fail to pay legally imposed income taxes.

When and how do we test whether a law or its application is moral, given our starting assumption that it is moral to follow the law, but our unwillingness to simply equate legality with morality? There are two kinds of situations in which one might question the link between morality and obedience to a given law. One is a matter of degree, and the other involves the basic values expressed in a law. A driver who is exceeding the speed limit by one mile per hour is technically in violation of the law. However, neither the driver nor the policeman behind her is likely to consider that she is doing anything wrong, in the moral or even the legal sense. We can and do argue about how much over the speed limit and under what conditions fast driving becomes a violation of law and/or ethics, but at the very margin, we do not generally maintain that the tiniest infraction of a law constitutes an immoral action.

In marketing, claims for a product or a service that just slightly stretch the truth are almost expected. Many consumers consciously or unconsciously scale down the claims made in advertising when forming their own expectations. However, outright material lies about a product are not considered acceptable, either legally or morally.[30] Such matters of degree trouble some individuals more than others. Individuals differ in their tolerance for ambiguity. Some prefer rules, whether they are laws or ethical prescriptions, to be simple and clear. Others feel that life as we live it is not simple, so ambiguity must be allowed for and expected in the rules by which we live our lives. Anyone who fulfills the role of manager for any length of time will find that, in the real world of organizations, ambiguity abounds. Further, simple clear-cut cases seldom are presented to managers; they are resolved by subordinates. Individuals with high needs for clarity and simplicity in their decision-making often have trouble succeeding in the role of manager because of the inherent ambiguities in the task of managing.

The second and more unusual kind of situation when the link between following the law and being ethical must be tested involves laws which express or enforce values that are not consistent with an individual's or society's sense of morality. There is much that can be said about the role of ethics in evaluating laws that is beyond the scope of this book.[31] However, the issue does sometimes arise in various business settings, and some thoughts on it may prove helpful. Under the law, neither ignorance nor disagreement is a valid excuse for violating a law. A moment's thought will show that it could not be otherwise. If laws did not apply to those who were not familiar with them, anyone could plead innocent to anything, and in order to apply the law and its sanctions, the knowledge of the offender would become the key turning point in legal proceedings. Proving what someone knows or does not know is a very difficult thing to do. If laws only applied to individuals who agreed with them, anyone could plead innocent to any offense by simply stating their disagreement with the law in question. Clearly a society could not operate on such a basis. Business people cannot know all of the laws and regulations that apply to them in detail, yet they are not excused from compliance by ignorance of a given law or regulation. They are expected to be generally knowledgeable about laws and regulations applying to their business. They are also expected to have access to and make use of specialists (generally speaking, but not always, these specialists are attorneys) who can identify and interpret applicable laws and regulations.

Business people, like other citizens, can and sometimes do disagree with a given law or regulation and can work to change it. The *Wall Street Journal* has for many years been the most widely read newspaper of business. On its editorial pages, the *Journal* often criticizes current laws and regulations and argues why and how they should be changed.[32] However, the *Journal* does not advocate that its readers, who include a good many managers, should ignore or fail to comply with laws or regulations that it disagrees with. Companies hire lobbyists, make political donations and engage in other forms of political activity with the intention of shaping laws and regulations in ways that favor their business. They often advocate changing present laws or regulations. Yet, they generally acknowledge the need to comply with those laws or regulations until such time as they are changed.

The decision that a law is unethical or immoral, and that an individual is compelled by his sense of morality to disobey that law, is relatively rare. This is a quite different thing than deciding that one thinks that a given law is based on bad reasoning, or supports the wrong values, or cannot be fairly and reasonably enforced. Going so far as to say that an individual's sense of morality requires him to disobey the law carries consequences. In the case of civil disobedience, such as that practiced by civil rights leaders of the 1960s in the United States, some individuals did decide that they were morally required to disobey laws that denied ethnic minorities certain rights. These individuals for the most part knew what they were doing and accepted the consequences. When they were jailed or fined for disobeying the law, they accepted the punishment. They did not judge it morally right, but they did acknowledge the existence of the law and its consequences.

Historically, few if any business people have concluded that a business law is immoral and that they are obliged by their personal sense of morality to disobey the law and accept the consequences. Many business people have disagreed strongly with some law or regulation, and have worked to change it, but this is a large step short of concluding that they are morally obliged to disobey the law and accept the consequences. It appears that, in the case of scandals involving Enron, Adelphia, HealthSouth and other major firms, individuals broke laws. They obviously did not feel that observing the laws was the best thing to do. However, it appears that their judgment was instrumental rather than moral. In other words, they concluded that their company could make more profit or attain other corporate goals more effectively if they broke a law. They did not do this, apparently, because of their views about the immorality of the law or their ethical obligation to break the law and accept the consequences.

Earlier in this chapter, we showed that there are several reasons for not simply equating ethics and the law. Reference was made there to the frequent defense against charges of corporate wrong-doing that whatever action is being challenged complied with existing laws or regulations. The point was made that an action is not automatically moral because it is legal. Are managers, then, sometimes morally obliged to go beyond the letter of the law? The short answer is yes. However, since this seems to many managers (and their attorneys) to be naïve, unrealistic, and soft and squishy in a world where the prescribed managerial reading includes *The Art of War*,[33] *Jack: Straight from the Gut*,[34] Machiavelli's *The Prince*[35] and other non-naïve, realistic titles, we need to discuss the issue a bit further.

Ethics and Managers

Most textbooks on Business Ethics or Business and Society include a chapter on the role of the corporation in modern society. Since corporate decisions are made by managers, this topic can be seen as the role of the manager in modern society. The chapter in question almost inevitably includes reference to and quotations from a very famous piece written by Milton Friedman for the *New York Times Magazine* in 1970 entitled "The social responsibility of business is to increase its profits." In this piece, Friedman, a Nobel Prize-winning economist, argued that the role of the manager is to act as the agent of the owners of the business that he or she manages, namely, the stockholders.

Friedman says that the manager as agent of the owners:

> ... has direct responsibility to his employers. That responsibility is to conduct the business in accordance with their desires, which generally will be to make as much money as possible while conforming to the basic rules of society, both those embodied in law and those embodied in ethical customs.[36]

If this is not the strongest statement of a manager's responsibility being not to himself but to his stockholders, it is certainly the most quoted. Even in Friedman's statement, there is explicit reference to ethical customs as well as to the law. In reaction to the sentiments expressed in Friedman's article, a good deal of discussion has ensued around the notion that corporations and their managers have responsibilities to stakeholders. R. Edward Freeman, a professor, has written extensively on the notion of stakeholders. He gives a narrow definition of the term stakeholder as describing "those groups who are vital to the survival and success of the corporation."[37] He also gives a wide definition which "includes any group or individual who can affect or is affected by the corporation."[38]

Earlier, we defined ethics as the discipline that studies interpersonal or social values and the rules of conduct that derive from these values. Certainly the decisions of managers do affect other people, including their subordinates, others within their organizations and various people beyond the organization, including but not limited to the stockholders or owners. Managerial ethics, then, must of necessity examine the impacts of the actions of managers. This examination cannot be limited to the compliance or noncompliance of those actions with laws and regulations.

A somewhat different way of looking at this is to ask what the individual manager, as a person, considers important and valuable. When I was a manager, I felt better about myself and my job at the end of some days than others. I cannot remember ever looking back on a day with satisfaction and saying to myself or anyone else, "I had a really good day today—I complied with the law!" When one reads the biographies or autobiographies of managers, one gets the sense that they enjoy meeting competitive challenges successfully. Many of them also seem to derive genuine pleasure from the development of subordinates and from maintaining or expanding company traditions. It is interesting that a great number of academic studies have been done on a wide variety of topics relating to management and leadership, yet there are very few studies on what motivates managers, other than those that study compensation in its various forms.[39]

There is a large amount of writing on leadership. Almost none of it refers to complying with the law as a characteristic of a successful leader. It is assumed that good leaders do not run afoul of the law, but it is not at all assumed that compliance with the law is the same as good leadership. Not all managers are leaders, but both managers and leaders have interaction with others as a significant part of their job. How we interact with others has already been defined as central to ethics. Good leaders, like good managers, are generally viewed as having a concern for the total impact of their actions. They are generally thought to carry out their own duties and to show concern for the rights of others. Fairness is high on the list of traits of both good managers and good leaders. These characteristics of good leaders and good managers have already been identified as central to the three basic approaches to ethics. It should not be surprising if we define good leaders and good managers as ethical individuals. Being ethical does not, by itself, make one a good leader or manager, but being unethical might be argued to prevent one from being either a good leader or a good manager.

There are unethical managers. Some of the executives of the companies involved in past scandals enriched themselves by tens or hundreds of millions of dollars while managing their companies in ways that were dishonest and value-destroying for stakeholders. Jimmy Cayne, the chairman of the board of directors of the large investment bank Bear Stearns, spent the last week of the company's independent existence, while it was fighting for its life, at a bridge tournament. He had to be summoned from a bridge game to vote (by phone) on approving the company's bankruptcy.[40] Some of these managers were simultaneously lying to their own directors, to regulators and to others about the true state of their companies. It certainly appears that much of the conduct of the top managers of these companies was unethical. For a period of time, their companies were widely praised and held up by the business press as models for others to follow. In the end, though, a manager who lies, enriches himself at the expense of stockholders and lenders, and manages his company into bankruptcy cannot be judged to be either a good or an ethical manager. This judgment holds true even if such a manager is never found guilty of breaking any law.

In describing previously the basic approaches to ethics, virtue ethics was briefly mentioned. As indicated there, we will not consider this as a basic approach to ethics for purposes of this book because virtue ethics has major difficulties in showing what the ethical action would be in a given situation, and why. However, there is one point from the virtue ethics approach that bears on our current discussion. Virtue ethics defines the moral act as the act that a virtuous person would perform. In some ways, this appears to be a case of circular reasoning. However, when we say that an unethical person who is not found guilty of breaking the law still cannot be judged to be a good manager, we are using the approach of virtue ethics.

Aristotle, the first proponent of **virtue ethics** and still the most quoted on this subject, said that the virtuous person is the one who does virtuous things. His point here is that we can discern a person's ethics by observing that person's actions over time. Many philosophers would set out to discern a person's ethics by discussing this subject with the person, asking both about his theories of ethics and how they might be applied in particular situations. In fact, all three of the approaches to ethics that we will consider at length in the following chapters concern themselves either with individual acts and their consequences or with the way that systems distribute resources. Aristotle concerned himself with people. In his major work on ethics, *The Nicomachean Ethics*,[41] Aristotle described the virtuous person as the one who observes moderation in all things. He discusses at length such virtues as courage, liberality, self-restraint and friendship. Throughout his discussions of the virtues, he uses examples constantly, showing what the courageous person or the true friend would do. The basis of all his discussion is that the virtuous person will show consistency and moderation in his actions.

Managers, as noted above, play various roles in their lives. Psychologists and social theorists tell us that individuals have trouble dealing with inconsistency. It is hard for the same person to be warm and nurturing with spouse and children, and cold and impersonal with subordinates at work. The ethical or virtuous person, according to Aristotle, is the person who shows consistency and moderation in all their dealings with others, be they family or friends, or peers, or subordinates. This is a point worth considering. We will examine, in the following chapters, specific instances of decisions managers must make that have moral implications. Some will involve the hiring or terminating of employees, others the evaluation and rewarding of the work of subordinates, and others the respect for or invasion of the privacy of others. In all these individual cases, we will ask how each of the three major approaches to ethics would determine whether a given act is moral.

There is a tendency, in examining isolated acts, to ignore or forget that the same human makes the various decisions that we will examine, and many others. Yet, when we reflect on ourselves as individuals attempting to be moral, we find that consistency or its lack is a major issue. How can we be caring and sympathetic in one situation and rational and emotionless in another? How can we be seriously concerned about telling the truth to our spouse or children, yet go to work and mislead others? How can we balance the time demands of our job with the time demands of our family? To Aristotle, these were important and reasonable questions. Yet, in much of the writing on business ethics, such questions are nowhere to be found.

Humans are sometimes inconsistent. Aristotle recognized this. Many of the best plays and novels ever written have this as a central theme. Totally predictable individuals are not generally valued as friends or as advisors. After all, if someone is totally predictable, once we have gotten to know them, we know in advance what they will say or recommend in any situation. Most people are not totally predictable. In other words, most people are, at least sometimes, inconsistent. We cannot predict their response in every situation because they cannot predict their response. However, most people do show patterns in their behavior and in their decision-making. These patterns are the basis for virtue ethics as an approach to morality. The just person typically acts justly. Typically does not mean always, but it does mean that a pattern of just actions can be perceived over time, and so for the other virtues. If individuals are truly free to choose different courses of action at least some of the time, then the pattern of their choices helps us to decide whether they are virtuous. As we examine individual choices in the following chapters, this is an important point to bear in mind.

Most people would not praise a person who habitually acts with no thought or concern for the consequences of his actions. We would apply terms such as thoughtless, heedless and reckless to such a person. None of these terms is complimentary. As we examine utilitarianism in the next chapter, we will see that the central point of this approach to ethics is concern for the consequences of actions. Most people would also not praise a person who habitually acts with no sense of responsibility toward others. We might apply such terms as selfish, uncaring and egomaniacal to such a person. Again, none of these terms is complimentary. In the chapter where we examine rights and duties, we will see that the central point is that other individuals do in fact have rights and that these rights often impose duties on us to take their concerns into account. Finally, little or no praise will come to the individual who habitually acts with no concern for the relative impacts of his actions on some people versus others, and with no sense of proportion between actions and their consequences for others. In the chapter where we examine fairness and justice, we will see that the relative impacts of our actions on others constitute a central concern of ethics, along with a sense of proportionality.

We have now considered a number of concepts concerning what ethics is, and what it is not. As a branch of philosophy, ethics shares the basic concerns of philosophy for clear thinking and accurate naming of things and for using reason rather than emotions or authority (divine or human) in reaching conclusions. We have seen that ethics often involves values that are shared by religious and legal systems, but that it is not identical with either of these kinds of systems. [...]

Notes

1

> If ... I tell you that to let no day pass without discussing goodness and all the other subjects about which you hear me talking and examining both myself and others is really the very best thing that a man can do, and that life without this sort of examination is not worth living, you will be even less inclined to believe me.
>
> (Plato, The apology, in Hamilton, E. and Cairns, H. (eds.) (1963). *Plato: The collected dialogues*. New York: Pantheon Books, p. 23)

2 Aristotle's answer to this question, which provides a good example of his approach in understandable language, comprises Book I of the *Nicomachean ethics*. This work is currently available in a number of versions; the one I have used is Aristotle, *The Nicomachean ethics* (translated by H. Rackham) (1990). Cambridge MA: Harvard University Press.

3 There is an approach to ethics known as egoism which maintains that the moral act is the one that satisfies my own individual desires. Even this approach, though, becomes somewhat complicated because it must deal with instrumental goals as well as direct goals. For instance, I choose to pay money and allocate time and energy to obtain an MBA because accomplishing this personally costly goal will help me attain something that I want badly enough to sacrifice for it. For a good basic description of egoism and challenges made to it, see Sober, E. (2000). Psychological egoism, in LaFollette, H. (ed.), *The Blackwell guide to ethical theory.* Malden MA: Blackwell Publishers, pp. 129–148.

4 As noted in the first chapter, the words "ethical" and "moral" are used interchangeably in this book.

5 For discussions of virtue ethics, see McGuire, S. (1997). Business ethics: A compromise between politics and virtue. *Journal of Business Ethics*, 16, 1411–1418 and McIntyre, A. (1981). *After virtue.* Notre Dame IN: University of Notre Dame Press.

6 Weaver, G. & Trevino, L. (1994). Normative and empirical business ethics. B*usiness Ethics Quarterly*, 4, 129–144.

7 Wilson, J.Q. (1993). *The moral sense.* New York: The Free Press.

8 Pinker, S. (2002). *The blank slate: The modern denial of human nature.* New York: Penguin Books.

9 Brooks, D. (2011). *The social animal: The hidden sources of love, character and achievement.* New York: Random House.

10 Hauser, M. (2006). *Moral minds: The nature of right and wrong.* New York: HarperCollins.

11 The ideas of moral development, or the influence of people and experiences on an individual's sense of ethics, and of early roots of adult traits have been explored widely. Wilson, in his previously cited book, *The moral sense*, considers these ideas at length. Among classic works on these subjects are Kohlberg, L. (1981). *The philosophy of moral development.* San Francisco: Harper & Row and Rest, J. (1986). *Moral development: Advances in research and theory.* New York: Praeger. Biographers have also had perceptive things to say about the development of an ethical or moral sense in individuals. Robert Caro, in the first volume of his extraordinary biography of Lyndon Johnson, has this to say about Johnson's drive for power:

> ... the more one learns—from his family, his childhood playmates, his college classmates, his first assistants, his congressional colleagues—about Lyndon Johnson, the more it becomes apparent not only that this hunger was a constant throughout his life but that it was a hunger so fierce and consuming that no consideration of morality or ethics, no cost to himself—or to anyone else—could stand before it.
>
> (Caro, R. (1982). *The path to power.* New York: Knopf, p. xix)

12 As Caro discusses extensively in his previously cited biography of Lyndon Johnson, the failures of Lyndon's father late in his life seem to have resulted in a strong drive on the part of the son to control the kind of circumstances that so hurt his father. Children (and adults) are sometimes strongly motivated to be unlike their parents.

13 McLean, B. and Elkind, P. (2003). *The smartest guys in the room: The amazing rise and scandalous fall of Enron*. New York: Penguin Group, and Swartz, M. with Watkins, S. (2003). *Power failure: The inside story of the collapse of Enron*. New York: Doubleday.

14 Halberstam, D. (2001/1969). *The best and the brightest*. New York: Modern Library.

15 See, for example, Bookstaber, R. (2007). *A demon of our own design: Markets, hedge funds, and the perils of financial innovation*. Hoboken, NJ: John Wiley & Sons; Hudson, M. (2010). *The monster*. New York: Times Books; Kelly, K. (2009). *Street fighters*. New York: Penguin Group; Muolo, P. and Padilla, M. (2008). *Chain of blame*. Hoboken, NJ: John Wiley & Sons.

16 Attorneys wishing to be admitted to the bar in any state in the United States must pass a professional responsibility exam, and accountants wishing to become Certified Public Accountants must pass an ethics component of the CPA exam in order to attain the designation.

17 Piper, T., Gentile, M. and Parks, S. (1993). *Can ethics be taught?: Perspectives, challenges, and approaches at the Harvard Business School*. Cambridge MA: Harvard Business School Press.

18 Schein, E. (1992). *Organizational culture and leadership*, 2nd edition. San Francisco: Jossey Bass.

19 Enron, by all accounts, had a dysfunctional culture in its last years before bankruptcy. The books cited in note 13 above and other sources identify numerous instances of unethical behavior either practiced by or approved by senior management. Yet this company had a sixty-four-page Code of Ethics, which prescribed exemplary behavior in both general and particular terms. The culture (largely unspoken but widely recognized) seemed to prevail over the written word.

20 The Boston Red Sox were the last major league baseball team to hire a black player. Their recalcitrance in this area was not only morally repugnant (although accepted by the team's owner and executives at the time); it also probably cost them success on the field and in pennant races. See Finkelstein, S. (2003). *Why smart executives fail*. New York: Penguin Group, especially pp. 119–125.

21 For a thought-provoking treatment of this subject, see Donaldson, T. (1992). *The ethics of international business*. New York: Oxford University Press.

22 For an informed and thoughtful perspective on the major world religions and their views on morality, see Smith, H. (1991/1958). *The world's religions*. New York: HarperCollins. Some of the most striking moral views in the history of religion have come from so-called fundamentalists. For an informed perspective on this element of religion, see Armstrong, K. (2000). *The battle for God: A history of fundamentalism*. New York: Ballentine Books.

23 For a series of essays by one of the twentieth century's foremost students of culture, and the author of a number of influential books on this subject, see Geertz, C. (2001). *Available light: Anthropological reflections on philosophical topics*. Princeton NJ: Princeton University Press.

24 There is a continuing, lively debate among those who study the law as to just what it is. To vastly over-summarize, one group maintains that the law is the sum total of statutes passed by legislators and the accumulation of judicial decisions interpreting those statutes. Another group maintains that the law, in a given case, is whatever the judge involved says it is. For a discussion of this issue by a widely cited author who is himself a judge and clearly espouses one point of view, see Posner, R. (1990). *The problems of jurisprudence*. Cambridge MA: Harvard University Press. For a quite different viewpoint, see Dworkin, R. (1986). *Law's empire*. Cambridge MA: The Belknap Press of Harvard University Press.

25 I.F. Stone notes that:

> Homer gives us a rudimentary lesson in sociology and political science. He shows us what in his own time were already considered the hallmarks of civilization. Odysseus fears that he will meet a creature of great strength, "a savage man who knows nothing of justice or of law", the primary elements that characterize a civilized man.
>
> (Stone, I.F. (1988). *The trial of Socrates*. Boston: Little, Brown & Co., p. 24)

The Odyssey, to which Stone refers, was written more than 2,700 years ago.

26 Article 1, the longest article in the United States Constitution, describes legislative powers of the federal government and of local governments.

27 There are many examples in literature of the tension that can exist when law and morality do not coincide. In the classic Greek tragedy *Antigone*, the playwright Sophocles has Creon, the king, decree that the body of one of two brothers killed in battle shall be left unburied. Antigone, the sister of the two slain brothers, defies the king's decree (law) and suffers consequences that also bring ruin to the king. In Shakespeare's *Merchant of Venice*, Shylock forms a legally binding contract specifying that he will be awarded a pound of flesh from his debtor if the debtor defaults on a loan from Shylock. Much of the play is taken up with vivid discussion of the legality and morality of this arrangement and Shylock's insistence on collecting his legal due. Martin Luther King's "Letter from Birmingham Jail" is an eloquent and learned discussion of the moral obligation to violate segregationist laws.

28 For a thoughtful, extended discussion of the relationship between law and ethics, see Lyons, D. (1984). *Ethics and the rule of law*. Cambridge UK: Cambridge University Press.

29 How the executive makes that money is a different question. Andrew Fastow, the former chief financial officer of Enron, agreed to plead guilty to several criminal charges. As part of his punishment, he agreed to pay back almost $30 million in money that he made as a result of his illegal activities (as well as serving ten years in prison). This is a legal settlement, but moral sentiment does not

seem to condone his keeping money that he made illegally. Interestingly enough, various reports have placed his total gains from illegal transactions at amounts from $40 million to $60 million.

30 See Carson, T., Wokutch, R. and Cox, J. (1985). An ethical analysis of deception in advertising. *Journal of Business Ethics*, 4, 93–104.

31 Perhaps the most thoughtful, accessible work on this topic is Martin Luther King's "Letter from Birmingham Jail". Written while King was being held in jail by the racist sheriff of Birmingham, Alabama during Civil Rights demonstrations in 1963, King cites (from memory, since he had no reference material available to him in jail) sources as varied as Thomas Aquinas and Thomas Jefferson in his discussion. He argues that it is incumbent on thoughtful people (his letter addresses fellow ministers who objected to his tactics of protest and wanted him to go slowly in advocating integration) to consider whether some laws are moral and to take action if they are not.

32 In a letter from the publisher to readers, Karen House, the publisher of the *Wall Street Journal*, spelled out very clearly the paper's dual goals of objective reporting in the news sections and strong, clear advocacy in the editorial pages. In her words, "While our news pages are committed to informing our readers, our editorial pages are dedicated to advocating a consistent philosophy and positions that emanate from it." *Wall Street Journal*, January 8, 2004, p. A23.

33 Sun Tzu (1971). *The art of war* (Griffith, S., translator). New York: Oxford Press.

34 Welch, J. with Byrne, J. (2001). *Jack: Straight from the gut*. New York: Warner Books.

35 Machiavelli, N. (1992). *The prince*. New York: Knopf.

36 Friedman, M. (1970). The social responsibility of business is to increase its profits. *New York Times Magazine*, September 13. Reprinted in Donaldson, T., Werhane, P. and Cording, M. (2002). *Ethical issues in business: A philosophical approach*, 7th edition. Upper Saddle River NJ: Prentice Hall, pp. 33–38.

37 Freeman, R.E. (2002). Stakeholder theory of the modern corporation, in Donald-son, T., Werhane, P. and Cording, M. (eds.), *Ethical issues in business: A philosophical approach*, 7th edition. Upper Saddle River NJ: Prentice Hall, p. 42.

38 Ibid.

39 In his biography of Steve Jobs, Walter Isaacson makes it clear that Jobs was a highly motivated manager—one might say driven—long after his financial situation was such that he did not need to work at all. See Isaacson, W. (2011). *Steve Jobs*. New York: Simon & Schuster.

40 Cohen, W.D. (2009). *House of cards*. New York: Doubleday, p. 60.

41 Aristotle (1990/1926). *The Nicomachean ethics* (Rackham, H., translator). Cambridge MA: Harvard University Press.

CASE STUDY

Two friends, Dave and John, have worked together in local government for 10 years. They are each assistant city managers for the same city (so they are considered peers) and enjoy spending a significant amount of time together outside of work. Their favorite hobby is fishing, so they commonly exchange fishing-related gifts for birthdays, holidays, etc. After 10 years, the city manager retires and Dave is promoted to the position, while John remains an assistant city manager. Dave is now technically John's boss, but they still continue their friendship as they have in the past. For Dave's next birthday, John finds a handmade fishing rod worth about $300 and cannot wait to give it to Dave. When Dave receives the gift on his birthday, he isn't sure what to do. In the past, he would not have even considered that it might be a problem, but now that he is John's boss, he is wondering whether it is ethical to accept such an extravagant gift from a subordinate. Dave doesn't want to hurt John's feelings, but he knows he must really consider not just what he thinks is ethical, but how this may be perceived by others in the organization. What do you think—is it ethical for Dave to accept the present? Why or why not? What if the gift were less expensive, like a fishing lure worth about $5? Is it always, sometimes, or never acceptable to accept gifts from an employee? Why or why not?

CHAPTER 3

Approaches to Ethics

SEE WHERE YOU STAND: 60 SECOND ETHICAL DILEMMA

Imagine that you are in the following situation and have one minute to make a decision about the most ethical course of action:

You are unexpectedly called to an urgent meeting, where your boss announces that your organization is facing a 10 percent budget cut, and an initial plan must be created by the end of the day. Programming activities will have to be cut, so she asks you to make a recommendation between supporting the local boys and girls club (school-age children) or a retirement center (older adults). She tells you that you will only be able to support one program, so you cannot split the money between both programs. Both populations benefit tremendously from these programs, so you don't know what to suggest. What do you do?

INTRODUCTION TO CHAPTER

This chapter introduces a central ethical question that has been asked by mankind for thousands of years: how does one have a good life? Describing what is a good life involves descriptive or empirical claims, after making which we can ask how we ought to live, a normative claim. Ethical claims are normative because they prescribe how one should act—what we should do and what we should not do. We can get advice about what it means to live a good life from art, religion, family, and institutions. The Ancient Greeks had a fundamental role in the development of ethical theory. Aristotle described the "good" life as one of achieving "happiness" in his *Nicomachean Ethics*. The Greeks believed the basic goal of a political community was to promote happiness. In the Declaration of Independence, it states that the pursuit of happiness is an unalienable right. This chapter discusses different branches of ethics that describe and prescribe how one lives a good life. This chapter also has a section on business ethics, which will give you an opportunity to compare ethical standards in the public and private sectors.

Approaches to Ethics

The Study of Ethics

By Lynn Sharp Paine

Ethics is a loaded subject—loaded with emotion and potential confusions. Some confusions which frequently arise in ethical or moral discussions can perhaps be avoided by considering what ethics or **morality** is about. What is a moral problem? Is it different from an ethical problem? How is it different from other types of problems faced in everyday life? What is ethical conduct? What is moral conduct? Are they the same thing?

The Subject Matter

Everyday usage of the terms "ethics" and "morality" is not a particularly useful reference point for defining the subject matter of ethics. Ordinarily, these words are used in a variety of loosely related senses, and on a particular occasion, they may be used to refer to any of the following:

- what is good and bad
- what is right and wrong
- how people ought to act
- generally accepted standards of individual conduct
- systems of mores
- beliefs about the purpose of human life
- dictates of conscience
- values
- virtues

- obligations and duties
- a set of prohibitions concerned with sex
- prohibitions, prescriptions, and other values sanctioned by religion
- principles for evaluating good and bad, right and wrong, generally accepted norms, or systems of mores
- the logic of moral language.

Confusion resulting from the absence of a commonly accepted and precise definition of the terms "ethics" and "morality" is complicated by the fact that there is no widely recognized philosophical or conceptual basis for differentiating the terms. Frequently, they are used interchangeably,[1] although philosophers sometimes stipulate a distinction for purposes of their own studies. Some philosophers apply the term "morality" to a particular part of ethics—for example, that part concerned with matters of urgent social control;[2] with matters affecting others' interests; with religious values;[3] or with right and wrong conduct, as distinct from questions of value. Others regard ethics as a higher order discipline, with morality or some aspect of morality as its subject matter.[4]

Lack of precision in the usage of the terms "ethics" and "morality" is not necessarily problematic, but it can occasion misunderstandings among persons using the terms in different senses. One who regards morality as a set of outdated prohibitions primarily concerned with sex may in this age of sexual freedom find it hard to take the study of morality seriously. Similarly, a secular-minded person who associates morality with religion is likely to have no interest in morality and to regard it as a technique for preventing people from having fun.

It is thus important to recognize that there is a broad spectrum of topics which constitute the subject matter of ethics and not to mistake any one topic for the whole field. In any ethical discussion the topic and terms of discourse must be clearly identified. And despite the absence of a generally accepted basis for distinguishing ethics from morality, it is sometimes useful for purposes of discussion to distinguish the concepts in a specified way.

The Point of View

A concern with ethics or morality can reflect a variety of points of view. One may, for instance, approach ethics from an anthropological point of view, from a moralist's point of view, from a psychological point of view, from a philosophical point of view, or simply from the point of view of one who wishes to do the right thing. Each point of view has its distinctive techniques and purposes. The moralist uses persuasion and exhortation to gain acceptance of particular values or principles. The anthropologist is interested in describing and understanding the mores of selected societies and cultures. The philosopher's concern is primarily with justifying and analyzing various types of ethical and moral judgments. The acquisition and implementation of ethical standards are issues which interest the psychologist.

The ethical or moral point of view which characterizes the person who wishes to do the right thing is often regarded as the ultimate and overriding perspective on all action. In contrast to the financial point of view or the aesthetic point of view, for example, the ethical point of view is paramount. Ethical or moral considerations, it is said, take priority over all others.

These various perspectives on ethics may well be, in the end, directed toward the same objective—perfecting or, at least, improving the quality of life. But it is important to recognize the distinctive characteristics of each point of view to avoid mistakenly rejecting ethics as a whole because of disagreement with a particular point of view on the subject. Rejection of the moralistic point of view, for example, does not entail rejection of the philosophical one.

Some Ethical Issues

A comprehensive view of the subject matter of ethics and of the possible approaches to the subject yields a broad conception of what counts as an ethical issue. Questions as diverse as the following may be regarded as ethical issues:

- What ought the central actor(s) to do?
- How should the central actor(s) decide what he ought to do?
- What values are at issue and are they important?
- How should one decide whether the values at issue are important?
- What, if any, generally accepted principles are applicable to the situation?
- Should these principles be applied?
- What principles should be applied if the governing general principles conflict or if no generally accepted principles apply?
- What values and beliefs generated the situation and are they justifiable?

The subject matter of ethics is thus quite varied. A skill which is critical for achieving a broad understanding of ethics is the ability to identify and relate particular ethical issues and points of view. This is facilitated by a comprehensive view of the subject to start with and by clarity and rationality in thought.

Making Ethical Decisions

Many ethical decisions are easy—so easy that they are not even regarded as decisions. It takes no deliberation to rule out torture as a technique for persuading subordinates to adopt your point of view. But ethical thinkers do not ordinarily focus on easy decisions. It is the hard cases which excite theorists and which often reduce practitioners to dogmatism or despair about the possibility of ethical reasoning at all.[5]

In fact, many moral decisions can be made simply by reference to familiar general principles of honesty, fairness, keeping promises, loyalty, doing good, avoiding harm, and obedience to the law. However, there are also situations where the familiar general principles are in conflict, or because of unusual circumstances they do not seem appropriate, or where there simply are no familiar guidelines. In these situations, guidance is needed. Even the most practical-minded need a little moral theory to give structure to these problems and perhaps to aid in resolving them.

The following thumbnail sketches describe some theories moral philosophers have proposed to aid in making ethically proper decisions. Each theory suggests a critical question which may be used as a "moral test" of a proposed action. The theories described are not necessarily incompatible with one another, although generally speaking each has its own special focus. Philosophical debates about the completeness and coherence of these various approaches are not addressed here. Instead a rudimentary description of each theory is supplied for purpose of testing its application to some concrete problems.

1 *Could you prescribe universal acceptance of the principle upon which you propose to act?*

The eighteenth-century German philosopher Immanuel Kant proposed a single principle to govern moral action: "I am never to act otherwise than so *that I could also will that my maxim should become a universal law*".[6] A modern rendition of this principle might go as follows: "Act only on those principles whose universal acceptance you could prescribe."

Kant illustrated his principle in a discussion of whether it is acceptable when in distress to make a promise with the intention of not keeping it. According to Kant, to determine the morality of making false promises when in difficulty one should ask, "Would I be willing to say that everyone may make a deceitful promise to extricate himself from difficulty?"[7] That is, could I prescribe universal acceptance of a principle permitting deceitful promises in these circumstances?

Kant concluded that he could not. He reasoned that a universal law permitting false promises would be self-defeating: promises would lose their intended effect if such a law were accepted. It would be impossible to make promises, since they would never be regarded as sincere. Thus, it would be wrong to make a false promise in difficult circumstances since such a practice could not be universally followed.

Kant argued for a clear distinction between prudence and morality. He believed that actions done from a sense of moral duty, but not those based on considerations of prudence, are of moral worth. Thus, he believed that the morally proper reason for rejecting a proposed action is the impossibility of prescribing its universal acceptance and not the disadvantages which might result.

Kant's proposed principle, although not without problems,[8] has a great deal to recommend it. Like the Golden Rule, it captures what Professor R. M. Hare of Oxford University has called one of the essential characteristics of moral judgments—their universalizability.[9] **Universalizability** is that characteristic of moral judgments that requires us, if we are logical, to judge like cases alike, and thus to treat others as we would like to be treated.

Professor Hare has recently advanced a two-level theory of moral thinking which clearly delineates the universal aspect of particular moral judgments, and its relation to general moral principles.[10] Moral thinking at the first level, the "intuitive level", proceeds by reference to the basic general moral principles to which most of us are firmly and deeply attached by virtue of our upbringing. According to Professor Hare, these relatively simple principles are necessary, but not sufficient, for all moral thinking. The limits of intuitive thinking are revealed when situations require judgment about the applicability of the level-one principles, as, for instance, when they conflict. There is no intuitive response when the principle of fairness and the principle of keeping promises conflict, because we have learned no simple principle to govern such conflicts. Because of the limits of intuitive thinking, the second level, the "critical level," of moral thinking must be invoked.

Critical moral thinking requires creativity, imagination, knowledge, and intelligence. The universalizability of moral judgments, which Kant emphasized and which Professor Hare has developed at length, is essential at the critical level of moral thinking. The thesis of universalizability, as noted, requires that if we make any moral judgment about a given situation we must be prepared, as a matter of logic, to make the same judgment about any other actual or hypothetical situation which is precisely similar, regardless of our own position in that situation.[11]

To take an example illustrating the role of critical moral thinking, suppose that as the successful elder child of a lower middle class family you gratuitously promise to pay your sister's college expenses for the year. After making the promise, however, your income declines significantly. Now you can keep your promise only by foregoing a long-awaited vacation with your spouse. What should you do? Several basic principles are in conflict in this situation. The principle of promise-keeping bids you pay the expenses and also, perhaps, to take the vacation. The principle of loyalty is also indeterminate. Should loyalty to spouse or younger sibling take precedence? Because intuitive moral thinking is not helpful, critical moral thinking must be exercised, and the universalizability thesis employed.

According to the universalizability thesis, only a judgment which you could prescribe universally, that is, regardless of your position in this situation—as promisor, sister, spouse—could be morally acceptable. Therefore, you must imagine yourself successively in the situation and having the needs, desires, and preferences of all those affected by your judgment. By imaginatively constructing the situations of all the stakeholders and considering the consequences for them of the alternative judgments, one determines which possible judgment is universally prescribable, and therefore which is morally correct.

2 *Does your action conform to principles that would be chosen behind a "**veil of ignorance**"?*

Impartiality is a critical moral concept closely related to the concept of universalizability. It plays a central role in the theory of justice developed by Professor John Rawls in his book *A Theory of Justice*.[12] The basic idea of Professor Rawls' theory is that we can identify correct principles of justice by imagining a convention of rational persons of equal liberty and status setting out to select the principles of justice which will govern their society. The situation in which the parties stand when they set out to choose the governing principles is what Rawls calls the "original position". To insure that the parties selecting the principles will not tailor them to fit their own individual circumstances, Rawls enshrouds each person in the original position with a symbolic "veil of ignorance".

The veil of ignorance, which is basically a device to insure impartiality, is designed to exclude from the decision process types of knowledge that tend to set people apart. In the original position behind the veil of ignorance, persons have no knowledge of their own social and economic status, their own natural assets and abilities, their own life plans, and even their own special psychological traits such as aversion to risk. In addition the veil of ignorance excludes knowledge of the particular circumstances of each person's own society, as well as knowledge of his generational position.

While persons in the original position lack information about particular individual situations, they do know general facts about human society. They understand the bases of social organization and the laws of human psychology, as well as principles of politics and economics.

As defined by Professor Rawls, the problem of choosing principles of justice is to determine what principles rational persons operating behind the hypothetical veil of ignorance would choose.[13] Professor Rawls' general program is to design a decision procedure for selecting principles of justice which reflects generally acknowledged constraints on moral argument.

Although his concern is with fairness, Rawls' theory may be applied to other ethical problems by following his general framework of determining what general principles would be chosen behind a "veil of ignorance" to govern the situation.

3 *What are the consequences of your decision for all the parties affected?*

"**Consequentialism**" is the name given to the view that the consequences of actions affect their moral value. Although it is widely believed that consequentialist and non-consequentialist moral theories are fundamentally opposed to one another, there is reason to doubt that the division is so clear-cut and antithetical. In fact, there are both consequentialist and non-consequentialist aspects involved in most theories and in most ordinary moral thinking.

Act utilitarianism and **rule utilitarianism** are probably the best known and most widely held of the numerous consequentialist theories. The nineteenth-century British philosopher and political reformer Jeremy Bentham was a vociferous advocate of act utilitarianism. John Stuart Mill, another nineteenth-century British philosopher, was also a proponent of utilitarianism, though whether he favored act utilitarianism or rule utilitarianism is a matter of debate.

Act utilitarians hold that an action is right if it produces consequences better than those of all the available alternatives.[14] As expressed by Mill, "actions are right in proportion as they tend to promote happiness, wrong as they tend to produce the reverse of happiness".[15] The act utilitarian is concerned with the consequences for everyone involved, not solely with the consequences for the actor. The effects for all the persons affected by the decision are relevant. Indeed the act utilitarian considers his own interests and desires as on an equal footing with those of the other persons affected. In other words, the actor's interests receive no special weight because they are *his*. This notion is captured by Bentham's formula "everybody to count for one, nobody for more than one".

Deciding which set of anticipated consequences is better than another requires a standard of evaluation. There is wide variation among consequentialists as to the appropriate standard. Some argue that happiness is to be maximized; others believe that maximization of peoples' welfare is paramount. Further disagreement exists as to how "welfare" should be understood—as satisfaction of desires, preferences, or interests. Conceivably, though, an act utilitarian approach could be linked with the promotion of almost any value.

It is noteworthy that most accounts of act utilitarianism assume that the very general moral principles of conduct with which most of us were brought up are of no real importance, and that it is perfectly conceivable that we might operate exclusively on a case by case basis in evaluating consequences.[16] The moral principles of the act utilitarian are very specific ones tailored to the circumstances of a particular choice. For this reason, act utilitarians are frequently regarded as without principles at all by those who believe that principles, by definition, are of wide generality (e.g., "Always tell the truth").

It should also be noted that act utilitarians regard the morality of an action as distinct from and independent of the morality of the actor. Provided that the consequences of an action are better than those of any available alternative, the action is right. The motives and attitudes of the agent are irrelevant to the moral value of the action except insofar as they affect its consequences. Moreover, according to act utilitarianism one can do the right thing by accident—if as a result of fortuitous events the consequences turn out better than could have been anticipated.

4 *What are the consequences of general adherence to the general rule upon which you propose to act?*

Another form of consequentialism associated with nineteenth-century British philosophy but still widely discussed today is rule utilitarianism. John Stuart Mill and Henry Sidgwick[17] are probably the best-known exponents of rule utilitarianism, although, as noted earlier, Mill is regarded by some as an act utilitarian.

As the name indicates, rule utilitarians believe that general rules, as opposed to highly specific rules, have a central function in morality. In contrast to act utilitarians, rule utilitarians believe that the consequences of following general rules or principles are paramount—not the consequences of individual actions. Accordingly, rule utilitarians are concerned with determining which general rules or principles would, if widely accepted, have best consequences, and with applying those rules in particular cases.

The different orientations of the act and rule utilitarian result in different views of the process of making moral decisions. Act utilitarians believe that making moral decisions is a matter of anticipating the likely consequences of the available alternative actions, and selecting the action most likely to have best results, taking into account the interests of all those concerned. Rule utilitarians tend to rely on general rules which have survived utilitarian scrutiny as a reference point for making moral decisions. Typically, rule utilitarians find that many conventional moral rules are justifiable on utilitarian grounds and thus provide sound guidance in the ordinary case.[18] Thus, for instance, the rule utilitarian rarely needs to decide whether to tell the truth by considering the various alternatives to doing so. Since the general principle of truth-telling has a sound rule utilitarian basis, one simply follows the rule in practice. Theoretically, it would appear that the act utilitarian is required to do a utilitarian analysis of every particular instance where lying is a possibility.

The rule utilitarian approach of following justifiable general rules breaks down when those rules conflict or when a situation falls outside their scope. In such situations two alternative approaches are possible. Act utilitarian reasoning may be applied directly, or a new general rule may be formulated. It is critical to notice again that act utilitarian reasoning is not unprincipled. Its principles, however, are of a very high degree of specificity. The principles of rule utilitarianism are, in contrast, usually relatively general.

One rationale behind the rule utilitarian preference for general, as distinct from specific, principles is seen in situations where cooperation is required to accomplish a desired result. For example, suppose that five people are riding in a car which stalls at the foot of a hill. In addition, suppose that all five passengers want to get the car up the hill and that at least four people are required physically to move the car. Under these circumstances the general rule "Everybody push" is likely to be the only effective rule.[19] If each potential pusher applies act utilitarian reasoning to his choice between pushing and not pushing, it could well work out that not enough people would push. More than one person might in isolation determine that he is not required to push under a more specific principle excluding, say, the tired, the sleepy, the hungry, or the frail. Of course, this example is contrived. The group is so small that no one would in fact be deciding what to do in isolation. Someone who felt his non-participation was justifiable could present his case to the group for consideration. In larger groups, however, such interaction may be impossible, and strict adherence to the general rule might be the most feasible way of achieving the coordination necessary for the desired result.

Rule utilitarians have differing approaches to evaluating the moral worth of individual actions. Some rule utilitarians judge an action's moral value on the basis of its actual consequences and treat general principles simply as guides to what is probably right. Other rule utilitarians regard an action as right if it conforms to a justifiable general rule, regardless of the actual consequences of that action. In either case, the critical issue from a practical point of view is identifying and following the appropriate general rule.

5 *How would a person of character behave in your situation?*

All the preceding approaches to ethical decision-making emphasize the moment of decision and the choice of a course of action to satisfy the immediate situation. A somewhat different approach, which was highly developed by **Aristotle** in the *Nichomachean Ethics* and which has received relatively little attention from contemporary thinkers, focuses instead on the virtues, certain desirable character traits or dispositions of the actor. Aristotle divided the virtues into two categories: the intellectual virtues, such as prudence, understanding, and knowledge of how to achieve one's goals; and the moral virtues, such as courage, truthfulness, temperance, and friendliness.

The emphasis on character draws attention to the importance of *how* we act, as well as *what* we do. Aristotle believed that virtuous action proceeds from the right motive, in the right way, and at the right time. Thus, neither a grudging donation to charity nor a true statement made to inflict harm is virtuous. Neither fulfills all the conditions of virtuous action despite the fact that both conform to conventional rules of moral conduct.

Aristotle believed that individuals can cultivate desirable character traits by habitually acting as someone who genuinely has the character traits would act. Thus, one can become courageous in the full sense—that is, with the right attitudes and motives—by doing courageous acts. For Aristotle, at least part of the point of acting courageously, or in accordance with any other virtue, is to cultivate that virtue in oneself. Aristotle did not try to give reasons for trying to become virtuous, but he did believe that virtuous actions are in themselves satisfying.

Considering particular ethical issues from the point of view of the character traits involved may not provide much guidance for someone who lacks a developed conception of the virtues, comparable in fullness to that of Aristotle. After all, even if one wants to act courageously, the difficult part of some choices is deciding which action would in the circumstances be more courageous. To make that decision, one needs a conception of courage. Nevertheless, one can think of people whose lives and actions exemplify certain valuable character traits, and when in difficulty it may be fruitful to reflect on what that person of wisdom, of integrity, or of courage would do in the situation one faces.

In addition, focusing on the character traits which created a situation necessitating moral choice can lead to long-term solutions. Analyzing the likely consequences of the available alternative courses of action may lead to a right decision under the circumstances, but an understanding of how to avoid the necessity of making some difficult decisions can come from understanding the circumstances, including the behavior and character traits, that gave rise to the situation.

Not all of the test questions suggested by these theories will be appropriate for every ethical decision, and some ethical decisions may require formulation of new test questions. However, these questions may provide a framework for analyzing some of the recurrent types of ethical choices.

Notes

1 E.g., Peter Singer, *Practical Ethics*, N.Y.: Cambridge Univ. Press, 1979, p. 1.

2 Joel J. Kupperman, *The Foundations of Morality*, Boston: George Allen & Unwin, 1983, p. 12.

3 Ethics Resource Center, a project of American Viewpoint, Inc., *Common Sense and Everyday Ethics*, Washington, D.C., 1980, p. 16.

4 R. M. Hare, *The Language of Morals*, N.Y.: Oxford Univ. Press, 1964, p. v.

5 This observation invites speculation: Why is it that equally hard cases do not reduce scientists or financial experts to despair about the possibility of scientific reasoning or financially sound decisions?

6 Immanuel Kant, *Fundamental Principles of the Metaphysic of Ethics*, trans. by Thomas Kingsmill Abbott, 10th ed., London: Longmans, Green and Co. Ltd, 1969, p. 21.

7 *Id.* at 22–23.

8 How, for instance, should the principle of a proposed action be formulated? How should the concept of a "universal law" be understood?

9 R. M. Hare, *The Language of Morals*, New York: Oxford Univ. Press, 1952.

10 R. M. Hare, *Moral Thinking*, Oxford: Clarendon Press, 1981, esp. Ch. 3.

11 *Id.* at 42.

12 John Rawls, *A Theory of Justice*, Cambridge, Mass.: Belknap Press, 1971, pp. 136–137.

13 Rawls concludes that the conception of justice that would be chosen would reflect the idea that all primary social goods—liberty and opportunity of income and wealth, and the basis of self-respect—would be distributed equally unless unequal distribution would be to the advantage of the least favored.

14 An alternative version holds that an action is right if it is *likely* to produce consequences better than those of all the available alternatives.

15 J. S. Mill, *Utilitarianism*, as found in *Essential Works of John Stuart Mill*, ed. Max Lerner, New York: Bantam Books, 1971, p. 194.

16 E.g., J. J. C. Smart, "An Outline of a System of Utilitarian Ethics", in *Utilitarianism For and Against*, J. J. C. Smart and Bernard Williams, Cambridge: Cambridge Univ. Press, 1973.

17 Henry Sidgwick, *The Methods of Ethics*, republication of 7th edition, New York: Dover Publications, Inc., 1966.

18 E.g., G. E. Moore, *Principia Ethica*, Cambridge: Cambridge University Press, 1903, Ch. V.

19 This example is borrowed from David Lyons, *Forms and Limits of Utilitarianism*, Oxford: Clarendon Press, 1965.

CASE STUDY

Maya is the director of admissions for a large public university. The state legislature has significantly reduced the funding allocated for the university, so they increasingly rely on private donations to maintain their high-quality education and provide scholarships. She has come to the end of the admissions cycle and there are only a handful of decisions left to make. Two of the students have nearly identical records: same GPA and test scores, similar extracurricular activities, and even same declared major. There is just one major difference: one of the students is the son of a wealthy businessman, who will likely give a significant amount of money to the university if his son is admitted; the other student is from a middle-class family that would not be able to make that type of contribution. There is an absolute cap on admissions, so she can only accept one of the students. Maya isn't sure what to do. On the one hand, she doesn't think that a student should receive an advantage because their parents could donate money to the university. On the other hand, she knows how much good that money could do for other students in the university, particularly for scholarships for students who could not otherwise afford to attend. What should she do? What ethical dimensions does she need to consider?

CHAPTER 4

Toward an Ethics

SEE WHERE YOU STAND: 60 SECOND ETHICAL DILEMMA

Imagine that you are in the following situation and have one minute to make a decision about the most ethical course of action:

You have just started working in a city's economic development office after finishing your MPA degree. Part of your job is to make recommendations about what projects should or should not be supported. The elected mayor walks into your office and says, "Jane, here is the go/no-go list. The people and companies on the go list are political supporters and should be given preferential treatment. The people and companies on the no-go list supported my rival and should have to jump through extra hoops." You are an at-will employee and he is your boss, so you don't want to get fired, but you aren't sure this is ethical. What do you do?

INTRODUCTION TO CHAPTER

In this chapter, the author addresses the ethical dimensions of building a wall in general and, more specifically, on the border between the United States and Mexico. Although this author focuses on the 2006 debate, it is just as relevant to contemporary discussions about what a potential wall should look like between the United States and Mexico, and more broadly, how we should be imagining borders and crafting immigration policy. What is the wall supposed to accomplish? These questions are often thought of as political, but as the author notes, they have important ethical consequences. If we put on our "veil of ignorance" advocated by John Rawls in the last chapter, would we look at the wall differently than we do as people living in the United States? Remember that the wall is also a metaphor for us to understand how we decide whether or not something is "good" or "bad". How do we decide if a wall (or anything else) is ethically acceptable? What are the questions we have to ask to make that determination? As you read this chapter, try to consider the very different perspectives that people may have on each side of a wall and how that may change to what extent they view a particular wall as ethical or unethical. Although the case study at the end of this chapter doesn't deal with an actual wall, it is designed to help you understand how challenging it can be to put on your "veil of ignorance" and be impartial when you may be personally affected by the outcome of a decision.

READING 3

Toward an Ethics

By Thomas Oles

In the summer of 2006, as the political debate over the construction of a fence along the border with Mexico was reaching its height, the editors of the *New York Times* solicited from prominent designers in the United States and Mexico proposals for a "national wall." The editors were assuming—correctly, as it turned out—that the border fence would be built, and that it was important to begin a discussion about the form it would take. They provided no instructions other than to think in new ways about how a wall dividing two countries might look and perform, with a view toward crafting "solutions that defy ugly problems [and] create appeal where there might be none."[1]

Some of the designers the *Times* approached refused to participate, one noting that design of walls was best left to "security and engineers." Others alluded to their personal ambivalence about the exercise. Among these was Enrique Norten, an architect from Mexico City who proposed a system of "infrastructure and connectivity that would allow our two countries to get closer." Norten's drawing showed multiple elevated highways spanning the national boundary. Los Angeles–based designer Eric Owen Moss suggested a giant linear earthwork covered with illuminated glass tubes that would "give [the boundary] a prominence over a distance." And architect Antoine Predock proposed a rampart of "tilted dirt [that] would be pushed into place by Mexican day laborers" and vanish like a mirage in the desert heat.

But perhaps the most provocative proposal was submitted by landscape architect James Corner. Rather than try to disguise the "fortified condition" of the boundary, Corner suggested that the border fence should take on "all the accoutrements of power and fortification and surveillance" that the term "national wall" implied. His drawing of this fortification—a massive sloping wall of mirrored glass—resembled a Renaissance bulwark more than a boundary between two modern states. But sheer mass was not all there was to Corner's proposal. He also suggested "turn[ing] the whole thing around to see if this new structure could have a benevolent and positive aspect." The wall not only would mark the meeting of two nations but would become a "solar power energy production line" for the United States and Mexico, as well as an entrepôt for goods traveling back and forth across the border. Closer inspection revealed ranks of long-haul trucks at the wall's base and photovoltaic panels arrayed along its surface.

Corner's design attempted to recover aspects of walls that were almost entirely lost in the debate over the border fence, which focused only on its capacity to separate the United States and Mexico. The new boundary he envisioned called into question the very idea of discrete nations in an age of international flows of people, goods, and energy. The wall would be a site of exchange in the form of commercial activity, nurture in the form of energy production, and dwelling in the sense that such a monumental installation, like Hadrian's Wall and the Great Wall of China before it, could not be maintained without a permanent human presence. The wall was not a fortification but an **ecology**. Though its form seemed to suggest the dominance and impregnability of a powerful nation, its prime function was to stage human congress at, and across, the border. Corner's design used a symbol of sovereignty to challenge the idea of sovereignty itself.[2]

The Limits of Property

Among the changes in almost every aspect of human thought that mark the shift to modernity, perhaps none is more significant than the notion of ***natural right***. In the seventeenth and eighteenth centuries, sovereignty ceased to be seen as a matter of arbitrary power and began to be conceived as the birthright of all people. The text most closely associated with this idea of original sovereignty is Locke's *Second Treatise on Government*. But Locke did not stop with the notion that people were their own sovereigns. In one of the fateful elisions of modern times, the *Second Treatise* also posited a necessary and inevitable relation between sovereignty over the body and the sovereignty over land and objects called ***property***. Because it represented the mixing of the labor of one's body with the common, property, too, was a natural right, as inalienable as the right to the body.

Many people continue to think of property in Lockean terms, as a clear and incontestable right. Yet Locke himself recognized that absolute rights of property were not workable in any real polity. Since all people have, in theory at least, equal rights to enclose parts of the common, they create civil government to balance these rights so that the rights of one do not curtail those of another. Even in Locke there is no such thing as ***absolute* sovereignty** of property; instead, the sovereignty of one person is limited by that of others through political agreement.

This notion has been expanded by recent scholars of property, who have challenged Locke's assumptions about its origins. They argue that property is not a single inalienable "right" at all, but rather a "bundle of rights" that are constantly being taken away, curtailed, or renegotiated in the context of larger political and social goals. As political scientist John Meyer has written, property is "a disaggregable and changeable collection rather than a unitary and near-sovereign object."[3] Lawyer Carol Rose calls property a "kind of speech, with the audience composed of all others who might be interested in claiming the object in question."[4] Urban planning scholar Harvey Jacobs has noted that notions of ownership in relation to land parcels or "sites" have "always been issues of intense social contention."[5] And in a similar vein, legal scholar Eric Freyfogle, discussing property rights in the United States, argues that claims of the inviolability of property "rest upon a poor understanding of how the law has defined landowner rights over the course of America's history.... Private property is made possible by law, police, and courts: it is a social institution in which public and private are necessarily joined."[6] In other words, there is no inalienable right to property that precedes law, because it is through law, custom, and communication that property comes into existence.[7] Property is the product not of naturally given sovereignty, but of politics.

This understanding of property has clear implications for the disposition of the physical environment. Writing half a century after Locke, Jean-Jacques Rousseau lamented the primal act of enclosure that created property:

> The first person who, having fenced off a plot of ground, took it into his head to say this is mine and found people simple enough to believe him, was the true founder of civil society. What crimes, wars, murders, what miseries and horrors would the human race have been spared by someone who, uprooting the stakes or filling in the ditch, had shouted to his fellow-men: Beware of listening to this impostor; you are lost if you forget that the fruits belong to all and the earth to no one![8]

As in Locke, here the boundary of an enclosure expresses the claim to sovereignty over territory. But unlike Locke's position, it in no sense embodies a "natural right." On the contrary, in Rousseau's vision the act of making a physical boundary to establish property could be, and ought to be, *contested.*

Such contestation is all around when one begins to look for it. This is perhaps easiest to see in the case of boundaries of national, rather than individual, sovereignty. The 700-mile border fence of the United States, for example, was completed only after years of litigation and political debate. But one need look no further than the fences and walls in the everyday landscape to see how boundaries are continually constrained by politics. Communities throughout history have adopted standards and regulations for the shape, size, and location of boundaries, from the fencing rules of the medieval open-field village, to the fencing bans of nineteenth-century suburbs, to restrictions on the material composition of walls, fences, and hedges in many cities and towns today. The "right" to mark a parcel with a high hedge, a gated community with a wall, or indeed a country with eighteen-foot-high corrugated steel panels may appear absolute in theory, but in fact this "right" is subject to ongoing curtailment in the interests of wider notions of the public good.

Regulation or deliberation prevents the construction of many bad walls, though by no means all. The problem that arises is one of scale and extent. Because the modern landscape is the result of land subdivision and alienation into privately controlled parcels, it teems with walls and fences of all shapes and sizes. Most of these walls result from countless small decisions by individuals and groups. It is not feasible in this context to deliberate *every* boundary politically. Yet the mere fact that a wall is not brought into the realm of public debate does not mean it is justified. A homeowners' association in a gated community may be within its rights to build a high fence between the neighborhood and the city around it, but this does not mean that that boundary is defensible. Many actions that are *legal* within a given system of property relations may be *unjustifiable* when judged by other standards. The question is, What are those standards, and where do they come from?

More Questions to Ask a Wall

> Before I built a wall I'd ask to know
> What I was walling in or walling out,
> And to whom I was like to give offense.

These lines from "Mending Wall" represent a common and widely accepted standard for judging the goodness or badness of a given wall. No wall that has been made without asking this question, the poem suggests, can be considered justifiable. It is not that walls should not wall people in or out, for they do this by their nature, but that they must do so in a way that consciously responds to the particular situations in which they arise.

The central message of "Mending Wall" is fundamentally *ethical*. Derived from the Greek ***ethos***, "habit" or "custom," ethics is concerned not with the truth or falseness of given propositions about the world, but with the desirability of particular actions. In Aristotle's terms, ethics is that "practical wisdom" people use in order to know what constitutes good action in a given situation.[9] It is both a guide for actions that have not yet occurred—means—and a standard for judging the results—ends. Ethics is anything but abstract; it is grounded in solid things and real behavior and is practical in nature and object. In the words of philosopher Martha Nussbaum, it is a form of "complex responsiveness to the salient features of one's concrete situation."[10]

In the philosophy of both Plato and Aristotle, the primary device of any ethics is the question. It is through relentless questioning that one arrives at good action. Frost, scholar of the classics that he was, knew this. His narrator does not attempt to determine whether the wall should exist based on some abstract, universal criterion or a rational calculus about whether walls *in general* are good or bad. Such a determination, as Frost's own comments on his poem suggest, is impossible. Rather, the narrator asks, Why *this* wall when there are no cows? What purpose does *this* wall serve? Why does *this* wall make good neighbors? The ethics of the poem lies not in the answers to these questions (finally, as in any poem, there is no one answer) but in the questions themselves. The ethical difference between the two men in the poem is that the narrator asks them while his neighbor does not.

Many people who make walls today are too much like Frost's neighbor and not enough like his narrator. They are accustomed to thinking about walls within the confines of ideas about property and sovereignty that are little more than three centuries old as though these ideas were somehow "natural." Boundaries have been made by people for millennia, but the assumptions about their function and meaning have become so constricted that to build them without questioning virtually guarantees that they will act as expressions of these ideas. Like the neighbor whose unthinking dictum about good fences remains the most quoted part of "Mending Wall," people all too often engage in automatic thinking when they set about marking a boundary.

Automatic thinking is exactly what an ethics of enclosure resists. It asks questions rather than repeating proverbs. But as "Mending Wall" also shows, it is not enough merely to ask the right questions. One must pose these questions again and again, adapting them to each new situation where a wall or fence is built and fashioning new questions when the old ones no longer offer guidance. An ethics of enclosure does not end, then, with the questions of "Mending Wall." It only begins there.

Question 1. Should There Be a Wall?

This is perhaps the most fundamental question one might ask about any wall anywhere, yet it is asked far less often than it should be. It is the question that lies at the heart of "Mending Wall": Frost's narrator wants to know whether the wall should be there at all when it no longer fulfills its original function. The disappearance of that original benefit opens the possibility that the two men should allow the wall to disintegrate into nonexistence.

In some of the cases discussed in these pages, this question seems to yield a very clear answer. It is certainly possible to make an argument against the United States border fence or the Israeli "seam line obstacle" on grounds of utility: they damage political relationships, complicate travel, and increase the costs of trade. But it is equally possible to reject these walls on purely ethical grounds. One might plausibly argue that walls grounded in such a disparity of power between the people who build them and the people who experience them are simply unacceptable, whatever the details of their form, extent, or duration. This radical position shuns cost-benefit thinking and submits that certain walls in the world simply should not exist. In many cases this ethical stance can be heard in the political debates surrounding a particular wall. During the debate over the United States border fence, for example, a number of senators asked their colleagues to consider whether, on building a given wall in a given situation, a person or group is prepared to accept the possibility of a world in which others build similar walls.

If the answer to this question is no, then the wall, regardless of the particular circumstances of its construction, is ethically unjustifiable.

The problem is that most of the time such clear ethical sanction is not possible. This is particularly true for most walls and fences in the urban landscape, or the boundaries of parcels rather than nations. It is indisputable that the walls and fences of gated communities degrade many urban environments, setting up an unequal relationship between people inside, who claim the right to determine the shape of that boundary, and people outside, whose lives are affected and sometimes disrupted by it. And yet it does not follow from these statements that every gated community wall is ethically unacceptable, if for no other reason than that most people likely would wish to preserve their ability to construct such walls if it were in their interest to do so. One reason it is easier to condemn national walls on ethical grounds is that their benefits, if any, are remote and unseen, while their costs are obvious and high. It is much easier to imagine the benefits that might redound from a fence built around one's own house or garden.

In most cases, then, it is not possible, or even desirable, to exclude a wall or fence on ethical grounds simply because it marks territory. But this does not mean these cases should not be subject to other forms of ethical speculation. Rather, the question whether a given wall should *exist* must yield to a more nuanced set of questions about how it *performs*. Unlike the position that a wall should not exist, such an approach implies weighing up costs and benefits: disruption to social and ecological relationships against new forms of interaction the wall might foster. And in some cases it may even mean making ethical distinctions among walls whose existence one does not condone.

Question 2. Is the Wall Contestable?

In *Discipline and Punish*, a wide-ranging history of the modern prison, Michel Foucault argued that power in the modern era has increasingly taken forms that are invisible, elusive, and insidious. Foucault connected this change to the emergence of "panopticism": "In order to be exercised ... power had to be given the instrument of permanent, exhaustive, omnipresent surveillance, capable of making all visible, as long as it could itself remain invisible. It had to be like a faceless gaze that transformed the whole social body into a field of perception."[11]

The notion that there is an inverse relation between degrees of power and degrees of visibility is important when considering the ethical justifiability of a given wall. As the continued aversion to walls among political progressives suggests, there is a widespread tendency to equate absence of physical boundaries with openness and freedom. Yet in the modern era, lightness and invisibility have often been the handmaidens of power. In enclosure-era England, the concealment of boundaries using the device of the ha-ha naturalized a contingent set of property relations. In the American West, the capacity of barbed wire to disappear made it an ideal instrument of territorial control. And the aptly named Israeli Ministry of Defense emphasizes that the separation barrier is a "fence" rather than a "wall," part of a public relations strategy designed to make the barrier seem tenuous and impermanent. The most effective wall is, more often than not, the one that cannot be seen at all.

Ironically, then, real walls are often more contestable than their invisible counterparts. A sheer concrete wall like that of Berlin or Jerusalem is a clear and unambiguous statement of an unequal power relationship. But it is also exceedingly vulnerable to public opposition. Walls, quite simply, are easy targets. They can be painted on, things can be thrown against them, they provide instantly recognizable spaces for meeting and protesting, and as Artists Without Walls discovered, they are an ideal surface for projecting all manner of images. For this reason the sections of the separation barrier that are solid concrete, primarily in Jerusalem, have been the focus of political protest even though the wall is just one, and arguably not the most disruptive, part of an elaborate system of territorial control. The same was true in Berlin, where the concrete portion of the fortifications that imprisoned the western half of the city served as a touchstone for political resistance and artistic expression.

These two cases bring up another aspect of contestability: the lateral extent of the area on either side of the wall. A wall is contestable only to the degree that people are permitted to approach and physically interact with it. This is often as important in determining its contestability as the character of the wall itself. All "no-man's-lands," demilitarized zones, and "killing grounds" are enemies of contestation. Protesting the "seam line obstacle" outside Jerusalem is effectively impossible because of the system of trace roads and motion-sensing guns along it. The same can be observed with the United States border fence, where contestation is possible only on the Mexican side, the American side having been turned into a semi-militarized zone patrolled by border agents and now automated drones.[12] These are just two examples of a centuries-old practice that began in the Renaissance, when the sheer urban curtain walls of the Middle Ages were replaced by increasingly elaborate and extensive systems of fortification in response to the development of cannons, a transition that imposed "a dreadful social burden upon the protected population" because of their inflexibility and cost.[13] This essential change restricted not only the mutability of the wall, but also how much it could stage other forms of human interaction.

Contestability is best thought of, then, as a continuum along which various kinds of walls and fences at different scales can be arranged. In assessing this continuum, physical characteristics do not always correspond in clear and simple ways to degrees of justifiability, and transparency does not always equal benignity. It may often turn out that the most contestable parts of a wall are those that at first appear most ruthless. Determining a wall's justifiability based on its contestability will therefore often involve making uncomfortable distinctions among walls one views as unethical. It is possible to compare two equally misplaced walls—two walls that, according to the first question above, should not exist—and *still* determine that the form of one is more open to protest, and hence more ethically justifiable, than the form of the other. In other words, it is possible to construct an ethics in which the justifiability of a given wall can be measured by how far it reveals and makes explicit the particular forms of social and political control it enforces, and how far it offers a target to those who would resist that control.

Question 3. Does the Wall Foster Exchange?

No wall is impermeable, no matter how solid it may appear. Like the walls of cells, every wall in the landscape is a filter rather than a barrier. Every wall has apertures of various sizes, allowing certain things to pass and blocking the passage of others, in either direction. The difference between a cell wall and a wall in the landscape is that with the latter it is often people who control that passage. National governments set the location and hours of manned checkpoints along a border; developers decide on the location and number of gates in a fence around a planned unit development; owners choose where to place gaps in a hedge in an urban neighborhood or a rural field.

Walls can therefore help or hinder exchange, but they can never stop it entirely. The ethical question is therefore one of porosity, of the extent and type of exchange the wall allows or encourages. Such exchange must respond to the particular context in which the wall rises if it is to be deemed ethically justifiable. As with cell walls, too much porosity is not always a good in a landscape wall. For example, one reason many security forces prefer chain-link fences to concrete panels is that the former can be shot through and allow oversight of what is happening on the other side. This is a case where porosity actually *increases* sovereign control through a particular, and socially corrosive, form of exchange. By contrast, John Harbison's fence shows that a wall can be minimally permeable but still invite transactions between owner and passersby.

The term "exchange," then, is ethically neutral; it says nothing about the relative desirability of what is exchanged. This tension is highlighted by the national walls discussed here. James Corner's proposal emphasized exchange along the border in the form of trade and thus attempted to recover the vital role of walls as sites of cultural and economic interaction. The "placeless" form of this interaction in some ways suggested the universality of this impulse, freeing it from the particular conditions along the border and thus depoliticizing it. The same cannot be said of the border ceremony at Wagah, where exchange takes the form of sublimated violence; the messages sent back and forth are so particular, and so politically charged, that the experience can be disorienting for outsiders unfamiliar with the history of enmity between the two countries.

Despite their obvious differences, however, all the walls in these pages are unified by a single overarching characteristic: they are sites of intensive social production. As with the notion of contestability, one must inevitably make distinctions among particular kinds of social production when determining if a given wall is justifiable. The exchange of a "peace museum" or a demonstration using video cameras and drums is arguably more ethical than the exchange of a performance of violence. However, it is also possible to assert that any exchange, whatever form it takes, is almost always preferable to its absence. As American sociologist Lewis Coser suggested in the 1950s, in most cases, most of the time, social *conflict* is better than no *contact*.[14] Only in the most dramatic instances of violence, such as the sectarian conflict that exploded in Iraq in the years after the American invasion of 2003, might one argue that segregation is preferable to exchange.[15] It is thus necessary to construct a secondary continuum of ethical justifiability, one that considers, first, *whether* the wall fosters or prevents exchange and, second, the *kind* of exchange it stages. As with the Israeli "seam line obstacle," built in part to prevent suicide attacks, making this determination will often involve arbitrating the rights of those who build the wall and the rights of those whose lives and livelihoods are forever changed by it.

For the most part, however, the persistence of rituals along and across walls in the modern world illustrates how walls, even today, are not so much arbiters of social and political rights as "scenes for the drama of responsiveness, hospitality and responsibility."[16] In often unseen or unnoticed ways, walls and fences act as sites of all those small transactions that give depth and richness to life lived in common, particularly in urban environments. Considering the ethical justifiability of a given wall means considering how far it enables or forecloses such dramas. Along this continuum, the walls of John Harbison, Aspen Farms, and the *yardas* can be considered more "ethical" forms of enclosure. In each case, the exchange that unfolds along or near the wall is not incidental to other functions but is a central reason for the wall's existence. The owners of the wall, those who had a legal right to construct it in virtually any way they chose, nevertheless thought carefully about the kinds of exchange they wanted to stage with their surroundings, whether by using simple materials in new ways or by designing exchange into the structure of the wall itself. Such consideration need not mean erasing boundaries altogether, but rather entails thinking about the ways a given wall works itself into the fabric of life around it and subjecting the public side of the wall to the same intent and care as is afforded the territory it marks. And this suggests perhaps the most important standard by which to judge a wall or fence: its relation to the ecology of the place where it rises.

Question 4. Does the Wall Support Ecology?

The word "ecology" derives from the Greek *oikos*, "house" or "home." It thus shares a root with "economy." Coined in the late nineteenth century, this word originally designated the study of the relationships of living organisms to one another and to their physical surroundings. More recently, however, the definition of the term has grown to encompass not just the study of those relationships, but the relationships themselves. As is now widely accepted and increasingly apparent, humans are just one part of ecology, enmeshed in a thick web of relationships with the biological and physical world. To damage one part of that web is to threaten the home of the whole. An essential ethical standard when judging a given wall is thus how much it strengthens or undermines that home.

The past two centuries have seen many walls disrupt social ecology, from hedges that deprived villagers of ancient rights of access and use in the parliamentary enclosure era, to barbed wire that obliterated the economy of the Plains Indians in the 1870s, to the United States border fence that cuts through cities, towns, and Indian nations today. These are well-known cases of a physical boundary's undermining complex relationships built up over centuries between people and the places they inhabit. But what is perhaps less known about these same cases is how they also compromised natural ecology. In the American West, barbed wire was instrumental in eliminating the bison; in England, parliamentary hedges included few plant species compared with their medieval predecessors; and the American border fence has seriously compromised the habitat of endangered animal species such as the ocelot and jaguarundi and has sliced in half nature reserves owned by the Audubon Society and Nature Conservancy that contain the last two remaining stands of sabal palms in the United States.[17]

In many cases this disruption of social and natural ecology is the result of walls that obey the arbitrary logic of parcel boundaries or the boundaries of nations. Yet evidence suggests that it is also possible to strengthen ecology even in the subdivided world that most people have inherited as part of their patrimony. It has been estimated that the hedge networks of Britain are as important as national parks in providing habitat for threatened species. Because they are exposed to the sun on both sides, hedges are "probably richer in woodland edge insects than are woods."[18] Large-scale hedge networks, it is increasingly being found, are essential corridors for the movement of animals across the landscape.[19] Hedges are also important for increasing a sense of collective identity and place among those who come in contact with them. Objects that mark parcel boundaries thus arguably support human and natural ecology at least as often as they compromise it.

Sometimes, however, strengthening ecology entails either ignoring or challenging legal boundaries. Such is the case with the Great Green Wall of the Sahara, which necessarily diverges from national borders in order to improve the ecology of an entire continent (and arguably the world). This example is striking because of its sheer ambition, but similar processes happen all the time in less dramatic ways, as when two landowners agree to divert a fence or wall around an old tree. Thinking about the relation between walls and ecology means questioning the invisible structure of legal parceling within which most people live and confronting the reality that the boundaries of parcels are economic and political fictions in ways that walls and fences are not. By constructing *Running Fence*, Christo and Jeanne-Claude called attention to the fundamentally arbitrary nature of legal boundaries in the modern world. But they did so in a way that created its own, albeit brief, social ecology—one that has remained in the memories of the people who experienced it three decades ago.

One way to think about this capacity of walls and fences to support the relationship between physical boundaries and natural and social ecology is the ecotone. According to landscape ecologist Richard Forman, an ecotone is "the overlap or transition zone between two plant or animal communities." Ecotones often occur along boundaries, which "exhibit distinctive characteristics unlike the adjacent ecosystems, and [may] thus be considered a system itself."[20] The physical boundary is not simply a membrane regulating passage between areas on either side, but a distinct and invaluable ecology in itself. An example of this in the natural world is the lee of a hedge, which is inherently favorable to particular birds and insects. But ecotones do not exist only in natural ecology. As the *faubourgs* of the Middle Ages and the Byker Wall show, walls also create new zones of social activity, fundamentally *distinct* in the people they house and the activities they stage.

Conceiving of walls as areas rather than as objects requires striking a critical balance between *width* and *porosity*. If a wall is to support ecology to the maximum extent, it needs to be thick enough to support the functions associated with that ecology but thin enough, and porous enough, to foster exchange between its two sides. The combination of these two aspects, ecology and exchange, adds up to nurture.

Question 5. Does the Wall Nurture?

Walls have always created the conditions for human societies to survive and thrive. The walls of Skara Brae, the earthen banks of Cornwall, the great wall of Uruk—all were central to creating and sustaining the distinct ecology where they arose, whether a Neolithic village, an Iron Age sheepherding culture, or the urban civilization of Sumer. For millennia, walls have provided nurture in the form of shelter from the environment, or even offered shelter within themselves, as the story of Rahab illustrates.

Little has done more to degrade the nurturing capacities of walls in the modern landscape than their close association with property rights. Walls continue to nurture, but the beneficiaries of such nurture are usually the individuals or groups that hold title to the land they enclose. In this context, a wider notion of nurture is needed in the way walls are built and judged. The cases discussed here show that such a wider notion is possible even within a highly parceled environment. Often this means returning to older forms of bounding, like the medieval hedge that bore edible fruits and provided many of the basic materials necessary to life. There is no reason such offerings cannot be made in the modern landscape, as the gardeners of Aspen Farms showed with their edible fence.

Yet fruits and vegetables were never more than an accessory benefit in West Philadelphia. The real nurture the fence provided was social and even spiritual. Such spiritual sustenance is no less a part of the story of walls than are power and dominance. From the temple walls of Ur and Uruk, to the walls that fused the living and the dead at Çatalhöyük, to the Western Wall, from which the "divine Presence" is said never to depart, walls have ever been sites of numinous experience. Nor are these cases relics of the ancient past. The Vietnam Veterans Memorial, for many, is holier than any cathedral, more nurturing than any shrine. There is no reason to think the walls and fences of a subdivided landscape cannot also begin to serve such functions, as the rich topography of religious images mounted in East Los Angeles lot fences demonstrates.

Nurture is thus another standard for determining the justifiability of a given wall. It makes it possible to say, for example, that a garden hedge composed of diverse plant species that offer their fruit to passersby is in some sense more ethical than a hedge made of hawthorn and nothing else. The key to recovering these nurturing aspects of walls, both social and spiritual, is considering how well they nurture not only people in the insides they mark, but also outsiders.

In short, it is no longer ethically sufficient, if it ever was, for a wall to nurture only those it encloses, protects, enfolds. Its benefits must extend to the larger society around it. John Harbison's fence and the walls of *yardas* show that, given ongoing attention, this is possible, even simple. The nurture a wall provides will always be closely related to the care put into its making. In other words: an ethics of enclosure comes down, ultimately, to craft.

Question 6. Is the Wall Craft?

At the center of ethics as Aristotle understood it was what he called *kalon*, a word that could mean "beautiful," "noble," or "fine." For Aristotle, *kalon* had to do with the making of good artifacts: artifacts from which nothing could be taken away and to which nothing further could be added without degrading their "virtue."[21] Aristotle saw such virtue—which extended to poetry, music, and drama—as very close to ethical virtue. A well-crafted artifact or a well-crafted project were by their very definition both ethical and *kalon*. *Kalon* was thus part of an ethical standard that Aristotle saw as applying to the making and shaping of any thing.

This Aristotelian notion of craft would come to inform much thinking about the nature of art in the Renaissance; Michelangelo is said to have claimed he created the *David* by subtracting material until the perfect essence of the statue emerged. Yet there is also something static, even lifeless, in this idea. Once a thing is *kalon*, the process of craft is complete; indeed, it *must* stop, for to pursue it further would be to degrade the "virtue" of the thing made. There is little room in this vision for the messiness, mistakes, and blind alleys of human life. In short, most people, for most of their lives, cannot hope to live up to Aristotle's standard.

But there is another way to think about craft, one that has less to do with the perfection of actions or objects and more to do with their making. Sociologist Richard Sennett has described this kind of craft as "pride in one's work." In this notion of craft, the important things are circumspection, learning, reflexivity, and increasing skill. Slowness is an important corollary of this notion, since all these things, by definition, take time: "Craftsmen take pride most in skills that mature. This is why simple imitation is not a sustaining satisfaction; the skill has to evolve. The slowness of craft time serves as a source of satisfaction; practice beds in, making the skill one's own. Slow craft time also enables the world of reflection and imagination—which the push for quick results cannot."[22]

Both these visions of craft suggest what is wrong with the walls of the modern landscape. It is certainly true that in the first sense many walls fail to meet an Aristotelian standard of *kalon*. The United States border fence is in many places little more than a collection of refuse and military surplus arranged along the national boundary, and many of the walls of the urban landscape are not much better. Fences like John Harbison's stand out precisely because they are the products of careful design and craftsmanship. By contrast, most of the walls now built are mass-produced objects that fundamentally resemble each other all over the world.

But it is in the second sense of craft, as ongoing making, that the walls and fences of the modern landscape fail most seriously. Walls are now easily bought, hastily built, and quickly ignored. Such speed is the handmaid of forgetfulness, the nemesis of ethical speculation. Frost was able to think about the ethical justifiability of the wall on the edge of his field precisely because that wall *was never finished*. The very act of lifting and setting stones year after year occasioned and provided the temporal and physical space for the questioning any ethics is ultimately based on. Were the stone wall transformed into a low-maintenance chain-link fence, such questioning would likely cease.

This is why craft, in some sense, is the key to all the other ethical standards here. For it is through the very process of making and shaping actual walls that an ethics of enclosure is likely to emerge. Carefully crafted walls are prone to be contestable, since a long course of making is more likely than a short one to be public and manifest. The slowness that craft demands also fosters exchange between the builder of the wall and his surroundings, as I discovered with my own living fence. Such slowness also is likely to yield results that strengthen rather than undermine social and natural ecology. And finally, lengthy crafting makes it more probable that a given wall will nurture the particular place where it is built and the people who dwell there.

This is not a romantic vision of craft. It is a call to recover the process of ethical speculation through making things. The crucial point is that craft takes time. One must come back to the wall again and again, refining, improving, tearing down, and rebuilding. One must never take walls as finished objects; they should be seen as processes. Parcel by parcel, territory by territory, recovering the wall as craft will mean rethinking the boundary as a stage for ethical reflection, a site no longer of forgetfulness, but of care.

We are All Outsiders

These are not the only questions one could ask of a wall. They will not be answered the same way by all people. They cannot provide flawless guidance in every case, as Aristotle knew no ethics could. Like "Mending Wall," this book is only the beginning of an ethics that will always—can only—remain unfinished. The questions it asks will always invite more nuanced questions. For example, if a wall fosters exchange, it will be desirable also to ask about the nature of that exchange and to make judgments about its character. A wall that functions as a stage for a peaceful ritual that builds the relationship between two communities is more ethical, one might argue, than a staged confrontation such as the one at Wagah. But one might equally argue that such confrontation, in almost all cases, is itself preferable to a zone, like the DMZ of Korea, that divides people and actively suppresses ongoing exchange.

Answering these questions thus will not describe most walls as *absolutely* ethical or unethical. Instead, it will help to arrange walls—both walls that exist and walls that are planned or imagined—along a continuum of justifiability. Few walls will do all the things described in this book; others will do different ones at different times. But one might postulate that the more of these questions one can answer in the affirmative, the more justifiable a given wall may be said to be. The first question—Should the wall be there?—is actually a function of the other ethical questions asked here: one cannot answer yes to it and no to all the subsequent questions. Similarly, one cannot answer no to the first question and yes to all the others. But it is not enough to ask these questions only once. Like Frost's narrator, it is necessary to return to them again and again. A wall might be porous enough for its environment one year but need to be changed the next in response to new circumstances. Boundaries, like the landscape as a whole, are dynamic, always changing, constantly in flux. Walls must have built into them the possibility, the inevitability, of that change.

This book has focused largely on thinking in new ways about the walls many people encounter every day. Most of the walls in the modern landscape are walls of property; yet there are few standards available for judging the performance of those walls that go beyond what are seen as absolute rights associated with this particular, and relatively new, form of sovereignty. Inevitably, then, recovering the wall will involve detaching the discourse about walls in the landscape from the discourse about property. We need a new attitude toward walls that recognizes them as common property. By contrast, the "ownership model" of walls, in which a single uncontested individual or group retains the right to determine the shape and character of the boundary, must be abandoned. Material boundaries impinge on the public world; thus they, like landscapes as a whole, inevitably have a moral, as well as a political, dimension.[23] However, it will not be possible to legislate such a new attitude when the economy of land and property has been built up around the entrenched myth of sovereign rights. The only way this will happen is through actual *behavior*. It is not a matter of first changing notions of property, then having property practices follow. Rather, it is only through thinking and making real things that ideas of property as absolute sovereignty will themselves, in time, be changed.[24]

An ethics of enclosure can begin to guide this thinking and making. The legacy of its absence is a landscape of bad walls, not so much because they are immoral as because they have been built unthinkingly, automatically, murmuring the same incantations as Frost's neighbor. The questions here are necessary not because they are final or complete, then, but rather because they begin to provide a common standard for what every wall, wherever it is, should do. It is on such standards that the quality of the landscape as a whole, slowly but decisively, will rise or fall.

Perhaps the ultimate standard one might adopt when building or judging a wall comes down to this: a call for concern beyond it.[25] Such a standard is built on the simple principle that for much of their lives people are more often outsiders than insiders. The modern landscape is one where nearly every territory, nearly every piece of land abuts and affects others in enormously complex ways. Most of the walls people encounter in that landscape are keeping them out, controlling their experience, and restricting their movements rather than offering protection or nurture. An ethics of enclosure recognizes this. It says that, rather than not building walls at all, it is better to expand the scope of concern to the outside, in the walls we judge and the walls we build.

In many ways this vision is similar to what French philosopher Emmanuel Lévinas called "infinite responsibility," an open-ended moral obligation to extend generosity to an unknown other.[26] But one might also argue that Lévinas's vision is not workable in practice because it fails to recognize and value our legitimate allegiance to those people and places closest to us. It fails to acknowledge that while we might extend generosity to the outside, this is an intellectual exercise; our emotions remain forever tied to the inside, to the enclosure, to the protected realm within the wall.

A better philosophical model, then, is the "**veil of ignorance**" described by philosopher John Rawls. According to Rawls, when constituting a political community it is necessary that each person operate from the position that "no one knows his place in society, his class position or social status, nor does any one know his fortune in the distribution of natural assets and abilities, his intelligence, strength, and the like."[27] Rawls called this stance the "original position." Only when people think about political arrangements from the original position, he argued, would any lasting form of social justice be achieved.

It is possible to perform the same mental exercise when building or judging any wall. One must ask, always, "What would my view of this wall be were I in the least advantageous position with respect to it? What benefits would it still offer?" Answering this question means adopting the Socratic position of the outsider, the stranger from another land who tries to remove her own interest from the calculus of ethical justifiability. This is a simple idea, but like many simple ideas it will be hard to implement in practice. It requires a fundamental reconception of what walls should do and what walls are. It asks people to think of walls' capacity not to separate, but to bind, not to enforce sovereignty, but to stage exchange. It requires us to think of walls not as objects that mark difference and distinction, but as the very things that bind the landscape and the people who make it up, together.

Our original position may have been inside the wall looking out, but that position has shifted. In the modern landscape, we are all, for much of our lives, just outside the wall, strangers passing by, glimpsing a life unfolding inside. Thinking and making from that position is one sure way to build landscapes that are more justifiable and more just.

Notes

1 William L. Hamilton, "A Fence with More Beauty, Fewer Barbs," *New York Times*, June 18, 2006, sec. 4, 14.

2 All quotations in this section are cited in Hamilton, "Fence with More Beauty."

3 John Meyer, "The Concept of Private Property and the Limits of the Environmental Imagination," *Political Theory* 37, no. 1 (2009): 117.

4 Carol M. Rose, "Possession as the Origin of Property," *University of Chicago Law Review* 52 (Winter 1985): 79.

5 Harvey Jacobs, "Claiming the Site: Evolving Social-Legal Conceptions of Ownership and Property," in *Site Matters*, ed. Carol J. Burns (New York: Routledge, 2005), 19.

6 Eric T. Freyfogle, *The Land We Share: Private Property and the Common Good* (Washington, DC: Island Press, 2003), 2.

7 Jeremy Bentham expressed much the same idea: "Property and law are born together, and die together. Before laws were made there was no property; take away laws and property ceases." Bentham, *The Theory of Legislation*, chap. 8, cited in ibid., 4.

8 Jean-Jacques Rousseau, *A Discourse upon the Origin and the Foundation of the Inequality among Mankind*, pt. 2, cited in Freyfogle, *Land We Share*, 4.

9 Aristotle, *Nicomachean Ethics* 6.5, trans. David Ross (Oxford: Oxford University Press, 1980), 142–43.

10 Martha Nussbaum, *Love's Knowledge: Essays on Philosophy and Literature* (New York: Oxford University Press, 1990), 55.

11 Michel Foucault, *Discipline and Punish: The Birth of the Prison* (1977; repr., New York: Vintage Books, 1995), 214.

12 On the use of drones along the United States border with Mexico, see William Booth, "Keeping Watchful Eye on Border, but Staying Out of Sight," *Washington Post*, December 22, 2011, sec. A, 8.

13 Lewis Mumford, *The City in History* (New York: Harcourt, Brace and World), 358. More recently, W. G. Sebald wrote about this same transition in the novel *Austerlitz*: "It is amazing ... to see the persistence with which generations of masters of the art of military architecture, for all their undoubtedly outstanding gifts, clung to what we can easily see today was a fundamentally wrong-headed idea: the notion that by designing an ideal tracé with blunt bastions and ravelins projecting well beyond it, allowing the cannon of the fortress to cover the entire operational area outside the walls, you could make a city as secure as anything in the world can ever be." W. G. Sebald, *Austerlitz* (London: Penguin Books, 2002), 17.

14 See Lewis Coser, *The Functions of Social Conflict* (Glencoe, IL: Free Press, 1956).

15 This is precisely the argument made by the occupying American authorities, who ordered the construction, virtually overnight, of a concrete wall three miles long and twelve feet high—the "Great Wall of Adhamiya"—between the Sunni and Shia neighborhoods of Baghdad in 2007. See Ewen MacAskill, "Latest US Solution to Iraq's Civil War: A Three-Mile Wall," *Guardian*, April 21, 2007, Home, 1.

16 Clive Barnett, "Hospitality and the Acknowledgement of Otherness," *Progress in Human Geography* 29, no. 5 (2005): 16.

17 Dan Barry, "A Natural Treasure That May End Up without a Country," *New York Times*, April 7, 2008, sec. A, 14.

18 Ernest Pollard et al., *Hedges* (New York: Taplinger, 1974), 119.

19 Richard T. T. Forman, *Land Mosaics: The Ecology of Landscapes and Regions* (Cambridge: Cambridge University Press, 1995), 195.

20 Ibid., 85.

21 Aristotle, *Ethics* 2.6, 38.

22 Richard Sennett, *The Craftsman* (New Haven, CT: Yale University Press, 2008), 295.

23 Nicholas Blomley, *Unsettling the City: Urban Land and the Politics of Property* (New York: Routledge, 2004), 77.

24 Meyer, "Concept of Private Property," 113.

25 See David M. Smith, "How Far Should We Care? On the Spatial Scope of Beneficence," *Progress in Human Geography* 22, no. 1 (1998): 15–38.

26 See Emmanuel Lévinas, *Totality and Infinity: An Essay on Exteriority* (Pittsburgh, PA: Duquesne University Press, 1969).

27 John Rawls, *A Theory of Justice* (Cambridge, MA: Harvard University Press, 1971), 12.

CASE STUDY

Emily works as an attorney for an environmental agency, and a significant part of her job is reviewing the legality of potential regulations. One day she reviews a potential regulation that would significantly increase the gas mileage requirements for car manufacturers. She knows that the regulation would be within the agency's jurisdiction, but she also knows it will require significant modifications from car manufacturers. Her husband happens to be the CEO of a car manufacturing company, and when she gets home and he asks her how her day was, she isn't sure what to say. This information is not classified, but it is also not yet public. She knows that if she gives this information to her husband, his company will have more time to determine how to adjust their gas mileage specifications to meet the new requirements, which would benefit his company and, ultimately, their family. However, she also knows that she would be giving him information that other companies do not currently have access to. What should she do? Is it ethical for her to use this confidential information for a purpose that is not part of her official job duties?

PART III

ETHICS AND THE LAW

CHAPTER 5

When the Umpire Throws the Pitches

SEE WHERE YOU STAND: 60 SECOND ETHICAL DILEMMA

Imagine that you are in the following situation and have one minute to make a decision about the most ethical course of action:

You have just been appointed to lead a state agency, and your new position includes a monthly stipend for a car. Your assistant says that he knows a local car dealership that has prices within the state's requirements. As you walk out the door, your assistant mentions that the owner of the dealership is his childhood best friend. You pause, wondering whether or not it is ethical to procure your car from the dealership. You don't want to hurt your assistant's feelings, but you don't want it to appear that you are using state funds to do a personal favor. What do you do?

INTRODUCTION TO CHAPTER

How much involvement is too much? Does a person's intent for that involvement matter? Virtue ethics, for example, suggests that the individual's intent is critical for determining whether or not an action is ethical. This chapter explores the ethics of Supreme Court justices taking a more active role in the judicial process, particularly for making decisions about the kind of questions they think should be answered. Whether or not you agree with the Court's decisions, consider what the appropriate role of the Court should be. Do the justices' intentions for this more active approach (i.e., pursuing a personal agenda versus helping guide lawyers to the key constitutional issues) matter? Although the author of this chapter has a strong opinion on this shift in the Court's approach, reflect on whether or not you think this more active approach is ethical and whether or not their intentions are even relevant to an ethical discussion.

READING 4

When the Umpire Throws the Pitches

By Pamela S. Karlan

During his confirmation hearings, Chief Justice Roberts famously compared judges to umpires. The analogy was designed to convey an image of judicial modesty: judges, like umpires, play a "limited role," impartially applying rules made by others rather than serving as partisans for one team or another. And he assured the Senate that he would "remember that it's my job to call balls and strikes and not to pitch or bat."

Umpires leave the tactical choices to the teams. That kind of reserve led Alexander Hamilton, in *Federalist* No. 78, to describe the judiciary as the "least dangerous" branch of the government. It has "no direction either of the strength or of the wealth of the society; and can take no active resolution whatever," Hamilton wrote.

In recent terms, however, the Roberts Court has been taking a more assertive stance. Many observers have remarked upon the Court's decisions striking down important government policies ranging from federal campaign finance laws to local school boards' desegregation plans. Although the Court generally grants review to resolve conflicts among the lower courts, it has taken cases involving hot-button issues such as affirmative action even in the absence of disagreement.

A second form of assertiveness has been less noted: the Court is not simply deciding which cases to hear, but is also directing the parties to address issues the justices want to take up and reaching out to decide issues never addressed by the parties.

To be sure, the Court sometimes acts appropriately in raising issues the parties have chosen not to. The 2012 challenge to the individual mandate in the Affordable Health Care Act provides an example. Both the challengers and the federal government wanted the Court to decide the question immediately. But a federal statute (the

Anti-Injunction Act) bars courts from entertaining certain kinds of challenges to federal taxes before those taxes have actually been collected. So the justices properly directed the litigants to address whether they had the power to decide the case before the Act came into force. So too with the 2013 challenge to California's marriage restriction. Both the challengers and the private citizens who had sponsored the ballot initiative limiting marriage to opposite-sex couples were hoping for a definitive ruling from the Court on the constitutionality of marriage restrictions, but the Court properly held that that once the state had declined to appeal the trial court's ruling requiring marriage equality, no party had standing to seek further review.

At other times, however, the Court ranges far afield in forcing the parties to address issues they may deliberately have chosen to forgo. And the Roberts Court has shown a troubling tendency to use this tool to overturn precedent.

The most striking examples involve scheduling cases for re-argument so that the justices can consider issues the parties didn't originally press. Consider ***Citizens United v. Federal Election Commission*** (2010). A request for re-argument transformed the case from a narrow inquiry into a particular application of the McCain-Feingold campaign finance law into a high-stakes examination of *all* corporate political spending. The Court directed the parties to brief and argue about whether it should overrule its decision in *Austin v. Michigan Chamber of Commerce* (1990), which held that restrictions on campaign spending could be justified by the government's interest in preventing "the corrosive and distorting effects of immense aggregations of wealth that are accumulated with the help of the corporate form and that have little or no correlation to the public's support for the corporation's political ideas." It then issued a bitterly divided 5–4 decision freeing all corporations and unions to use general-treasury funds for any kind of election-related speech and setting the stage for the rise of super PACs. (I discuss the case in more detail earlier, particularly in Chapter 8.)

In the 2012 term, the Court ordered re-argument in another case involving corporate conduct, ***Kiobel v. Royal Dutch Petroleum Co.*** The plaintiffs in *Kiobel*, former residents of the Ogoni region of Nigeria, claimed that the defendants—including the Shell oil company—provided logistical and financial support to government security forces that engaged in a series of human rights abuses, including extrajudicial killing and torture. The case was brought in the United States under the Alien Tort Statute (ATS), which gives federal district courts jurisdiction over tort claims by aliens for "violation[s] of the law of nations." The ATS was enacted by the first Congress in 1789 and, after lying dormant for the next two centuries, was resurrected in *Filártiga v. Peña-Irala* (1980) to permit foreign victims of particularly egregious and universally condemned human rights abuses to sue the perpetrators in U.S. courts.

The question on which the Supreme Court initially granted review—the question raised by the parties before it—was whether corporations can be sued under the ATS or whether it permits lawsuits only against natural persons. The answer to that question was potentially quite important. The individual corporate employees involved in human rights violations might not themselves be subject to the jurisdiction of U.S. courts, which can adjudicate claims only against defendants who have had sufficient contacts with the United States. So a foreign employee who commits a wrongful act overseas may not be subject to suit here. And even when foreign individuals can be sued in the United States, it may be hard to collect on any judgment. By contrast, it's relatively easy to sue a multinational corporation that also does business domestically, and the company will have assets to satisfy a judgment. (One might be forgiven, in light of the Court's decision in *Citizens United*, for seeing something ironic about the argument that corporations are sufficiently like persons to be entitled to constitutional speech protections while being sufficiently different to avoid liability for human rights violations.)

But the Court upped the ante even further with its order for re-argument. A week after it heard oral argument in the original case, the Court told the parties to file new briefs addressing whether the Alien Tort Statute allows U.S. courts to hear cases "for violations of the law of nations occurring within the territory of a sovereign other than the United States." That order raised the possibility that the Court, beyond shielding foreign corporations from being sued in U.S. courts, would hold that under the ATS *no one* can be sued for human rights violations that occur outside the United States unless they occur on the high seas or in some no man's land. In short, the Court's rewritten question asked whether plaintiffs in *Kiobel* and similar cases can use the ATS to sue torturers who committed their violations on dry land, even if the plaintiffs—as in *Kiobel* itself—or the defendants are now living in the United States. (Disclosure: In *Kiobel*, I submitted amicus briefs on behalf of more than a dozen individual plaintiffs as well as a nonprofit public interest law firm that had brought suits under the ATS against individual human rights violators who had subsequently moved to the United States and were later sued here.)

Chief Justice Roberts's opinion for the Court answered that question by holding that the "presumption against extraterritorial application" governed suits under the ATS. In other words, only if the violation of international law has occurred within the United States or on the high seas will U.S. courts have the power to hear a plaintiff's case. If the violation occurred in another nation's territory, then the ATS provides no basis for U.S. courts to hear the plaintiff's case. In Kiobel's case, Chief Justice Roberts found that "all the relevant conduct took place outside the United States," and thus the presumption against extraterritorial application prevented suit. But the chief justice cautioned that even "where the claims touch and concern the territory of the United States"—as they might when a U.S.-based corporation makes decisions about its activities overseas—they still "must do so with sufficient force to displace the presumption against extraterritorial application."

By contrast, in his concurrence in the judgment, Justice Breyer, joined by Justices Ginsburg, Sotomayor, and Kagan, would have held that the ATS permits U.S. courts to hear cases not only when the alleged violation occurs on American soil, but also when either the defendant is an American national or when "the defendant's conduct substantially and adversely affects an important American national interest," including the interest "in preventing the United States from becoming a safe harbor (free of civil as well as criminal liability) for a torturer or other common enemy of mankind." Justice Breyer's approach would apparently leave open the possibility of ATS lawsuits against individual defendants found in U.S. territory, even if their human rights violations occurred overseas.

The difference in these approaches is hardly academic. Consider the case of Edgegayehu Taye. She was imprisoned and tortured for more than ten months in Ethiopia. The abuse was personally supervised by Kelbessa Negewo, an official of the military dictatorship. After her release, Taye fled to the United States, where she went to work in a hotel in Atlanta. Some years later, she encountered Negewo, who was working in the same hotel. She and other victims filed suit using the ATS, and she obtained a verdict for $200,000 in compensatory damages and $300,000 in punitive damages. Under Chief Justice Roberts's approach, the presumption against extraterritoriality would presumably bar her suit; under Justice Breyer's it clearly would not. In a cryptic concurrence, Justice Kennedy suggested that the chief justice's opinion, which he had joined in full, left open a significant number of questions, but he neither identified those questions, nor suggested how he would answer them.

Kiobel is just one example of the Court dictating which points litigants will argue. The Court used *Kiobel* to force a question not presented by the litigants, and the majority made the most of the opportunity, effectively rewriting the existing doctrine. That's a lot of responsibility for an unelected, self-described umpire.

CASE STUDY

Janine is the manager of a local post office, where Corinne has worked for the past five years as a clerk. Corinne is a single mother of two children and struggles to pay her bills on her relatively meager salary. She has always been a great employee, but recently Janine has noticed that Corinne's till has not matched the receipts for her register. The differences are not huge—five dollars here, 10 dollars there—but given that there are repeated discrepancies, Janine asks Corinne to meet with her. When you confronted her with the information, Corinne breaks down in tears and admits that she took the money in order to pay her rent and prevent her family from becoming homeless. Technically, Corinne has embezzled money and her crime should be reported to the police, but Janine isn't sure what the best course of action is. She has three options: (1) report Corinne to the police; (2) don't report her to the police, but fire her and create a plan to pay back the money; (3) don't report her to the police, don't fire her, and create a plan to pay back the money. What should Janine do? What is the most ethical action? Why?

CHAPTER 6

Gideon's Muted Trumpet

SEE WHERE YOU STAND: 60 SECOND ETHICAL DILEMMA

Imagine that you are in the following situation and have one minute to make a decision about the most ethical course of action:

You are a city manager in a state with a very rigid sunshine law that does not allow any private deliberative decision making by public officials. You have just finished a city council meeting, and the city council members have invited you to go out with them and socialize. You soon realize that they are now discussing council business, which violates the sunshine law, but you don't want to upset them, given that you technically report to them. What do you do?

INTRODUCTION TO CHAPTER

What bar must we meet for our legal and moral obligations? This chapter articulates the often woefully inadequate public representation provided for indigent people. The Court declared in *Gideon* that states must provide attorneys to defendants who cannot afford them, but this chapter asks the question, how good does that representation have to be? The numbers demonstrate a stark reality—individuals with attorneys are much less likely to be convicted of a crime, but what happens when the public attorneys are so overburdened they can only dedicate 30 minutes per case? Does this meet our ethical expectations for representation? There are some nonprofit organizations and programs that have tried to alleviate this burden, such as the Gates Public Service Law Program at the University of Washington, which provides a full scholarship in return for five years of public service after graduation. However, given the significant debt of recent law school graduates and the much more lucrative private-sector pay, these programs can make only a limited impact on the number of lawyers entering public service. So, what should we as a society do? Consider whether or not you think that meeting the legal obligation is enough to satisfy our ethical obligation.

READING 5

Gideon's Muted Trumpet

By Pamela S. Karlan

Last spring marked the 50th anniversary of ***Gideon v. Wainwright***, in which the Supreme Court considered the Sixth Amendment's guarantee that "in all criminal prosecutions, the accused shall enjoy the right ... to have the Assistance of Counsel for his defence." The Court unanimously interpreted the Amendment as requiring that states provide attorneys for defendants who lack the resources to hire them privately. The "noble ideal" that "every defendant stands equal before the law," Justice Hugo Black's opinion declared, "cannot be realized if the poor man charged with crime has to face his accusers without a lawyer to assist him." Given an attorney for his retrial, Clarence Gideon was acquitted.

Today, the vast majority of criminal defendants depend on appointed counsel to represent them, and the quality of representation varies wildly.

At one end of the spectrum, indigent defendants represented by some public defender organizations receive counsel every bit as expert as the most well-heeled client could buy. But the majority of the states that operate public defender services fail to meet the federal government's standards for attorneys' maximum caseloads. And many defendants receive dreadful representation: a shockingly high percentage of defendants sentenced to death were represented by lawyers who were either disciplined or disbarred at some point in their careers, often within a few years of the defendants' trials. Indeed, there are enough instances of lawyers who literally slept through their clients' trials to produce a grotesque jurisprudence regarding when somnolence rises—or sinks—to the level of a Sixth Amendment violation.

The Supreme Court has recognized that just any counsel isn't good enough. But the Court's standard for constitutionally ineffective assistance, announced in *Strickland v.*

Washington (1984), makes it extremely hard for a defendant to argue that his lawyer failed him. A defendant challenging his conviction not only has to show that his lawyer's performance fell below a relatively deferential bar, but also has to prove prejudice—that is, a reasonable probability that, but for the errors, the outcome would have been different. By contrast, for most other constitutional violations, the burden is on the government to show the error was harmless. And although in recent years the Court has been somewhat more vigilant in enforcing the Sixth Amendment—requiring in *Padilla v. Kentucky* (2010), for instance, that lawyers provide accurate information to noncitizen clients about the immigration consequences of pleading guilty—its promise all too often goes unfulfilled.

Consider two powerful illustrations of how *Gideon*'s trumpet—to borrow from the title of the late Anthony Lewis's superb 1964 book about the case—has been muted.

One is ***Boyer v. Louisiana***. Boyer, who has a borderline I.Q., a third-grade reading level, and a history of mental illness, had admitted under police interrogation to killing the victim, but his statement did not match the physical evidence in several relevant respects. There was also at least one other plausible suspect. Nonetheless, the state charged him with capital murder in 2002.

Louisiana has a long history of underfunding its indigent defense system, and at the time Boyer was charged, the state provided no resources to indigent defense. Local indigent defender boards were funded essentially by revenue from traffic tickets, which fluctuated dramatically from year to year.

In Boyer's case, the public defender was unavailable due to a conflict of interest. So the judge drafted a practitioner from a small firm to represent Boyer. But there were no funds available to compensate the lawyer for the hundreds of hours he would be required to devote to the case or for out-of-pocket litigation expenses. The next five years were consumed by proceedings trying to obtain those funds. Those proceedings were repeatedly postponed to await decisions in parallel cases also involving unfunded indigent defense.

When Boyer's attorney moved to dismiss the charges against his client for violation of a different provision of the Sixth Amendment—the right to a speedy trial—he was forced to abandon that claim because, in a Kafkaesque twist, the very lack of funds that had caused the delay had also prevented him from showing why the delay had impaired his ability to mount an effective defense.

In the end, the state abandoned the capital charge against Boyer so that it could proceed against him on a lesser charge for which he could be represented by a less experienced attorney. By the time of the trial, in 2009, a number of potentially relevant witnesses had either died or gone missing. Boyer was convicted by a non-unanimous jury (a practice permitted only in Louisiana and Oregon) and sentenced to life in prison without the possibility of parole.

On appeal, the state appellate court recognized that the extraordinary delay in bringing Boyer to trial raised a red flag under the Supreme Court's foundational speedy trial case, *Barker v. Wingo* (1972). But in another twist, it held that the "funding crisis" was a "cause beyond the control of the state," and therefore the prosecution had proceeded properly.

While the Supreme Court originally agreed to hear Boyer's claim that he had been deprived of his right to a speedy trial, it later dismissed his petition as "improvidently granted." Thus the Court avoided confronting the question of whether Louisiana's entire system is constitutionally deficient.

Another example of the Sixth Amendment's false promise arises from more mundane sources than Boyer's murder charge: misdemeanor cases. A decade after *Gideon*, in *Argersinger v. Hamlin* (1972), the Court extended *Gideon*, which applied only to felony cases, to all criminal prosecutions, including misdemeanors, in which jail time is imposed. The government can prosecute misdemeanors without providing counsel to indigent defendants, but unless the defendant waives his right to counsel, the judge cannot order the defendant to serve time if he is convicted.

And yet, as a practical matter, misdemeanor defendants may face a cruel dilemma. A 2009 investigative series in the *San Jose Mercury News* discovered that in Santa Clara County, California, defendants charged with misdemeanors were not provided attorneys at arraignment, generally their first court appearance. Instead, they faced the option of asking for a lawyer—in which case they might be kept in custody until one is appointed—or of pleading guilty on the spot. Without a lawyer at arraignment, many defendants will find it difficult to get pretrial release, as the legal scholar Douglas Colbert has shown.

The upshot is that unrepresented defendants often end up getting the equivalent of a jail sentence, only they serve it *before* they've been convicted.

And in many cases, they might never be convicted if they receive competent counsel. A *Mercury News* study of roughly 250 defendants charged with resisting arrest found that while almost half of the represented defendants had their charges reduced or dropped altogether, only one in ten self-represented defendants did. Moreover, defendants who plead guilty simply to avoid being locked up while they wait for a lawyer to be appointed will be stuck with criminal records and all the consequences they entail.

Underfunding misdemeanor defense creates its own problems. In Detroit, according to a 2008 National Legal Aid & Defender Association report, lawyers spend around half an hour, on average, on each misdemeanor case.

Misdemeanor cases may not be as striking as Jonathan Boyer's, but they too demonstrate the significant costs inflicted by the failure to honor *Gideon*. As Justice Black put it 50 years ago, "Lawyers in criminal courts are necessities, not luxuries."

CASE STUDY

Kevin is a senior-level manager at NASA and has 12 employees he directly supervises. One of his employees, Richard, has worked at NASA for the past 10 years and has been quite successful in his position as head of research and development. However, recently Kevin learned that Richard started also working as a consultant for a rocket booster company that provides rockets for NASA and other private space exploration companies. Technically, his job does not preclude him from working as a consultant for a private-sector company, but he didn't disclose his involvement. When confronted with the information, he continued to deny that he should have to disclose his work, despite NASA's requirement that all employees disclose potential conflicts of interest. Richard has become combative and continues to claim it is not a conflict of interest. Nevertheless, he remains fairly popular in his department and with external stakeholders. Kevin knows that he cannot let Richard continue in his position, but he also doesn't want to generate a lot of internal conflict in the organization. Kevin is considering two options: he can fire Richard for violating NASA's policy, or he can tell Richard that if he leaves quietly he will give him a positive recommendation for a future job. If he fires Richard, he will not have to lie about his performance, but he may create significant turmoil within the organization. If he allows Richard to leave on his own terms with a positive recommendation, it won't create any upheaval in the organization, but he isn't sure it's ethical to lie about Richard's performance. What do you think? What should Kevin do? Why?

PART IV

ETHICS IN PUBLIC ADMINISTRATION

CHAPTER 7

Big Questions from Cooper and Rohr

SEE WHERE YOU STAND: 60 SECOND ETHICAL DILEMMA

Imagine that you are in the following situation and have one minute to make a decision about the most ethical course of action:

You work for a local government and are attending a city council meeting. Your boss (the city manager) is discussing an issue you have been working on for six months. You realize that he is only presenting one side of the story, and the council members cannot really make an informed decision based on what he is saying. When he is done, they ask you if you have any additional comments. You think they should know the truth, but you know if you publicly contradict your boss, you could risk your participation in future important projects. What do you do?

INTRODUCTION TO CHAPTER

The first reading in this chapter is a lecture delivered by Terry Cooper at the annual meeting of the American Society for Public Administration in 2004. The focus of the lecture is ethical studies that have been conducted by public administration researchers. Without making any normative claims about how public administrators should behave, Cooper asks five questions about the scholarship that informs the state of the discipline of administrative ethics. As you read the chapter, think about the literature that you have read in your studies. Are new questions being asked? Are Cooper's calls for the advancement of the discipline being answered?

READING 6

Big Questions in Administrative Ethics

A Need for Focused, Collaborative Effort

By Terry L. Cooper

INTRODUCTION[1]

I have argued elsewhere that administrative ethics as a significant field of study is only about 30 years old, dating from the mid-1970s, largely instigated by the work of the New Public Administration, and reflecting developments in thought about public administration dating back into the 1930s.[2] During these few decades, scholarly work on administrative ethics and its application to practice have expanded with enormous speed and rich diversity, both in the United States and around the world. The number of journal articles, books, courses, conferences, and training exercises have proliferated beyond anyone's wildest expectations. More than a passing fad, administrative ethics has demonstrated its sustainability and its centrality to the field (Cooper 2001, 1–36).

What is lacking with respect to these developments is anything like a focused effort by groups of scholars to study specific sets of significant research questions in a sustained and systematic fashion. There is an enormous amount of interesting but highly disparate scholarship on administrative ethics reflecting the diverse and often episodic interests that capture our attention. The existence of this rich diversity of work is not bad at all; rather, it indicates lively intellectual engagement and the multifaceted nature of the field. It also may be viewed as a necessary scoping of the field in its early stages, the product of an energetic exploration of the range of concerns in the study of administrative ethics.

After approximately three decades, however, there is very little that manifests ongoing scholarship by working groups based on specific theoretical perspectives,

Terry L. Cooper, "Big Questions in Administrative Ethics: A Need for Focused, Collaborative Effort," *Public Administration Review*, vol. 64, no. 4, pp. 395-407.

sets of related problems, or significant issues.[3] Without collaborative efforts to fix our gaze on the most fundamental and vexing questions that are essential to moving administrative ethics forward, there is a risk that the creativity and energy now being directed to the subject will dissipate, and that our field will fail to earn the sustained prominence in journals, curricula, and professional development it deserves. Without this kind of concentrated work, administrative ethics may remain an interesting but peripheral concern.

None of us can define the elements and boundaries of such concentrated efforts; that needs to become a matter in which many of us invest ourselves. We need to work at building consensus among those interested in administrative ethics about sets of research questions that, in some sense, define the heart of the field. Not intended to preclude or exclude other work on other questions, the call here is for the establishment of a center of gravity for the development of administrative ethics around some focused collaborative efforts. Diversity of interests articulated by many from various areas in public administration are needed to keep the field fresh and lively; focused efforts of those mainly committed to studying administrative ethics may be required to provide sustainability, coherence, and sufficient weight to advance it solidly into the core of public administration.

This essay should be viewed as the first bid in a conversation about those "big questions" around which some focused, sustained, and collaborative activity might be organized. It began with an invitation I sent out to the ASPA Section on Ethics Listserv on September 27, 2002. In that message, members of the section were asked to offer their nominations for the "big questions" in administrative ethics. Thoughtful responses were received from 10 persons, with excellent proposals for questions of central importance. These questions reflected a wide range of perspectives on the field and helped to provide a sense of the scope and types of questions on the minds of others interested in ethics.[4] However, I do not attribute my big questions to any of those respondents, but appreciate the stimulation they provided.

Some Big Questions in Public Administration Ethics

These questions are presented in no particular order of importance, nor are the relationships among them addressed. They are laid out simply as an attempt to identify significant topics that have not been fully explored, but are deemed essential to the development of administrative ethics as a field of study. *My intention is to stimulate discussion about the big questions of the field, not to urge others to simply adopt the ones I have advanced.*

What are the Normative Foundations for Public Administration Ethics?

This question has plagued all who have attempted to engage in research, education, and training in administrative ethics. Usually it is framed less formally, often simply posed as, "**whose ethics should we adopt** in making ethical decisions in government?" Typically the questioner assumes all we can turn to are our own personal ethical perspectives rooted in religion, political commitments, secular philosophies, or some highly personal ethical orientation that has been improvised through socialization, life experience, and coping with the world of work. The notion that there is another category of ethics—in addition to one's own personal perspective—called "professional ethics" seems not to have been acknowledged and understood generally among students and practitioners of public administration (Adams 2001). This is probably because there is no clear consensus about what the normative substance of a professional public administrative ethic might be.

Also, the lack of a strong professional identity for public administration has left most thinking only of their employment role rather than understanding with clarity the difference between the obligations of employment by an organization and those associated with being a member of a profession.[5] This lack of professional identity leaves public administrators vulnerable to dominance by organizational and political imperatives; hence, the question "whose ethics should we adopt?" is an appropriately innocent one that still deserves responses. As we search for answers, it is important to keep in mind that we are looking for normative foundations, not in the sense of ultimately given in the nature of things (ontologically), but in the sense of a social construct that fits a particular context—American, in our case.

As we consider where we might turn for the normative touchstones of a profession or "practice" (MacIntyre 1984) of public administration, the literature of the last three decades suggests several perspectives are vying to become answers to this vexing question. I see five major alternatives that have been advanced in the literature over the last 30 years: (1) *Regime values, constitutional theory, and founding thought* seem so closely related they are worthy of being treated together rather than as separate streams; (2) *citizenship theory* is somewhat related to these, and not inconsistent with them, but sufficiently different to require distinction; (3) *social equity*, often of a Rawlsian variety, is a third alternative originally associated with the so-called New Public Administration of the late 1960s and early 1970s; (4) *virtue, or character-based ethics* provides a different kind of answer that is also not incompatible with the other perspectives; and finally, (5) the *public interest* is still a way of grounding normative ethics for public administration ethics that emerges from time to time. I will comment briefly on each of these perspectives without any attempt at an exhaustive or even representative review of the literature for each.

Regime Values, Constitutional Theory, and Founding Thought. In public administration this general stream of ideas is most clearly associated with the work of John Rohr. Rohr's path-breaking book, *Ethics for Bureaucrats: An Essay on Law and Values* (1989), first published in 1978, argued that public administration ethics ought to be grounded in the American constitutional tradition and the regime values upon which it rests. Rohr maintained these regime values are to be found in the U.S. Constitution and the U.S. Supreme Court's interpretations of it. The three regime values he identified are freedom, equality, and property, although he indicated this is not an exhaustive list. Rohr called for public administrators to steep themselves in this evolving tradition of constitutional values because when one accepts employment in a regime, it is extremely important to be clear about its core values and whether one can uphold them.[6] That is the fundamental professional ethical problem to be resolved, and addressing it does not require the full range of knowledge and skills expected of moral philosophers.[7] Thus, taking a job in government is an ethical decision, as well as an economic and career decision. Others affirmed Rohr's work and developed this way of grounding administrative ethics beyond the Constitution. They examined other founding documents in addition to the Constitution in an attempt to broaden the field of regime values. Among those scholars are Richardson and Nigro (1987a, 1987b), Vetterli and Bryner (1987), Hart (2001; Hart and Smith 1988), Frederickson (Frederickson and Hart 1985), and Chandler (1987).

Citizenship Theory. Also historical in its approach, this body of thought generally views the citizen's role in the American political tradition as providing the normative foundations for public administration. It is the area in which I have focused my efforts to contribute to the ethics literature. The public administrative role is viewed as derived from that of the citizen, thus making administrators representative citizens, professional citizens, fiduciary citizens, or citizens in lieu of the rest of us. Public administrators hold the role of citizen in trust as they conduct the public business previously done by citizens, but now handed over to professional citizens who have the time, technical training, and resources to carry it out. Their ethical obligations are associated with the good citizen in American society. Thus, there is discussion of the importance of being responsive to citizens, encouraging their participation, being accountable to them, viewing them as the locus of ultimate administrative loyalty, respecting the dignity of the individual, fostering reasoned deliberation, and encouraging civic virtue and concern for the common good. Administrators may be employed by the police department, the water department, the health department, or the public schools to undertake certain specialized tasks, but they work in those places on behalf of the citizens they represent. Administrators work in bureaucratic organizations where hierarchical bonds and obligation are important, but they also need to cultivate horizontal bonds and obligations among the citizenry for whom they are surrogates.

H. George Frederickson published the first journal article on this subject in 1982, but the citizenship perspective emerged significantly in the administrative ethics literature following a conference on citizenship and public administration organized and led by Frederickson in March of 1983 preceding the national conference of the American Society for Public Administration. The papers were published in a special issue of *Public Administration Review* in March of 1984. Among those addressing citizenship as a normative foundation for administrative ethics were Frederickson and Chandler, Gawthrop, Hart, Rohr, and Cooper.

Since the 1983 conference and the special issue of *PAR* in 1984, there has been a steady stream of articles and books examining, critiquing, developing, and applying the citizenship foundation for public administration ethics. Among the authors contributing to this literature are Stivers (1988, 1990a, 1990b, 1991, 1994, 1996), Cooper (1991), Timney (1998), King and Stivers (1998), Foley (1998), Box and Sagan (1998), and Kalu (2003). As with the work on regime values, constitutional theory, and founding thought, this perspective has not risen to a dominant position, but remains one of the normative orientations that continue to be of interest.

Social Equity. This single ethical principle was the normative perspective around which administrative ethics as a field of study was first focused in the early 1970s. John Rawls's *A Theory of Justice* (1971) argued that justice is the central organizing principle of government and set forth a fully developed argument for specific criteria for establishing social equity. The New Public Administration movement, which found its first organized expression at the Minnowbrook Conference in 1968, claimed Rawlsian social equity as its core ethical principle (Marini 1971).[8] Rawls's work was the subject of special issues and symposia in scholarly journals in virtually every discipline and field of study. Public administration was among them, with a special issue of *Public Administration Review* in 1974 that included six articles on administrative ethics. These essays by McGregor, Chitwood, Porter and Porter, White and Gates, Harmon, and Hart addressed a number of administrative areas such as personnel management, fiscal federalism, the use of statistics in service delivery, and social service productivity. Two pieces amounted to clear and significant contributions to administrative ethics: Harmon's "Social Equity and Organizational Man: Motivation and Organizational Democracy," and Hart's "Social Equity, Justice, and the Equitable Administrator." The other essays offered specific concrete applications, but these two addressed the use of the concept more generally.

Although New Public Administration is no longer an identifiable movement, its contributions to administrative ethics were crucial in the development of a field of study. Social equity never achieved acceptance in the field as the single central ethical principle, but clearly it has become one of the major normative touchstones for administrative ethics. This seems to have been exemplified by the offering of a panel session at the 2003 conference of the National Association of Schools of Public Affairs and Administration, "Reflections on Teaching Social Equity."[9] Perhaps indicative of the status of social equity as a guiding principle for public administration ethics was that, although the session attracted 25–30 people, much of the discussion had to do with the importance of social equity as a touchstone for the field at present. No one suggested it is no longer relevant, but some argued it is associated too much with the New Public Administration of the 1970s and projects such as affirmative action to be used generally. Others maintained that social equity clearly rises above those episodic events, but is just another ethical concept in our tool kit, not the central one. I would argue that it clearly antedates New Public Administration and affirmative action and, as one expression of the principle of justice, should occupy a position of great prominence in any ethic associated with democratic government. However, it is equally clear that it is not the cornerstone of the administrative ethics edifice.

Virtue. The early work on administrative ethics during the 1970s focused mainly on reasoning about ethical decisions and the appropriate normative orientations for cognitively resolving ethical dilemmas faced by administrators. In 1981, Mark T. Lilla launched a frontal attack on the rational analysis approach to ethical decision making, which he characterized as simply training administrators to rationalize whatever suited them at any given time. He inveighed against focusing on the analysis of ethical quandaries as lacking any normative foundation, and therefore likely to be manipulated to serve the interests of the analysts. Instead, Lilla argued for the cultivation of a democratic ethos in public organizations that would be conducive to the formation of character appropriate for public service.

This challenge was followed shortly by Pincoffs's more extensive critique of what he called "reductivism" in professional ethics. After a critique of analyses of ethical quandaries, he joined Lilla in calling for a focus on virtue understood as character. Pincoffs maintained this could be accomplished by "judging" the lives of others. He did not mean to encourage pronouncing judgment from some presumed position of moral superiority, but rather regularly reflecting on the character of others, as one of their fellows, by examining them biographically and assessing their character. Pincoffs argued that being able to weigh the character of others in a given community—even a community of practice—is an essential moral skill. He asserted, "It is our daily business to assess, to appraise, to judge persons." He went on, "It is a task so important and central in life that it takes on a life of its own; it is the central stuff of drama, film, literature, and history and of several psychological and social sciences and arts" (1986, 166–67).

A number of other authors followed the lead of Lilla and Pincoffs in asserting the importance of virtue understood as character. Hart was one of the leading voices in calling attention to virtue, not as the sole focus of administrative ethics, but as an essential element. In "The Virtuous Citizen, the Honorable Bureaucrat, and 'Public' Administration,'" (1984) he outlined the desired character traits of public administrators as superior prudence, moral heroism, caring or love for humanity, trust in the citizenry, and a continuing quest for moral improvement. In "The Moral Exemplar in an Organizational Society" (1992), a chapter in *Exemplary Public Administrators: Character and Leadership in Government*, Hart set forth a framework for assessing character that focused attention on "moral episodes" and "moral processes." Within the broad category of moral episodes, Hart identified two subcategories of action, which he termed "moral crises" and "moral confrontation." Under the scope of moral processes, he specified two subcategories called "moral projects" and "moral work."

Hart's framework for reflecting on character was used by the authors of the character studies in Cooper and Wright's *Exemplary Public Administrators: Character and Leadership in Government* (1992). Radey (1990) argued for the importance of stories in developing professional ethics. Vitz (1990) maintained more specifically that life stories were particularly important because they can be understood as "the laboratory of moral life." Because assessing character seems to imply a biographical focus, with the assistance of Wright, I invited a group of scholars to identify someone, living or dead, whose character they could study biographically in chapters for the edited volume. The book finally included 11 character studies that were developed using Hart's framework. I concluded the book with "Reflecting on Exemplars of Virtue," in which I drew some tentative conclusions (Cooper and Wright 1992b). The main one was that in all of the lives studied in that volume, the pursuit of moral processes (moral work and moral projects) in the daily routines of practice provided a foundation for dealing with the more dramatic moral episodes such as moral confrontations and moral crises. Character, understood as the predisposition to behave consistently with one's espoused values and principles, is built slowly and consistently over time, not all at once when confronted with a dramatic challenge.

Virtue, or character, is clearly one of the elements of the normative foundations of public administration ethics. All of the rational analysis of morally charged situations, ethical principles, citizenship obligations, and regime values will come to naught without the courage of our convictions. Absent the strength of character to "walk our walk" and "practice what we preach," ethics is ultimately an empty exercise. However, it is still unclear how, and even whether, we ought to see a role for ourselves in cultivating character, evaluating the character of specific individuals for hiring and appointment decisions, or in creating organizational environments that uphold character.

The Public Interest. This is probably the most widely recognized and most generally espoused normative touchstone for public administration ethics. There is an enormous literature on the public interest (Friedrich 1962; Flathman 1966), but it has received little attention by scholars of administrative ethics. Charles T. Goodsell noted in 1990 that he had been unable to find any "serious advocacy of the notion in the literature which is avowedly public administrationist" since 1957 (97). Goodsell attributed the ignoring of the public interest concept to a critique by Glendon Schubert in the same year. Although Schubert's biting attack on the use of the public interest concept may well have had a significant impact on thought in the mid-twentieth century, the apparent longer-term reason is that the concept is so broad and diversely understood that it has little operational value. The public interest has a number of somewhat specific meanings, but these tend not to be indicated when the term is used—usually in a vague manner, as though it conveys particular meaning when it does not.

Goodsell's "Public Administration and the Public Interest" (1990) and Douglas Morgan's "The Public Interest" (2001) are notable exceptions in recent years to the lack of attention to the concept by scholars of public administration ethics. Goodsell reviews four different perspectives on the public interest and attempts to apply them to public administration. Morgan develops the public interest concept historically in the American context. After a treatment of its origins around the end of the seventeenth century, he traces the evolution of the public interest through the American founding debate, the rise of Jacksonian democracy, populist reform, the Progressive movement, and more recent formulations.

My own view is that the public interest has a place in the construction of a normative administrative ethic as our moral compass, orienting us to a fundamental obligation. It serves a symbolic purpose by raising an important question before every administrative and policy decision: "Are you acting on behalf of broad shared interests or limited particular ones?" The public interest concept is most useful in reminding us that as public managers, our ethical obligation is to the former rather than the latter. It is often raised retrospectively when it is clear that something has gone seriously wrong in a particular situation and we are trying to redefine what should have been done in the past and what should be done in the future. When confronted with scandal and gross misconduct, the idea of the public interest provides an intuitive navigational beacon that points us in the right direction. It was raised during crises such as Watergate and the Iran-Contra hearings, and many others. Goodsell observes that "the words *public interest*—despite their poor academic reputation—remain in use in the realm of *practical* government. They are found sprinkled throughout the statutes practitioners administer, the memoranda they write, the testimony they give, and the verbal speech with which they articulate their points of view" (1990, 97).

So, we have these four approaches to establishing normative foundations for public administration ethics. They do not seem to be incompatible, but they have not been clearly integrated into a coherent and operational administrative ethic. That work remains to be done.

How Do American Administrative Ethical Norms Fit into a Global Context?

After reviewing the options that seem to be under consideration for normative ethics in the United States, it is clear that much of this work is being constructed out of the American experience and tied to our history and political culture. This is especially true for the regime values and citizenship perspectives. Whether or how these fit with the administrative ethics of other political communities and traditions around the world is an increasingly pointed question. Do administrative ethical norms have to be created specifically for each nation? Is there anything one could call a global administrative ethic? If administrative ethics is socially constructed and the world is experiencing greater global interdependence due to trade, travel, and communication (including especially the effects of the Internet), might there be an emerging global ethic for public administration?

This is one of the more intriguing and newer questions that administrative ethics faces, to which the answers are few and only suggestive at best. However, in my experience this question is raised with increasing frequency, both in international meetings and in cities such as Los Angeles that are truly global in their population and cultures. Gilman and Lewis published the first attempt to address this question in the public administration literature in 1999. Subsequently, I was invited to a small conference on globalization in Seoul in the summer of 2000 and asked to address the question, "Is there an emerging global ethic for public administration?" Diane Yoder and I attempted an answer by carrying forward the path-breaking work of Gilman and Lewis. We examined a large number of international treaties, pacts, agreements, conventions, and programs going back to the 1970s in an attempt to identify the core values that were explicitly advocated or implicitly assumed. We also tried to examine the reasoning connected with such values. Why were they deemed important?

In "Public Management Ethics in a Transnational World," we identified self-determination, freedom, honesty, trust, and stability as the values that are clearly central to the initiatives we examined (Cooper and Yoder 2002). Recognition of an increasingly interdependent world and a growing worldwide commitment to market economies and democratic governance are the reasons given in these documents and programs to justify support for the five recurring core values. *Whether these values are enacted or just espoused is not known and goes beyond our study. However, we argue that the fact they are espoused international values indicates they are at least viewed as aspirations.* What we can say is that there *may* be an emerging consensus that these at least are the values which nations of the world believe they *ought* to say they support. The profession of them is significant.

The story that seems to run through these documents is that, in an increasingly interdependent world aspiring to democracy and market economies, stable governments are achieved by upholding and maintaining self-determination of the citizens of each nation and honesty in domestic and international affairs because these help to build trust, both internally within nations and among the nations of the world. Market economies do not work without trust, honesty, and stability, nor can democratic governance be achieved and maintained without these same values.[10]

Next comes the question of how these values mesh with the elements of the normative foundations of administrative ethics in the United States discussed previously. The short answer is that there appear to be no inconsistencies or conflicts. The long answer, yet to be explored, is that we do not know how seriously these values are being taken by the various nations of the world, and we cannot be certain of their congruence with U.S. norms without a lot more experience with concrete applications. Values have meaning only in specific contexts. Here, as in the case of our own domestic norms, we appear to be engaged in a process of socially constructing (on a global scale) a set of normative foundations for public administration ethics. Whether that will be successful remains to be seen. At best, we get glimpses from time to time about the reality of this process.

For example, one of the requirements frequently advocated as a basis for trust in government is a subsidiary value, *transparency*. Currently, it is as close to being a universally advocated public value as one can find. The importance of transparency for trust to exist within a nation and among nations was visible in China's handling of the SARS crisis in early 2003. When the Chinese government attempted to conceal the spread of SARS in Beijing, Shanghai, Hong Kong, and a number of other cities, trade, tourism, and business travel dropped precipitously. Considerable turbulence also occurred inside China. Distrust of the official reports threatened China's emerging market economy and its internal stability (*LA Times* 2003). A lack of transparency in this case appears to have had powerful negative effects that were understood only after China's leadership was confronted with the resulting domestic and international problems.

One caveat is that if such a social construction process is occurring internationally, that does not necessarily imply the diverse cultures of the world are being homogenized, westernized, or destroyed. There may be different overlays of culture that involve domestic life within a society and international relations as somewhat distinct entities. People may live and act within a culture at home while also engaging a global culture. Whether it is possible to maintain such a juggling act remains to be seen.

A serious concern worth noting is that commitment to social equity is not frequently found in the documents we examined. Amy Chua (2004) argues persuasively that market economies coupled with emerging democratic political systems can be an explosive mix.[11] If, as seems to be the case in many developing countries, the market is largely dominated by an ethnic minority, while the mass of the populace is moving toward democratic government, tension is created between political and economic access. Absent some commitment to social equity, these imbalances may create enormous instability and unrest.

How Can Organizations Be Designed to Support Ethical Conduct?

Since the 1960s, before the birth of administrative ethics as a field of study, we have had evidence that organizational structure and culture are not neutral with respect to ethical conduct. Our typical hierarchical bureaucratic organizations generally not only have failed to encourage ethical action by the people who work within them, but often have created serious impediments to their efforts to do the right thing. **Milgram**'s experiments at Yale in the 1960s and Zimbardo's prison simulation at Stanford in the 1970s made painfully clear how simple hierarchical arrangements and culturally determined organizational roles can shape behavior toward humanly destructive ends (Milgram 1974; Haney, Banks, and **Zimbardo** 1973).

Milgram was able to create a basic organizational structure in a laboratory setting that induced obedience among very large numbers of people of different ages, genders, religious orientations, occupations, and educational levels—even to the point of being willing to administer powerful, painful, and dangerous electrical shocks to other human beings. Some 980 subjects went through various versions of Milgram's experiments, and the majority did as they were told, even while protesting that they were being ordered to impose agonizing shocks on the other participants in the experiments. Milgram explained how this occurred as the "agentic shift," a series of gradual psychological transitions through which the subjects moved from being relatively autonomous individuals to becoming willing instruments of the experimenter, and in the process abandoned all responsibility for their actions.

Zimbardo discovered to his dismay that college students assigned roles in a simulated prison, with only the briefest explanations of the typical behavior associated with those roles, would become harsh prison guards and retaliatory prison inmates within a matter of a few days. The guards' treatment of the inmates became so inhumane and abusive that the inmates experienced emotional breakdowns, turned on each other, and reacted aggressively against the guards. Guards and prisoners alike were captured by roles associated with certain cultural and organizational norms that shaped their behavior. The experiment had to be terminated after six days instead of running the full two weeks planned at the outset.

During the late 1960s through the 1970s, the tendency of large bureaucratic organizations to stifle conscience and punish those who called attention to corruption and misconduct became painfully apparent. The case of Ernest Fitzgerald, a high-level executive in the Department of Defense, was probably the first widely known example of behavior that became characterized as "whistle blowing." Far from being a self-promoting publicity seeker, as has been obvious with some whistle blowers, Fitzgerald had been quietly working inside the department to call attention to the enormous cost overruns of a new cargo aircraft, the C5A. Finally, he was subpoenaed by a U.S. congressional committee and forced to reveal what had been going on. For testifying before Congress under oath and telling the truth, Fitzgerald lost his job and suffered retribution for years (Nader, Perkas, and Blackwell 1972). In 1978 Senator Patrick Leahy conducted hearings on 70 cases of legitimate whistle blowers who had experienced severe retaliation from their own employing organizations for reporting forthrightly to higher authorities the involvement of these agencies in serious misconduct (Leahy 1978).

Literature on the dominance of large hierarchical organizations also began to appear in the academic literature during these years. As early as 1956, William H. Whyte was writing about the tendency of modern organizations to create servile "organization men" whose loyalty was so fully tied to the wishes of its hierarchy that they simply did its bidding without question. By the 1970s, a flood of writings on this problem followed suit. In *Freedom Inside the Organization: Bringing Civil Liberties to the Work Place*, David Ewing (1977) lamented employees' surrender of most of their rights upon entering the workplace each day; he characterized large organizations as "minigovernments" and charged that "for all practical purposes, employees are required to be as obedient to their superiors, regardless of ethical and legal considerations, as are workers in totalitarian countries." Ewing proposed a legally enforceable employee bill of rights to deal with this problem of organizational dominance.

The problem of organizational dominance appeared quite early in the public administration ethics literature. William G. Scott and David K. Hart published *Organizational America* in 1979, raising the specter of a fascist state growing out of the oppressive nature of large bureaucratic organizations. Alberto Guerreiro Ramos argued for "organization delimitation" in *The New Science of Organizations: A Reconceptualization of the Wealth of Nations* in 1981 because organizations threatened to dominate their employees' lives with an emphasis on a narrow market mentality that would turn them into economic maximizers devoid of appreciation for the qualitative side of human existence outside the workplace. The first edition of my book *The Responsible Administrator* in 1982 called attention to the problem of organizational dominance. Six years later Kathryn G. Denhardt's book *The Ethics of the Public Service* (1988) developed the problems of the organizational context further.

More recently, the problem of organizations impeding ethical conduct has been manifested in two space shuttle catastrophes, when *Challenger* exploded during launch on January 28, 1986 (Cooper 1987), and *Columbia* on February 1, 2003. The executive summary of the accident report on *Columbia* includes the following revealing statement:

> The organizational causes of this accident are rooted in the Space Shuttle Program's history and culture, including the original compromises that were required to gain approval for the Shuttle, subsequent years of resource constraints, fluctuating priorities, schedule pressures, mischaracterization of the Shuttle as operational rather than developmental, and lack of an agreed national vision for human space flight. Cultural traits and organizational practices detrimental to safety were allowed to develop, including: reliance on past success as a substitute for sound engineering practices (such as testing to understand why systems were not performing in accordance with requirements); organizational barriers that prevented

> effective communication of critical safety information and stifled professional differences of opinion; lack of integrated management across program elements; and the evolution of an informal chain of command and decision-making processes that operated outside the organization's roles. (Columbia Accident Investigation Board 2003, 9)

The identification of organizational factors is much more explicit in the report on this second shuttle tragedy than in the *Challenger* report. We learned during that earlier investigation that shuttle engineers had been locked in an all-night struggle with NASA and Morton Thiokol management over whether it was safe to launch in the subfreezing temperatures that had prevailed through the night. The engineers insisted the O-rings that sealed the major sections of the booster rocket tank would not be sufficiently pliable in the cold temperatures to prevent the disastrous escape of superheated gases. There being no dissent channels in NASA for such expert judgments to be heard in time to prevent the launch, the engineers were finally told to take off their engineering hats and put on their management hats. The launch went ahead as scheduled on January 28, 1986, the external fuel tank exploded, and the crew was killed. In the report of the investigation that followed, it is clear the decision to launch was made by management over the protests of the engineers (Presidential Commission on the Space Shuttle Challenger Accident 1986).

We now have a substantial literature on the problem of organizations' tendency to deprive the people who work in them of the freedom to exercise their professional conscience, as well as considerable practical experience to confirm it. During my 27 years of conducting ethics training for public administrators in various parts of the United States, and even in Hong Kong during my year as a Fulbright professor there, at all levels of government, and in many different kinds of public and nonprofit organizations, my experience has been extremely consistent on this point.

Whenever I do ethics training for working practitioners, I require everyone participating to write a case about some ethical problem from his or her professional experience and submit it to me confidentially. I then select a set of cases around which I build the training session, maintaining anonymity for the authors unless they choose to identify themselves, which they do more often than not. There is no doubt that among those several thousand cases in my files, the single most frequent problem presented is one concerning an organizational hierarchy, and often an organizational culture, that impedes ethical conduct and punishes those who attempt to act ethically, and sometimes even those who suggest doing so.

The question that burns in my mind from these experiences is whether we can design public organizations in a way that provides for ethical concerns to be heard and supported by the organizations in which public employees work on our behalf. I have seen public administrators on the verge of tears years after they had faced the bleak choice of rectifying a wrong or retaining their jobs, and then had been vilified for attempting to act ethically. They were churning inside over something they and their peers—and even sometimes their bosses—knew was violating someone's rights, violating the law, draining the organization's resources into someone's pocket, demeaning someone inside or outside the organization, doing things that poisoned the environment and placed human life at risk, grossly abusing power for personal ends, or regularly lying to the public and their elected representatives. But, they had either felt impotent to act or had acted and suffered significantly.

As I have struggled with this question myself, I have often thought how ethicists and organizational development specialists in public administration need to be working together to design organizations that provide for effective dissent channels, include policies to encourage ethical conduct, and protect employees from retribution when they act with moral courage. I am not sure how this might be done, but the institutional design approach worked powerfully for the American Progressive reform movement at the end of the nineteenth century and the first few decades of the century. That movement created bureaus of municipal research that were independent workshops or think tanks in cities around the United States, the first of which was the New York Bureau of Municipal Research established in 1906. These bureaus were the front lines of reform to crack the hold of political machines on local governments and put in place organizational forms and processes designed to encourage efficiency. Perhaps we need to consider the establishment of places analogous to those bureaus of municipal research that could bring together engaged scholars of administrative ethics and organizational development with thoughtful practitioners to address the problems of organizational structure and culture in supporting ethical conduct at the beginning of the twenty-first century.

I advocated a design approach to ethics in the fourth edition of *The Responsible Administrator*, for which I am indebted to Carolyn Whitbeck's article "Ethics as Design: Doing Justice to Moral Problems" (1996). This way of thinking about ethics does not assume the problem to be simply one of analyzing an ethical concern toward arriving at a defensible ethical decision. Rather, it also requires thinking about what else is necessary to make the decision effective. As I have conducted ethics training for practitioners, I have increasingly encouraged them to arrive at a decision when presented with a case, but not to stop there. In the central exercise for these sessions, they are required to identify the characteristics of the organization that would encourage or impede the kind of action they advocate. And not to stop there, but go on to describe the kinds of management interventions that would be appropriate to make the changes necessary in the organization's structure and culture to support their desired conduct. This kind of thinking would be much richer and helpful if I were working in these sessions with colleagues with expertise in organizational development. Ethics is as much about organizational design as it is about analytical and decision-making skills.

When Should We Treat People Equally in Order to Treat Them Fairly, and When Should We Treat Them Unequally?

This is a question that has emerged from our assertively diverse society. During the first half of the twentieth century, we found ourselves under the sway of the Progressive reformers' assumption that in order to treat everyone fairly, it was necessary to treat everyone the same. This was a logical response to the dominance of machine governments at the state and local levels, which provided unequal treatment based on support for political bosses. If the problem was that some streets were swept because someone had voted the "right way" in the last election, and others did not because they had voted the "wrong way," then fairness dictated sweeping everyone's streets in the same way. Standardized services were to be delivered across a city by agencies that, "without fear or favor," treated everyone the same. (Ostensibly, that was the formula, although it is never the case that everyone really does get the same street sweeping, or any other service.) The Progressives found a nice congruence in their approach to reform between their commitment to a science of administration and rectifying inequity. By delivering services "scientifically," which meant based on presumed scientific principles that would apply to everyone in every place and every time, they could achieve efficiency and provide fairness (Mann 1963; Wiebe 1967; Nelson 1982; Kennedy 1971; Haber 1964; Warner 1971; Ekirch 1974; Caro 1974; Croly 1965).

However, soon after the middle of the twentieth century, American society became increasingly diverse and increasingly assertive about its differentiated needs and preferences. Social movements and organized reform advocacy groups emerged in the late 1950s and with increasing intensity through the decades that followed. They engaged in the full panoply of social change strategies and tactics. The civil rights movement, the antipoverty movement, the new women's movement,[12] the environmental movement, the student movement, the disabled movement, the gay rights movement, the Chicano (later Latino) movement, and an array of other ethnic movements were all manifestations of a burgeoning of assertive diversity in American society.

This plethora of demands for particularized treatment based on special circumstances has forced us to recognize that the all-too-easy formula of the Progressives—treat everyone the same and you will treat everyone fairly—simply does not work so well given the realities of the late twentieth and early twenty-first centuries. Organizational systems based on rationalization understood as standardization have had difficulty responding to a diverse citizenry and its differential needs and preferences. The result is that many, if not most, citizens frequently feel unfairly treated at the hands of large, centralized bureaucracies with standard ways of delivering services.

The key ethical problem that emerges from this conflict between an assertively diverse society and public organizations that attempt to treat everyone the same is that sometimes we need to treat everyone the same, but at other times we need to treat them differently in order to provide fairness. However, the criteria for sorting these two ways of offering fair treatment are not clearly understood and result in considerable conflict among us. The contours of how to justify differential treatment for the sake of fairness are better understood and supported in some cases than in others. For example, public policy concerning the disabled appears to be less contentious than when it concerns race, ethnicity, or gender. Providing handicapped parking spaces, curb breaks and ramps, wheelchair lifts for buses, and special restroom arrangements seems to be generally accepted and supported. However, affirmative action for members of our society who have experienced the disadvantages of racial discrimination, or for women who have confronted the barriers of a male-dominated workplace, is among the most hotly contested strategies in recent decades. The challenges are equally difficult for educational, policing, and health care services.

And so the question hangs there before us: When should we treat people differently to be fair and when must we treat them the same? We should have no illusions about the efficacy of ethicists in actually resolving these problems through ethical analysis because they are also matters of power, passion, and politics that are not likely to give way to reasoned argument. However, ethicists may have a modest role to play in helping make explicit the values and principles that are implicit in policy alternatives.

If the most fundamental formulation of the justice principle is something like, treat equal cases equally and different cases unequally, the problem is always to identify the attributes that should be treated differently or similarly. Gay and lesbian members of our society are aggressively asserting their right to marriage based on fairness arguments. They insist their commitments to faithfulness to each other should be treated the same as any other such lifelong commitments between two people. Sexual identity should not be the basis for treating them differently. Those who oppose state recognition of these unions argue that marriage is for heterosexual couples only, and, at best, gay and lesbian committed relationships should be called something else. And so the battle rages on over which characteristics qualify one for equal treatment and which disqualify one for equality. Is it lifelong commitment that matters most or sexual identity?

Six years ago, when we set about reforming our city charter to create an official neighborhood council system to connect the people of Los Angeles to its governance processes, the same-versus-different-treatment question emerged at the center of a sometimes very heated debate. Should we create a set of standard boundaries based on equal population, or should we permit neighborhoods to create their own boundaries that may result in very different sizes for neighborhood councils? Should we impose a citywide set of standard bylaws and organizational structures for all of the neighborhood councils, or allow them to develop their own? Most of the city's administrative agencies argued for standardizing everything, and the justifications were ones we in public administration might expect—efficiency and order. The elected officials tended to argue similarly, but for reasons that were never articulated out loud—control and efficiency. Allowing citizens to create their own boundaries was held out as a prospect that would produce chaos.

In the end, we wound up—appropriately I think—with a combination of standardization and variety. Neighborhoods were allowed to define and justify their own boundaries, bylaws, and system of financial accountability in order to be fair to the diversity of Los Angeles. The slogan was "No cookie cutter solutions will work in L.A." However, the new charter did establish a certification process to which all of the neighborhoods had to submit. This process required a demonstration of active and comprehensive outreach to all of the stakeholders in their area, a set of bylaws that provided transparency and access to all stakeholders, and a system of financial accountability that was similarly transparent and responsible. So we wound up with some things standardized and some things different, both of which were means of providing fairness to the citizenry. I do not want to leave you with the impression that all is tranquil and fair now in the Los Angeles neighborhood councils, because it is not, but we have made our way through the initial minefields largely because people were willing and able to think of fairness in more textured and flexible ways even if they are somewhat inefficient, more than a little messy, and lacking in predictable order.

These knotty and often emotional public debates over the meaning of equity in a complex assertively diverse society are among the most difficult we in administrative ethics engage in. We certainly have to view ourselves modestly as one of the several kinds of players in these struggles, but I think our role is an important one nevertheless.

Conclusion

I conclude where I began—with a call for focused collaboration on the big questions in public administration ethics. My nominations for these are as follows:

1. What are the normative foundations for public administrative ethics?
2. How do American administrative ethical norms fit into a global context?
3. How can organizations be designed to be supportive of ethical conduct?
4. When should we treat people equally in order to treat them fairly, and when should we treat them unequally?

Are these some of the big questions in administration ethics? I think so, but they are offered here, not in the nature of a pronouncement, but as an invitation to dialogue among us to identify what *the* big questions are for us as a community of scholarship and practice. This dialogue should in no way be exclusive, but it does need to be focused and sustained. The interplay between this kind of ongoing work and divergent other scholarship could be creative, stimulating, and even exciting.

How might we go about engaging this kind of deliberation? One way would be to create working groups that would meet a couple of times during the year, perhaps prior to ASPA and just before NASPAA, for a day of work each time on sorting out some big questions for collaborative research. These then might become the thematic focus for ASPA Section on Ethics conferences or similar events. However we proceed, I hope we will do so. Much has been accomplished over the last 30 years, but much remains to be done to advance the study of public administration ethics.

Notes

1. Advancing a specific list of concerns identified as *the* big questions in administrative ethics is presumptuous, and maybe even hubristic. The only way that could be done

without sacrificing the requisite modesty of scholarship would be to characterize it as the first step in a collaborative process. It would have to be understood as an invitation to colleagues to participate in achieving focus in our collective work. It is in that spirit that this essay is presented.

2 The study of ethics has been with us since the beginning of civilization, but here the point is that the emergence of *administrative* ethics as a specialized field of study with a group of scholars devoted to its development, a significant and continuing stream of scholarly literature, conference presentations, and academic courses is far more recent. Its origins are found in the mid-1970s, as detailed in Cooper (2001, 1–36).

3 The notable exception would be the work being done from the theoretical perspective of cognitive moral development, rooted in the work of Lawrence Kohlberg, by Debra Stewart, Carole Jurkiewicz, Ann-Marie Rizzo, and Richard White.

4 I have not used any of the specific questions submitted in their original form, but they informed and stimulated my thinking in ways that were essential to the development of this essay. I wish to thank Charles Garofalo, John Rohr, Robin Bittick, Pamela Gibson, James Heichelbech, Leo Huberts, Eleanor Glor, Rod Erakovich, Bob Cunningham, and Daniel Williams for their contributions to my thinking, but also note that they bear no responsibility for what I have done with their ideas in this essay.

5 In my experience, this is contrasted with the strong professional ethical identity of students in social work who readily refer to their professional code and its meanings in particular situations.

6 Rohr dismissed the in-depth study of moral philosophy by public administrators as impractical.

7 Rohr also argued that attempting to train public administrators to be moral philosophers would be unrealistic.

8 New Public Administration was a movement to challenge the older understandings of the field rooted in assumptions that administrators carried out their work as technical professionals without much discretion according to the wishes of their political masters. New Public Administration rejected notions of administration as ethically neutral instrumental thinkers apart from the citizenry. Their work advanced the first significant treatments of the ethical obligations of public administrators and the importance of citizen participation in administrative decisions. Their first published work appeared in Marini (1971).

9 NASPAA is the national association of the more than 200 college and university professional education programs in public administration and the accrediting organization for the master of public administration degree.

10 This is not to imply that democratic governance is always stable. Indeed, it is often turbulent. What is intended here is a kind of dynamic equilibrium that may undergo frequent turbulence but adapt to the changes without destroying itself.

11 I am indebted to Patricia M. Nickel for this reference and insight.

12 I use the term "new women's movement" to distinguish it from that which began with organized effort in the 1840s and continued through the battle for the suffrage for women.

REFERENCES

Adams, Guy B. 2001. Administrative Ethics and the Chimera of Professionalism. In *Handbook of Administrative Ethics*, 2nd ed., edited by Terry L. Cooper, 291–308. New York: Marcel Dekker.

Box, Richard C., and D. Sagan. 1998. Working with Citizens: Breaking Down Barriers to Citizen Self-Governance. In *Government Is Us: Public Administration in an Anti-Government Era*, edited by Cheryl Simrell King and Camilla Stivers, 158–74. Thousand Oaks, CA: Sage Publications.

Caro, Robert. 1974. *The Powerbroker: Robert Moses and the Fall of New York*. New York: Vintage Books.

Chandler, Ralph C. 1984. Conclusions: The Public Administrator as Representative Citizen: A New Role for the New Century. *Public Administration Review* 44(Special Issue): 196–206.

Chandler, Ralph C., ed. 1987. *A Centennial History of the American Administrative State*. New York: Free Press.

Chitwood, S.R. 1974. Social Equity and Social Service Delivery. *Public Administration Review* 34(Special Issue): 29–35.

Chua, Amy. 2004. *World on Fire: How Exporting Free Market Democracy Breeds Ethnic Hatred and Global Instability*. New York: Anchor Books.

Columbia Accident Investigation Board. 2003. *Final Report on Columbia Space Shuttle Accident*. Washington, DC: U.S. Government Printing Office.

Cooper, Terry L. 1982. *The Responsible Administrator: An Approach to the Ethics of the Administrative Role*. Port Washington, NY: Kennikat Press.

_____. 1984. Citizenship and Professionalism in Public Administration. *Public Administration Review* 44(Special Issue): 143–49.

_____. 1987. Hierarchy, Virtue, and the Practice of Public Administration: A Perspective for Normative Ethics. *Public Administration Review* 47(4): 320–35.

_____. 1991. *An Ethic of Citizenship for Public Administration*. Englewood Cliffs, NJ: Prentice Hall.

_____. 2001. The Emergence of Administrative Ethics as a Field of Study in the United States. In *Handbook of Administrative Ethics*, edited by Terry L. Cooper, 1–36. New York: Marcel Dekker.

Cooper, Terry L., and N. Dale Wright, eds. 1992a. *Exemplary Public Administrators: Character and Leadership in Government*. San Francisco: Jossey-Bass.

_____. 1992b. Reflecting on Exemplars of Virtue. In *Exemplary Public Administrators: Character and Leadership in Government*, edited by Terry L. Cooper and N. Dale Wright, 324–40. San Francisco: Jossey-Bass.

Cooper, Terry L., and Diane Yoder. 2002. Public Management Ethics in a Transnational World. *Public Integrity* 4(4): 333–52.

Croly, Herbert. 1965. *The Promise of American Life*. Indianapolis, IN: Bobbs-Merrill.

Denhardt, Kathryn G. 1988. *The Ethics of the Public Service*. New York: Greenwood Press.

Ekirch, Arthur A., Jr. 1974. *Progressivism in America: A Study of the Era from Theodore Roosevelt to Woodrow Wilson*. New York: New Viewpoints.

Ewing, David. 1977. *Freedom Inside the Organization: Bringing Civil Liberties to the Work Place*. New York: Dutton.

Flathman, Richard E. 1966. *The Public Interest: An Essay Concerning the Normative Discourse of Politics*. New York: John Wiley.

Foley, Delores. 1998. We Want Your Input: Dilemmas of Citizen Participation. In *Government Is Us: Public Administration in an Anti-Government Era*, edited by Cheryl Simrell King and Camilla Stivers, 140–57. Thousand Oaks, CA: Sage Publications.

Frederickson, H. George, ed. 1974. Symposium on Social Equity and Public Administration. *Public Administration Review* 34(Special Issue): 1–51.

———. 1982. The Recovery of Civism in Public Administration. *Public Administration Review* 42(6): 501–8.

Frederickson, H. George, and Ralph C. Chandler. 1984. Citizenship and Public Administration. *Public Administration Review* 44(Special Issue): 99–209.

Frederickson, H. George, and David K. Hart. 1985. The Public Service and the Patriotism of Benevolence. *Public Administration Review* 45(5): 547–53.

Friedrich, Carl J., ed. 1962. *The Public Interest*. New York: Atherton.

Gawthrop, Louis C. 1984. Civis, Civitas, and Civilitas: A New Focus for the Year 2000. *Public Administration Review* 44(Special Issue): 101–7.

Gilman, S.C., and C.W. Lewis. 1999. Public Service Ethics: A Global Dialogue. *Public Administration Review* 56(6): 517–24.

Goodsell, Charles T. 1990. Public Administration and the Public Interest. In *Refounding Public Administration,* edited by Gary L. Wamsley et al., 96–113. Newbury Park, CA: Sage Publications.

Haber, Samuel. 1964. *Efficiency and Uplift; Scientific Management in the Progressive Era, 1890–1920*. Chicago: University of Chicago Press.

Haney, C., C. Banks, and P. Zimbardo. 1973. Interpersonal Dynamics in a Simulated Prison. *International Journal of Criminology and Penology* 1(1): 69–97.

Harmon, Michael. 1974. Social Equity and Organizational Man: Motivation and Organizational Democracy. *Public Administration Review* 34(Special Issue): 11–18.

Hart, David K. 1974. Social Equity, Justice, and the Equitable Administrator. *Public Administration Review* 34(Special Issue): 3–11.

———. 1984. The Virtuous Citizen, the Honorable Bureaucrat, and "Public" Administration. *Public Administration Review* 44(Special Issue): 111–20.

———. 1992. The Moral Exemplar in an Organizational Society. In *Exemplary Public Administrators: Character and Leadership in Government*, edited by Terry L. Cooper and N. Dale Wright, 9–29. San Francisco: Jossey-Bass.

———. 2001. A Dream of What We Could Be: The Founding Values, the Oath, and Homo Virtutis. In *Handbook of Administrative Ethics*, 2nd ed., edited by Terry L. Cooper, 207–26. New York: Marcel Dekker.

Hart, David K., and P. A. Smith. 1988. Fame, Fame-Worthiness, and the Public Service. *Administration and Society* 20(2): 131–51.

Kalu, Kalu N. 2003. Of Citizenship, Virtue, and the Administrative Imperative: Deconstructing Aristotelian Civic Republicanism. *Public Administration Review* 63(4): 418–27.

Kennedy, David M., ed. 1971. *Progressivism: The Critical Issues*. Boston: Little, Brown.

King, Cheryl Simrell, Camilla Stivers, and collaborators. 1998. *Government is Us: Public Administration in an Anti-Government Era*. Thousand Oaks, CA: Sage Publications.

Leahy, Patrick J. 1978. *The Whistle Blowers: A Report on Federal Employees Who Disclose Acts of Governmental Waste, Abuse, and Corruption*. Report prepared for the Senate Committee on Governmental Affairs. Washington, DC: U.S. Government Printing Office.

Lilla, Mark T. 1981. Ethos, "Ethics," and the Public Service. *Public Interest* 63(1): 3–17.

Los Angeles Times. 2003. A Lesson for China in SARS. Editorial, April 16.

MacIntyre, Alasdair. 1984. *After Virtue*. 2nd ed. Notre Dame, IN: Notre Dame University Press.

Mann, Arthur, ed. 1963. *The Progressive Era: Liberal Renaissance or Liberal Failure?* New York: Holt, Rinehart, and Winston.

Marini, Frank, ed. 1971. *Toward a New Public Administration: The Minnowbrook Perspective*. Scranton, PA: Chandler Publishing.

McGregor, E.B. 1974. Social Equity and the Public Service. *Public Administration Review* 34(1): 18–29.

Milgram, Stanley. 1974. *Obedience to Authority: An Experimental View*. New York: Harper and Row.

Morgan, Douglas F. 2001. The Public Interest. In *Handbook of Administrative Ethics*, 2nd ed., edited by Terry L. Cooper, 151–78. New York: Marcel Dekker.

Nader, R., P.J. Perkas, and K. Blackwell. 1972. *Whistle Blowing*. New York: Grossman.

Nelson, William E. 1982. *The Roots of American Bureaucracy, 1830–1900*. Cambridge, MA: Harvard University Press.

Pincoffs, Edmund L. 1986. *Quandaries and Virtues: Against Reductivism in Ethics*. Lawrence: University Press of Kansas.

Porter, D.O., and T.W. Porter. 1974. Social Equity and Fiscal Federalism. *Public Administration Review* 34(1): 36–51.

Presidential Commission on the Space Shuttle Challenger Accident. 1986. Report of the Presidential Commission on the Space Shuttle Challenger Accident. http://history.nasa.gov/rogersrep/genindex.htm.

Radey, Charles. 1990. Telling Stories: Creative Literature and Ethics. *Hastings Center Report* 20(6): 25.

Ramos, Alberto Guerreiro. 1981. *The New Science of Organizations: A Reconceptualization of the Wealth of Nations*. Toronto: University of Toronto Press.

Rawls, John. 1971. *A Theory of Justice*. Cambridge, MA: Belknap Press of Harvard University.

Richardson, William D., and Lloyd G. Nigro. 1987a. Administrative Ethics and Founding Thought: Constitutional Correctives, Honor, and Education. *Public Administration Review* 47(4): 367–76.

______. 1987b. Self Interest Properly Understood: The American Character and Public Administration. *Administration and Society* 19(2): 155–77.

Rohr, John A. 1984. Civil Servants and Second Class Citizens. *Public Administration Review* 44(Special Issue): 135–40.

______. 1989. *Ethics for Bureaucrats: An Essay on Law and Values*. 2nd ed. New York: Marcel Dekker.

Schubert, Glendon A. 1957. The Public Interest in Administrative Decision-Making: Theorem, Theosophy, or Theory. *American Political Science Review* 51(June): 114–15.

Scott, William G., and David K. Hart. 1979. *Organizational America*. Boston: Houghton Mifflin.

Stewart, Debra W. 1991. Theoretical Foundations of Ethics in Public Administration: Approaches to Understanding Moral Action. *Administration and Society* 23(3): 357–73.

Stivers, Camilla. 1988. *Active Citizenship in the Administrative State*. PhD diss., Virginia Polytechnic Institute and State University.

———. 1990a. Active Citizenship and Public Administration. In *Refounding Public Administration*, edited by Gary L. Wamsley et al., 246–73. Newbury Park, CA: Sage Publications.

———. 1990b. The Public Agency as Polis: Active Citizenship in the Administrative State. *Administration and Society* 22(1): 86–105.

———. 1991. Comments: Some Tensions in the Notion of the Public as Citizen. *Administration and Society* 22(4): 418–23.

———. 1994. The Listening Bureaucrat: Responsiveness in Public Administration. *Public Administration Review* 54(4): 364–69.

———. 1996. Refusing to Get It Right: Citizenship, Difference, and the Refounding Project. In *Refounding Democratic Public Administration: Modern Paradoxes, Postmodern Challenges*, edited by Gary L. Wamsley and James F. Wolf, 260–78. Thousand Oaks, CA: Sage Publications.

Timney, Mary M. 1998. Overcoming Administrative Barriers to Citizen Participation: Citizens as Partners, not Adversaries. In *Government Is Us: Public Administration in an Anti-Government Era*, edited by Cheryl Simrell King and Camilla Stivers, 88–101. Thousand Oaks, CA: Sage Publications.

Vetterli, Richard, and Gary Bryner. 1987. *In Search of the Republic: Public Virtue and the Roots of American Government*. Totowa, NJ: Rowman and Littlefield.

Vitz, P.C. 1990. The Use of Stories in Moral Development: New Psychological Reasons for an Old Education Method. *American Psychologist* 45(6): 709–20.

Warner, H. Langdon, ed. 1971. *Reforming American Life in the Progressive Era*. New York: Jerome S. Ozer.

Whitbeck, Carolyn. 1996. Ethics as Design: Doing Justice to Moral Problems. *Hastings Center Report* 26(3): 9–16.

White, Orion, and B.L. Gates. 1974. Statistical Theory and Equity in the Delivery of Social Services. *Public Administration Review* 34(1): 43–51.

White, Richard D. 1999. Public Ethics, Moral Development, and the Enduring Legacy of Lawrence Kohlberg. *Public Integrity* 1(2): 121–34.

Whyte, William H., Jr. 1956. *The Organization Man*. New York: Simon and Schuster.

Wiebe, Robert H. 1967. *The Search for Order, 1877–1920*. New York: Hill and Wang.

READING 7

On Cooper's "Big Questions"

By John A. Rohr

I had the good fortune to hear Terry Cooper present his paper on "Big Questions in Administrative Ethics" at the ethics workshop preceding ASPA's 2004 annual meeting in Portland. His remarks, though well received, did not escape close and penetrating questions, which he handled with the clarity and forthrightness we have come to expect from him. His call for "focused, collaborative effort," as announced in the paper's subtitle, fell on sympathetic ears. Anyone who has written in the field of administrative ethics has surely been appalled by the chaotic nature of the literature. We seem to have trouble building on one another's work. Cooper faced this problem directly and boldly identified four "big questions" that writers in the ethics field would do well to examine carefully. I will comment on them one by one in the order Cooper lists them toward the end of his article.

1. *What are the normative foundations for public administrative ethics?* To address this question, Cooper succinctly summarizes five approaches to administrative ethics that are most salient to the field. I have no quarrel with the five approaches he lists, but I am puzzled by the absence of any reference to the profound influence of Denis Thompson's work. Granted, Thompson's writ runs far beyond administrative questions, but such questions are certainly included in his wide-ranging writings across the broad spectrum of ethics in government. I have in mind especially his influential article "The Problem of Many Hands," which appeared in the *American Political Science Review* in 1981 and is still cited frequently in the literature. The omission of Thompson's work is particularly unfortunate because of the philosophical rigor that characterizes his work. I do not think I am telling stories out

of school when I say that philosophical rigor is not always apparent in much of the administrative ethics literature.

If I understand Cooper's position correctly, his five approaches to ethics are empirical rather than normative. That is, he is simply reporting what he has seen in reading the administrative ethics literature over a good number of years. My remarks on Thompson challenge Cooper's reading of the data. There is another serious omission for which I can not fault Cooper on empirical grounds: the absence of any discussion of the ethical issues in conflict-of-interest laws and policies and the financial disclosure regulations adopted pursuant to such laws and policies. The scarcity of articles on these topics in public administration journals is most unfortunate. It serves only to reinforce the unwholesome split between academics and practitioners for whom ethics often means nothing but conflict of interest and financial disclosure. Because Cooper's five approaches are empirically based, he is perfectly correct in omitting conflict of interest. It is unfortunate, however, that he is so correct. At the risk of upsetting the tidiness of Cooper's argument, I would enter a plea on normative grounds that we give far more attention to these legal questions, which can have enormous significance for administrators who run afoul of them. For openers, I would recommend careful attention to Andrew Stark's brilliant analyses of conflict-of-interest laws and policies.

2. *How do American administrative ethical norms fit into a global context?* Cooper addresses this question with considerable insight, especially his hard-headed insistence on the importance of articulating international principles, even when they are often disregarded in practice. Although a global administrative ethic, at least for now, smacks of utopianism, Cooper's emphasis on transparency is particularly well advised. This is a value that is taken seriously in many parts of the world and one that might serve as a foundation for further international cooperation in transforming today's utopias into tomorrow's realities. My only caveat touches on the use of the words *global* and *globalization*. These words have a nice, inclusive tone that makes us want to burst out in a chorus of Beethoven's *Ode to Joy*. The sad truth, however, is that globalization is not global at all. Africa leads the parade of those likely to be left out of whatever advantages will come from greater international cooperation. Ethical discourse on globalization is right and proper, but it is important for ethicists not to be trapped by the metaphors they use into seeing a far more hopeful world than the one we live in.

3. *How can organizations be designed to be supportive of ethical conduct?* Cooper's reply is thoughtful and persuasive. I would add only that those engaging in such organizational design pay careful attention to the work of the framers of the Constitution of the United States. Their elaborate scheme of checks and balances was not intended to make men virtuous, but rather to take them as they are—with all their warts and wrinkles—and to channel their self-interest and ambition along politically constructive lines that would support the demands of republican principles. Nowhere is this plan explained more

clearly than in the famous fifty-first *Federalist*. Here is a link between contemporary organizational design and the fundamental principles of the republic.

4. *When should we treat people equally in order to treat them fairly and when should we treat them differently?* Once again, Cooper's discussion is most enlightening, especially his engaging narrative of efforts to establish a neighborhood council system in Los Angeles. His puzzlement as to why some forms of discrimination are more acceptable than others would be considerably reduced if he would reflect on the ethical implications of the constitutional law governing such matters. Cooper wonders why "public policy concerning the disabled appears to be less contentious than when it concerns race, ethnicity, or gender." Special parking places for the handicapped do not produce the same anger and resentment as affirmative action programs for racial minorities.

The Supreme Court has developed a category called "suspect classifications" to address such questions. Although there has been considerable debate over just which categories are "suspect," one can rest assured that race is one of them and gender another, though less suspect than race. Classifying people as handicapped or disabled is not suspect. To pass constitutional muster, government agencies must show there was a "compelling state interest" for making use of a suspect classification—race, for instance—and the interest in question can be achieved by the "least restrictive means"—that is, by relying on race as little as possible without endangering the compelling interest. A less stringent test is used for discrimination based on gender, whereas the very relaxed test of "mere reasonableness" is used for nonsuspect classifications such as disability. This constitutional scheme does not answer all of the questions Cooper raises about unequal treatment, but it provides a solid foundation for further ethical reflection. In a word, Cooper exaggerates the severity of the problem by neglecting the steps that have already been taken to solve it.

Despite the misgivings I have mentioned, I am happy to follow Cooper's lead in bringing greater coherence to the field of administrative ethics without enforcing a rigid orthodoxy. I hope those who write articles for public administration journals (as well as those who review and edit them) will take Cooper's position seriously and show how their work either builds on one or more of the approaches he has identified, or addresses one or more of his "big questions." If they choose to follow neither path, they would do well to explain briefly their reason for failing to do so.

Bravo, Terry Cooper.

CASE STUDY

Helen is a physics professor at a state university. Additionally, she volunteers on the scholarship board for a major nonprofit organization that awards scholarships to students attending graduate school. When they give out scholarships, the board usually relies on a primary recommendation from the person who is the expert in the subject matter of the potential awardee (i.e., Helen usually takes the lead for students pursuing a graduate degree in physics). This year there are 10 physics students who have applied for a scholarship, and two of the students are from her university; in fact, she has had both of them in class and knows they are excellent students. She doesn't want to be subconsciously biased toward those students or give the appearance of having any bias. However, she is the only one on the board with a physics background, and her years of work with graduate students has made her an excellent judge of which students will be successful in graduate school. She worries that if she has someone else evaluate the physics students, they may not be able to do it adequately. What should she do? Should she avoid the appearance of a conflict, even if she believes she can be unbiased? Or should she participate in the evaluation but risk the potential impression of bias?

CHAPTER 8

Public Service, Ethics, and Constitutional Practice

SEE WHERE YOU STAND: 60 SECOND ETHICAL DILEMMA

Imagine that you are in the following situation and have one minute to make a decision about the most ethical course of action:

You are at a party and someone starts talking to you about your boss. They are insinuating that he is having an affair with a lobbyist who works closely with your organization. Your organization only has an intraoffice dating policy, so he isn't breaking any of the organization's rules, but if this is true and becomes public, it could damage the reputation of both your boss and the organization. However, if it's not true, bringing it up could create unnecessary turmoil. They then ask you if you are going to do anything about it. What do you do?

INTRODUCTION TO CHAPTER

This chapter directly addresses why ethical competency in public administration is so important. The author's argument is that bureaucrats are policymakers who exercise administrative discretion in nearly everything they do. In essence, public administrators make value judgments, which inherently involve ethical claims. Without focusing on the normative ethics of what administrators should or should not do, John Rohr describes where public administrators can go to find values. Public administrators, however neutral they attempt to be, make ethical choices nearly every day in determining who gets what and who does not. Moreover, as elected officials and their appointees come and go, career civil servants provide stability in governance. Because these civil servants are not directly subject to the levers of democracy, being grounded in and upholding the values of the public can promote an ethically competent bureaucracy that works in the public's interest.

Ethics for Bureaucrats

By John A. Rohr

This is the first article I wrote on public service ethics. Intended for a general audience, it tells the story of the rise and fall of the politics/administration dichotomy and relates that story to the emergence of administrative discretion as the most fundamental ethical problem for the career civil servant. Does today's reader think that administrative discretion is as pervasive now as it was in 1973?

The starting point of our ethical inquiry is the assertion that bureaucrats in our regime are policymakers. By "bureaucrats," I mean those tenured public officials who are neither elected nor politically appointed. "Tenured" means they can be removed only "for cause." Political appointment is distinguished from examination or some other "**merit**" mechanism as a means of selection. Thus, no congressman, president, cabinet officer, or federal judge is a **bureaucrat**. Neither are the ambassadors or commissioners of the independent regulatory commissions. Bureaucrats are those men and women with a "passion for anonymity" who gradually work their way up the various grades of the civil service, the foreign service, or the armed forces. They are the persons who provide stability to the regime as they remain in their posts while presidents and cabinet secretaries come and go.

To be sure, there is nothing startling in asserting that bureaucrats share in the governing power in our society. The assertion takes on some significance, however, when one reflects on the democratic thrust of American institutions and values. Since bureaucrats neither achieve nor lose their political power through the electoral process, this power is hard to square with traditional democratic theory. There is a certain bite to public complaints about a bureaucracy that is "insensitive" or "unresponsive." To the extent that this complaint is justified, it is a self-inflicted wound. In establishing a politically neutral civil service with entrance and promotion based on examination, merit, and seniority, the American people have deliberately isolated the bureaucracy from the electoral process and institutionalized the very "insensitivity" of which they complain.

The architects of the contemporary American bureaucracy were the civil service reformers of a century ago. Then, the Jacksonian principle of "rotation of office" had degenerated into a "spoils system," and public administration was all too "sensitive" to the political process. The need for reform was apparent, but a major obstacle was the theoretical argument that the spoils system, despite its abuses, was a more democratic way of selecting public officials. The merit system with its "good government" overtones was, nevertheless, an invitation to government by a ruling class.

The reformers' response to this argument was to structure a theory of a "science" of administration. This theory rested on a sharp dichotomy between politics and administration. Its leading proponent was Woodrow Wilson, then a professor of political science, whose famous article, "The Study of Administration," appeared in *the Political Science Quarterly* of June 1887. Wilson argued that administration was a science that could be learned by and entrusted to people who had the proper credentials and expertise. This dichotomy provided the theoretical justification for civil service reform. The people express their will through the electoral process; here, democracy reigns supreme. There can be no democratic administration, however, for the same reason there can be no democratic chemistry. If public opinion enters the administrative process, it will only prove "meddlesome." Administrators must be freed from politics if they are to apply their politically neutral techniques to the problems involved in executing the policies determined by the people.

Under the leadership of Wilson and his followers, the model of a politically neutral administrator dispassionately applying his scientific expertise became high doctrine. Max Weber's "ideal-type" bureaucracy, the "scientific management" movement, the Hatch Act, and the insistence of the Civil Service Commission upon "economy and efficiency" as the hallmarks of good administration reinforced the Wilsonian doctrine.

Shortly after World War II, however, political scientists began to examine the dichotomy of politics and administration more closely. They questioned the legitimacy of the inference that bureaucrats are isolated from the *political* process simply because they have been isolated from the *electoral* process. Soon, public administration literature abounded with case studies documenting the highly politicized role of the career bureaucrat.

The relationships between the railroad industry and the Interstate Commerce Commission, or the Agricultural Extension Service and the American Farm Bureau Federation, or the Army Corps of Engineers and the Rivers and Harbors Congress were only the most spectacular examples of "captured" government agencies. A dominant theme in studies of bureaucracy focused on the problem encountered by elected or politically appointed officials in their struggle to get real control over the bureaucrats who were subordinate to them on government organizational charts.

Theodore Lowi's *The End of Liberalism* (1969) has provided an enlightening explanation of the historical growth of the political power of the bureaucrat. The complexities of a modern industrial economy deterred Congress from regulating industry with detailed statutes; the legislative process was too cumbersome for this. An irresistible tendency developed for Congress simply to point out a problem area and to give administrators discretionary authority to develop substantive public policies. At first, the discretion of the administrators was carefully circumscribed by law. Thus, the Interstate Commerce Commission, created in 1887, was to regulate maximum rates for railroads. Railroads and maximum rates are concrete and specific areas of jurisdiction; so are the trusts that were to be regulated by the Sherman Act of 1890. Less concrete and specific, however, was the task given to administrators under the Food and Drug Act of 1906. Under this act, bureaucrats were directed to regulate substandard food, impure drugs, and immoral women. Such value-laden concepts broadened the discretion of the administrators and shifted the political thrust of the lobbyists from congressional committees to administrative agencies. The creation of the Federal Trade Commission (FTC) in 1914 was a further step in the same direction. This commission was to stop "unfair" competition. "Unfair" is as difficult a word to define as "impure" or "immoral," but prior to the creation of the FTC, bureaucrats were concerned with regulating concrete persons and things—women, drugs, food, and railroads. The FTC was given jurisdiction over an abstraction—competition.

Bureaucratic discretion continued to grow when Congress created the Securities and Exchange Commission in 1935 and charged it with the vague responsibility of maintaining a "fair and orderly market." This directive meant that the bureaucracy would regulate not only behavior within the market but access to the market as well. The power to determine what securities are marketable authorized administrators to determine who the players should be, as well as the rules by which they would play. The power enjoyed by the Federal Communications Commission to grant radio and television licenses as "the public interest, convenience, or necessity" dictates is another example of almost unfettered bureaucratic discretion to control access to a competitive market. The same could be said of administrators' licensing power in such diverse areas as the airlines, satellite communication, and atomic energy.

Perhaps the clearest example of the growth of administrative discretion (and therefore power) comes from contrasting what Lowi has called "old welfare" (Social Security Act of 1935) with "new welfare" (Economic Opportunity Act of 1964). The Social Security Act of 1935 is best known for its contributory system of old age insurance, but it also provided a noncontributory aid program for the aged, the blind, and dependent children. The statute defined the categories with some precision and specified the minimum grants to be given to persons falling within the categories. Thus, old welfare limited the discretion of bureaucrats responsible for the administration of the act. New welfare attacked poverty through community action programs rather than simply giving money to needy people in clearly defined categories. The massive political question, of course, was to determine which community action programs were to be the recipients of federal largesse. This decision was made by the bureaucracy.

Sargent Shriver, who served as the first director of the Office of Equal Opportunity (OEO), gave extremely broad discretion to his bureaucratic subordinates in deciding which programs would be funded. He maintained there was only one basic criterion—the community action program had to be "broadly representative of the interests of the community."[1] The funded programs could be public or private as long as they enjoyed the support of "the relevant elements of community government." Instead of specifying the kind of behavior required of programs seeking federal funding, Shriver's directive merely stated that "it is likely" that funded agencies would include activities "such as the following." He then went on to enumerate some fifteen activities that one might be "likely" to find in funded community action programs. By using the device of a "such as" clause followed by a nonexclusive list of acceptable activities, Shriver conferred tremendous discretionary power upon the field representatives (i.e., bureaucrats) of OEO in determining which community organizations would be funded. This, of course, is the very stuff of politics and illustrates clearly the reason behind the demise of the politics/ administration dichotomy.

The demise of the dichotomy destroyed the theoretical defense of the merit system advocated a century ago by civil service reformers. Their argument was that a civil service based on examination and merit rather than politics was not undemocratic because the civil service dealt with the "science" of administration, which was quite distinct from politics. Empirical evidence of the broad discretionary powers enjoyed by bureaucrats has demonstrated the inadequacy of the reformers' argument, but it leaves unsolved the problem they addressed—How can a democratic regime justify substantial political power in the hands of people who are exempt by law from the discipline of the ballot box?

I do not believe this question can be answered without some kind of public concern with the normative values of our bureaucrats. This is a hard saying. The McCarthy era stands as a somber warning of excessive public concern with the normative values of bureaucrats, and the civil liberties of bureaucrats must not be sacrificed on the altar of public concern. Experience has taught us the severe limitations on the wisdom and usefulness of loyalty oaths. It might be better if the public's concern with the personal values of bureaucrats were procedural rather than substantive. Rather than insisting upon bureaucratic orthodoxy in matters of public doctrine, it might be wiser to look for ways to encourage bureaucrats to reflect intelligently on the moral values involved in their policymaking role. Intelligent reflection, of course, is no guarantee of righteous behavior, but it is at least a starting point. Part of the problem of developing an ethic for bureaucrats is that they have been so deeply imbued with the civil service reform mentality—the dichotomy of politics and administration—that they fail to see themselves as policymakers. It is established doctrine in many government agencies that "we don't make policy." It is for this reason that ethical questions in government have for so long been limited to avoiding conflicts of interest, fairness in personnel decisions, a full day's work for a full day's pay, etc. To be sure, these issues are important, but no more so for the bureaucrat than for any conscientious person. The ethical questions do not come to terms with the policymaking aspects of the bureaucrat's role.

To suggest that bureaucrats be encouraged to reflect on the moral dimension of their role is not terribly bold or venturesome. Indeed, the reader may wonder why social scientists have not been doing this all along. The policy role of the bureaucrat has been a commonplace in political science for some time. The reason is that value-free social science was the prevailing orthodoxy in the academic community during the years in which political scientists were so ably documenting the policymaking role of the bureaucracy. Value-free social science provides the analytical tools to isolate and identify policymakers, but is quite inept at addressing the moral issues implicit in its findings. In exposing the sterility of the politics/administration dichotomy, value-free social science created an ethical void since "values" are mere whims or irrational passions that are not answerable to the rigors of the scientific method. In substituting a new dichotomy of facts and values for the older one of politics and administration, value-free social scientists were unable to provide moral leadership for solving the problems their research had discovered. The myth of the politically neutral civil servant was dissipated, but there was no adequate theory available to handle the fact that nonelected, **tenured** personnel have tremendous political power.

The political climate of the late 1960s challenged the complacency of value-free social science and demanded that the academic community become "relevant" and "involved." The most significant response was a collection of essays in *Toward a New Public Administration* edited by Frank Marini of the Maxwell School of Citizenship and Public Affairs at Syracuse University. The essays were written by young (under thirty-five) professors of public administration and delivered at a conference held at Syracuse in the fall of 1968. The summary remarks of the chairman of the final plenary session underscored the need for "greater emphasis upon normative concerns in public administration" as the primary theme of the conference. Since then, the "new" public administration has become an identifiable movement within the discipline. This movement is concerned with substantive policy issues and moral values rather than the discipline's traditional concern with planning, coordinating, and budgeting.

At the 1973 convention of the American Society for Public Administration (Los Angeles, April 1–4), several major papers were presented on such normative questions as the concern of administrators with "social equity." Notable among these papers was an attempt by Michael Harmon of George Washington University to apply John Rawls's A *Theory of Justice* (1971) to normative problems in public administration. These efforts were most encouraging, but I could not ignore the reaction of one administrator with whom I discussed the merits of considering normative questions. He thought it was fine for academics to be concerned with such questions, but he could not see how it concerned him as a practitioner. "Besides," he added, "I have nothing to do with policy; I work for the IRS." Old dogmas die hard; the bureaucracy seems to have learned its lessons from an earlier generation of political scientists so well that it is impervious to the counsel of the descendants of its erstwhile mentors.

We can, however, take some comfort from the fact that there are over ninety-eight schools of public administration in the United States with an enrollment exceeding 12,153. If the "new" public administration permeates these schools, we should be able to look forward to a more ethically alert bureaucracy in the future.

Note

Chapter One originally appeared as "Ethics for Bureaucrats," *America* 128 (May 26, 1973): 488–491. Reprinted with permission.

1 Theodore Lowi, *The End of Liberalism* (New York: W. W. Norton, 1969), p. 236.

The Problem of Professional Ethics

By John A. Rohr

Whereas the previous essay explained bureaucratic ethics to the general reader, this chapter explains professional ethics to the public administration community. It concludes with a hint that links the problem outlined in this chapter to the Constitution of the United States and thereby lays the foundation for the rest of the chapters in the book.

Professional codes and statements of ethics often engender cynicism and derision because these statements, couched in terms of broad and generous public spirit, frequently harbor self-serving sentiments that, when exposed, embarrass the professions and delight their critics. The purpose of this chapter is to explain why professional statements tend to be self-serving and to examine the ethics of public administration in light of this explanation. In so doing, I hope to illuminate an aspect of professionalism that should be of particular interest to the public administration community.

Universal and Particular

Popular discussion of ethical issues tends to be framed in the language of universals—do not steal, do not lie, love your neighbor, etc. This sort of language immediately creates problems for the discussion of professional life. That is, professional life deals with a particular aspect or role in one's life; it does not exhaust one's humanity. The limited (or particularistic) character of role morality immediately challenges the universal quality of most moral propositions. When we say one should not lie or steal or that one should love one's neighbor, we are usually thinking about human beings as such rather than as physicians, journalists, public servants, et al.

Principles v. Exigencies

Universal principles come under considerable pressure when they confront the exigencies of professional life. Familiar examples abound: May a physician lie to his or her patient if there is good reason to believe that the truth would considerably retard the patient's recovery? May an investigative reporter lie to "Deep Throat" to get information that will expose wrongdoing in Richard Nixon's White House? May a "double agent" lie to protect national security? Clearly, these are not the sorts of examples we have in mind when we announce as public doctrine the straightforward, moral principle that lying is wrong. Professional life demands exceptions from these universal moral principles and therefore becomes morally suspect. We fear that the exceptions may soon swallow up the rules and that the chaste simplicity of the moral principle—don't lie—will be fatally compromised by the "what ifs" of the professions' casuistry.

Role Morality

To be sure, it is not only the professions that put pressure on universal moral principles. In a certain sense, all moral acts in the concrete are examples of "role morality"—I act as spouse, parent, citizen, believer, consumer, voter, television viewer, neighbor, taxpayer, welfare recipient, etc. Circumstances may arise in each of these roles that call for an exception to a well-established moral rule—e.g., the familiar example of the parent who steals bread to feed a starving child.

The problem of professional ethics is particularly acute, however, for two reasons. First, there is the elite nature of professional life. Only the few can be physicians, attorneys, and engineers, but all of us are or can be spouses, parents, citizens, and consumers. As a democratic people, we are more comfortable with an exception that, given the proper circumstances, is open to all of us as opposed to an exception that is available only to the few. Better to trigger exceptions by circumstance than by status.

Second, the foundation of the professional's exception differs from the foundation of the exceptions demanded by ordinary persons engaged in ordinary activities. The latter usually rely on a "just this once" argument. The father steals bread today, but tomorrow he will have a job, or sell his wares, or visit the welfare office, or receive money from a rich uncle, or beg for the wherewithal to support the family. Quite literally, he practices *situation* ethics. A unique set of circumstances has conspired to override the rule that bids us respect the property of others, but the rule is overridden "just this once." If he were to institutionalize his behavior, we would say he had taken up a "life of crime"; that he was no longer a concerned parent but a thief. The point here is that moral character is usually determined by one's habits (virtues or vices) rather than by isolated actions.

Professionals, on the other hand, do institutionalize the exceptions they seek, and the exceptions are hailed as ethical principles of the profession. A successful defense attorney owes no apologies for making a clever argument that diverts the jury's attention from incriminating evidence and contributes to the erroneous verdict that a guilty defendant is innocent. Psychologists do not blush about the statement in their Ethical Standards that the use of deception in research is permissible if the knowledge cannot be generated in any other way. The spy who lies successfully to the enemy stands quite ready to do it again. Attorneys, psychologists, and spies do not appeal to a unique set of circumstances to justify their behavior. On the contrary, their behavior is based on a *principled* demand for exceptions from the rules by which the rest of us are supposed to live.

Public Interest and Self-Interest

The tension between universal principles and particularistic demands is crucial for understanding why professional codes, despite their public service language, are frequently in fact self-serving. The reason is that the justification for the exceptions the professions demand from universal moral rules is grounded in an implicit, utilitarian assumption that the profession itself can produce sufficient benefits to society to outweigh whatever harm is caused by its departure from customary morality. To clarify this point, let me cite several examples from the profession of law.[1]

- The client is the prosperous president of a savings and loan association. In leaner days he borrowed almost $5,000 from a man working for him as a carpenter. He now wishes to avoid repaying the debt by running the statute of limitations. He is sued by the carpenter and calls his lawyer (*Zabella v. Pakel,* 242 F. 2d 452 [1957]).
- The client has raped a woman, been found not guilty by reason of insanity, and institutionalized. He wishes to appeal the decision by asserting a technical defense, namely, that he was denied the right to a speedy trial (*Langworthy v. Slate,* 39 Md. App. 559 [1978], rev'd. 284 Md. 588 [1979]).
- A youth, badly injured in an automobile wreck, sues the driver responsible for the injury. The driver's defense lawyer has his own doctor examine the youth; the doctor discovers an aortic aneurism, apparently caused by the accident, that the boy's doctor had not found. The aneurism is life-threatening unless operated on. But the defense lawyer realizes that if the youth learns of the aneurism he will demand a much higher settlement (*Spaulding v. Zimmerman,* 116 N.W. 2d 704 [1962]).

In each of these cases, professional ethics would counsel counterintuitive judgments in favor of the banker, the rapist, and the driver. The reason, of course, is that the attorney's moral commitment to the client overrides broader principles of what our common sense tells us is right in each of the examples.[2] Such a commitment can itself be morally justified only on the grounds that (1) the integrity of the legal system demands it and (2) the legal system itself is so valuable to society that, on balance, we do well to tolerate occasional injustices because of the rich benefits the system provides.

Ethics and Self-Interest

Such an argument may well be challenged on empirical grounds, but for the purposes of this chapter it is the *structure* of the argument rather than its validity that is of interest. The justification for professional conduct that defies common-sense notions of right is necessarily grounded in an affirmation of the overriding importance of the profession itself. It is the necessity for making this kind of argument that forges the link between professional ethics and self-interest. Because of the tension between the particularistic demands of the professions and the universal character of moral discourse, the professions must argue that they are worthy of the moral exception they demand. In effect, they must argue that what is good for the profession is good for society, America, humanity, or whatever.

Needless to say, such an argument is freighted with peril. To invite attention to the close connection between the interests of one's profession and broader public interests can lead to keen embarrassment. Indeed, at times it can expose professional self-adulation as ludicrous and absurd.[3]

Overriding Value

I am not interested in the preposterous aspects of professional ethics. Suffice it to say that all professionals, poor sinners like the rest of us, suffer the thousand natural shocks that flesh is heir to. It is the *argument* for professional ethics, an argument rooted in the nature of professional life, that is instructive for our purposes. No matter how upright and decent the members of a profession might be, they will at times demand exceptions from ordinary rules of morality, and when they do, they must justify their demand in terms of the overriding value of their profession for the society whose rules they would transcend. Such an argument quite properly invites close scrutiny and not a little skepticism.

Public Administration as Profession

Codes of ethics for government employees labor under the suspicion of being self-serving statements. This suspicion can arise from several aspects of government service, but, for the purposes of this chapter, I shall narrow my focus to the ethical concerns over political manipulation of the career civil service. Such interference is, of course, anathema to our sense of professionalism.

Value-Laded Word

I have deliberately used the value-laded word "manipulation" to signal the improper nature of the political activity to which we object. We are, of course, to be "accountable" and "responsive" to the political leadership, but we should not be subjected to political interference, meddling, or partisan pressure—in a word, "manipulation." Language of this sort goes to the heart of the merit system and is thematic in public service codes of ethics. A reaffirmation of this position came from the first director of the Office of Personnel Management, Alan K. Campbell. In response to the charge that the creation of the Senior Executive Service (SES) would lead to the "politicization" of the civil service, Campbell replied that the SES would provide "appropriate responsiveness to the government's political leadership while resisting improper political influence."[4]

One might be tempted to dismiss Campbell's delphic utterance as question begging verbiage, but this would be a mistake—at least for our purposes. In scoring "improper political influence," Campbell proclaimed the ancient faith of civil service reform. Professional orthodoxy commits us to the belief that resistance to such influence is a cardinal principle of professional ethics. That is all quite obvious. What we tend to ignore, however, is the self-interested character of this principle.

Sphere of Autonomy

In saying that government officers or employees should resist improper political influence is to carve out for them a **sphere of autonomy** within the governmental process. Such autonomy is crucial for any group that aspires to professional status. The client does not tell the attorney how to cross-examine a hostile witness; the hospital administrator does not tell the physician what medicine to prescribe; the traveler does not tell the engineer when the bridge is safe; indeed, the baseball owner does not tell the manager when to change pitchers—unless the owner is George Steinbrenner.

In each of these examples, there is a sphere of professional autonomy that attorneys, physicians, engineers, and baseball managers guard jealously. It is in their interest to do so, but it is also in the interest of their client, patient, team, etc. So also with public administrators. It is in their interest to protect their administrative "turf," and in so doing, they make government more efficient and effective and thereby promote the public interest.

So the argument goes, and it's not a bad argument. To put a finer point on it, however, my position, reductively, is that in exercising certain aspects of governmental authority, government employees must be exempt from the democratic principle of subordination to political leadership and this in the name of democracy itself. To put the argument this way recalls the attractiveness of the old politics/administration dichotomy. Here was a conceptual tool that finessed the potential embarrassment in our claim to a sphere of autonomy from the elected leadership. Indeed, it defined the problem out of existence. The discretionary character of contemporary public administration has discredited the dichotomy and forced administrators to assert their autonomy in a more forthright manner.

The Law is Supreme

A remarkable example of this forthrightness appears in "Principles for the American Society for Public Administration" adopted by that body's National Council on July 12, 1981. The third of its ten principles reads as follows: "The law is supreme. Where laws or regulations are ambiguous, leave discretion, or require change, we will seek to define and promote the public interest."

To be sure, the law is supreme, but it is no secret that the hallmarks of contemporary public law are its ambiguity and its conferral of broad discretion on administrative agencies. Reduced to its simplest terms, the above statement is an announcement of our intention to share in governing the republic, for he who defines the public interest surely governs. The announcement is not a bureaucratic power play; it is a candid (perhaps too candid?) statement of what conscientious administrators have been trying to do for a long time. Given the fact of administrative discretion, what criterion other than the public interest is suitable for its exercise?

Not Uncommon

We should not be surprised to find such a statement in a code of ethics. As we saw earlier in this chapter, it is not uncommon for professional ethics to demand an exemption from ordinary societal standards. This is precisely what we are doing when we claim a sphere of autonomy from political leadership. The American Society for Public Administration's statement is simply a positive formulation of the more familiar negative proposition that the political leadership should not manipulate us in the exercise of our administrative discretion.

This is an example of a particularistic demand against the universal, democratic principle that all governmental activities should be accountable to the electorate. This self-interested claim is grounded in the long-term benefits the sound exercise of administrative discretion can bring to a democratic regime. Like other professional groups, we can make claims that are either plausible or outrageous. In this untidy world, they are usually a little bit of both.

Conclusion

If public administration resembles other professions in cherishing a sphere of autonomy, it also differs from them in some important ways. The precise grounds on which we base our claim for autonomy may be less clear for us than it is in other professions. The "learned" professions of law, medicine, and religion can point to a lengthy period of formal training that is followed by a certification process prior to admittance to the bar, ordination, etc. The profession of engineering is more relaxed than law, medicine, and some churches in determining who belongs to the profession, but, like the learned professions, engineering also bases its professional status on technical knowledge. The profession of journalism relies less on formal training than the other professions mentioned. The journalists' claim for exceptional ethical standards rests on the vital role they play in rendering operative the public's "right to know."

Our profession lacks these advantages. In the days of the politics/administration dichotomy, we could ground our profession in the administrative skills, which, by definition, were distinct from politics. The discretionary character of contemporary public administration has taken this argument from us. We know Carl Friedrich was right when he said (in his *Public Policy and Administrative Responsibility)* that to execute public policy is to make it. Our problem is that we are really claiming an expertise in governing, a claim that is not likely to fall on sympathetic ears in a democratic society. It is for this reason that I believe the question of professionalism in public administration will always be somewhat controversial in the United States.

There is one line of argument that might possibly legitimate our claim to share in governing the republic. In the famous 1803 case *Marbury v. Madison,* Chief Justice John Marshall developed an argument in support of the power of the federal courts to declare acts of Congress unconstitutional. The argument rested in part on the oath taken by judges to uphold the Constitution of the United States. Marshall's point was that it would be immoral for judges to enforce legislative enactments contrary to the Constitution they are sworn to uphold.

Marshall ignored the fact that not only federal judges but presidents, senators, representatives, state legislators, and "all executive and judicial Officers, both of the United States and of the Several States," are required to take an oath to uphold the Constitution. The significance of Marshall's argument is that it suggests a link between the oath of office and the legitimacy of exercising an otherwise questionable power—like that of judicial review of acts of Congress. Perhaps the statutory mandate that requires from federal public administrators an oath to uphold the Constitution could provide a glimmer of hope for legitimating a principled defense of professional autonomy.

Notes

Chapter Two originally appeared as "The Problem of Professional Ethics," *The Bureaucrat* 11 (summer 1982) and was reprinted in "The Best of *The Bureaucrat*" 20 (summer 1991): 9–12. Reprinted with permission.

1 These cases are taken from the *Report from the Center for Philosophy and Public Policy* 1 (summer 1982): 6. They are discussed more fully in David Luban, "Calming the Hearse Horse: A Philosophical Research Program for Legal Ethics," *Maryland Law Review* 40 (1981).

2 A good discussion on legal ethics can be found in Geoffrey Hazard, *Ethics in the Practice of Law* (New Haven: Yale University Press, 1978).

3 See *Virginia State Board of Pharmacy v. Virginia Citizens Consumer Council, Inc.,* 425 U.S. 748 (1976); *Bates v. State Bar of Arizona,* 433 U.S. 350 (1977); *Ohralik v. Ohio State Bar Association,* 436 U.S. 447 (1978).

4 *Public Administration Tunes 2* (August 1, 1979): 1.

CASE STUDY

Keaton works for a national security agency and has been assigned to travel with the director of the agency on an overseas trip. Although secrecy is paramount, his agency's outdated equipment makes it nearly impossible to conduct business remotely. The agency has technology that allows employees to access secure servers remotely, but it often does not work and it almost never allows someone to print documents. Keaton has been asked by the director to quickly print a critical document she just received electronically, and this document is so new that it does not yet have a classification. Keaton realizes he can't connect to the secure server, but he knows that it is critical to the director's mission that this document be printed right away, as she needs it for her next meeting. Keep in mind that he can't print it directly from a phone; he could print it from his personal email at the hotel computer, but the agency requires that all business transacted on its behalf be done on its encrypted systems (although Keaton knows that this last requirement is largely overlooked if one is helping the director with critical requests). What should he do? What ethical considerations does he need to contemplate?

CHAPTER 9

Ethical Problems in Public Careers

Lying

SEE WHERE YOU STAND: 60 SECOND ETHICAL DILEMMA

Imagine that you are in the following situation and have one minute to make a decision about the most ethical course of action:

You are the coach of a championship-winning high school soccer team. The success of the soccer team has resulted in many college scholarships for the athletes. You know that the players are often recruited because the team has a reputation for being hard working and well behaved, in addition to their athletic successes. The players vote for their captain, and you are now counting the votes after practice while the team waits. You realize that there is a tie between a player you know will continue to foster this positive reputation (which will ultimately benefit the entire team) and a player who is popular but often encourages his teammates to engage in questionable behavior, which could potentially hurt their chances of receiving college scholarships. The team is supposed to pick the captain, but you are worried about the potential outcome. What do you do? Do you announce that there is a tie and have another vote or announce that the preferred player has won? Why?

INTRODUCTION TO CHAPTER

From a deontological perspective, lying is inherently unethical, but the historical case studies in this chapter (some real and some imagined) will force you to consider whether or not it is ever ethical to lie. Even with the benefit of hindsight, some of these cases can challenge our understanding about what is the "best" course of action. Consider what framework (i.e., deontology versus utilitarianism) you are using to determine whether or not the decision to lie is ethical. Are you applying the same framework to every case? Why or why not? People have a tendency to reach a conclusion based on the outcome they would prefer and then later create a justification for that preferred outcome, but that is not the most systematic (or perhaps even ethical) way to make decisions. Can an outcome ever justify using only the facts that are convenient to support that outcome? Is it possible to generate a set of guidelines that could be applied to all situations equally? As you go through each of the cases, keep track of whether or not you think the decision to lie in each of these cases is right or wrong.

Ethical Problems in Public Careers

Lying

By Allison Graham and Lance M. Liebman

Participants in public life often face ethical dilemmas when they are called upon to transmit information. Honesty may in fact be the best policy, but does it apply in any and all situations? This is a matter of some controversy. This case starts from the recognition that prevailing practice in public life often condones—and sometimes requires—departures from any grand standard of "the truth, the whole truth, and nothing but the truth." It focuses on the issue of the public official's obligation to tell the truth: how strong is this obligation, to whom, and under what circumstances does it apply? When—if ever—is deception justified? And can any guidelines be formulated to help resolve the difficult ethical issues that regularly confront participants in public affairs?

This case is actually a set of ten minicases. In each, some participant in public life faces a decision of whether or not to tell the truth. Some, you will note, are entirely fictitious; others are drawn from actual occurrences. Some involve elected officials, some political appointees, and some nominally private citizens in public roles, such as journalists, lobbyists, and consultants. In each, you are asked to judge whether you believe the particular statement in question to be, on balance, morally right or wrong.

Read each case carefully and then circle the appropriate letter on the answer sheet following case #10. [...]

Ethical Hypotheticals

1. Analyst Muffles Uncertainties

It is January 1969. Governor Francis Sargent of Massachusetts is facing the issue of whether or not to approve plans for the construction of a state medical school. The school is supported by its proponents as a way to increase the number of practicing physicians in the state and as a means of expanding medical educational opportunities for Massachusetts residents. Plans call for the construction of a new 400-bed teaching hospital and a new classroom and medical sciences building in Worcester. The school is to enroll an annual class of 100 students.

Of major concern to Sargent, however, is the cost of the proposed school. Official estimates have recently raised the projected costs of construction from $80 million to $124 million. While it is hoped and expected that approximately half of this amount would come from the federal government, the state's share is still uncomfortably high. Moreover, the school's annual operating costs are projected to cost the taxpayers an additional $12 to $15 million indefinitely.

Despite its defects, the proposal has the solid support of the leadership of the state legislature and of organized labor. Sargent knows that to block the project he must have a convincing and workable alternative. He commissions a professor of management science at MIT to do a cost-benefit analysis of the proposal and of several alternatives to it.

During the course of his analysis, the professor comes to favor a system of "community medical schools," an innovative concept in which the basic medical sciences would be taught at one central facility, while clinical instruction would take place in existing hospitals scattered around the state. The analyst believes that, under this alternative, the cost per additional practicing physician might be less than half of the existing proposal. He knows that, as a new and untried method of medical education, the plan contains a large number of uncertainties, uncertainties that could substantially affect the estimated costs. To maximize the proposal's attractiveness, however, he deliberately understates those uncertainties, and instead presents his most optimistic estimate of its costs and benefits as if it were based on "hard" data.

Is the analyst's action right or wrong?

2. JFK, the "Deal," and the Denial

On Saturday, October 27, 1962, at the height of the Cuban Missile Crisis, President John F. Kennedy receives a letter from the Soviet government proposing to strike a deal. The Soviet Union, the letter offers, will dismantle and remove its missiles from Cuba if the United States agrees to a similar withdrawal of its nuclear-armed missiles stationed in Turkey. In fact, Kennedy twice ordered the removal of these obsolescent and vulnerable missiles in the months prior to the October crisis. But each time the Turkish government had objected, and so the missiles remained—an easy target for Soviet retaliation should the United States be forced to take military action against the missiles in Cuba.

Kennedy believes, along with virtually all of his advisers, that the Soviet offer is unacceptable. To back down under fire, he reasons, would be to demonstrate that the United States was willing to trade off European security for its own. It would undermine the credibility of America's pledge to defend Europe against Soviet attack, and would invite the Soviets to stage another missile crisis elsewhere—only this time in a situation where the military deck was not so heavily stacked in America's favor. But he also knows that tens of millions of Russians and Americans might soon be dead if he cannot find some other way to resolve the crisis.

Kennedy decides to ignore the Soviet proposal and to respond favorably to an earlier, private letter from Premier Khrushchev to himself, in which the Soviet leader had offered to withdraw the missiles in Cuba in return only for an American pledge not to invade the island. But to sweeten the deal, guessing that Khrushchev's colleagues may have subsequently raised the price of Soviet withdrawal, Kennedy has his brother Robert inform Soviet Ambassador Anatoly Dobrynin privately that, while there can be no Cuba-for-Turkey exchange made under pressure, the president had already ordered the removal of the American missiles in Turkey and would make sure the order was carried out speedily.

At a press conference on November 20, after the crisis had passed and after the congressional elections that were on Kennedy's mind during October 1962, the following exchange occurred:

> *Q.* Mr. President, in the various exchanges of the past three weeks, either between yourself and Chairman Khrushchev or at the United Nations, have any issues been touched on besides that of Cuba, and could you say how the events of these past three weeks might affect such an issue as Berlin or disarmament or nuclear testing?
>
> *The President.* No. I instructed the negotiators to confine themselves to the matter of Cuba completely, and therefore no other matters were discussed. Disarmament, any matters affecting Western Europe, relations between the Warsaw pact countries and NATO, all the rest—none of these matters was to be in any way referred to or negotiated about until we had made progress and come to some sort of a solution on Cuba. So that has been all we have done diplomatically with the Soviet Union the last month.
>
> Now if we're successful in Cuba, as I said, we would be hopeful that some of the other areas of tension could be relaxed. Obviously when you make progress in any area, then you have hopes that you can continue it. But up till now we have confined ourselves to Cuba, and we'll continue to do so until we feel the situation has reached a satisfactory state.

Was this answer sufficiently forthcoming?

3. Woodward Lies to Deep Throat

Investigative reporter Bob Woodward has uncovered a source on Watergate that he calls "Deep Throat." He has been getting information from Deep Throat for more than a month. Woodward has come to suspect that presidential aide H.R. Haldeman was deeply involved in the Watergate affair but has little hard evidence to back up his suspicions. He tries to get Deep Throat to fill him in on the extent of Haldeman's involvement, but Deep Throat is reluctant to reveal more than he already has. Therefore, trying to get Deep Throat to confirm his suspicions, Woodward falsely tells him that he and fellow reporter Carl Bernstein have a story for the following week saying that Haldeman was the fifth person in control of disbursements from a secret slush fund, and that the *Washington Post* has already decided to print the story.

Is Woodward's lie defensible?

4. The Election Debate

It is November 1969. John Lindsay is running for reelection as mayor of New York. His principal opponent is Mario Procaccino, a conservative Democrat. In a TV debate the Sunday before election day, Procaccino charges that Lindsay has "made a deal with the landlords." More specifically, he claims that (1) Lindsay has a secret report on housing in New York City, (2) the report states that rent control is at the heart of the city's housing problem, and recommends revisions of the rent control law which will result in massive rent increases, and (3) the report is being suppressed until after the election.

In fact, Lindsay knows that two city consultants (RAND and McKinsey) have done such a study for the Housing and Development Administration. He has not seen their report, but has seen a preliminary summary of their findings, which do find that rent control is aggravating the city's housing shortage, and do recommend substantial revision of the rent control law in such a way that many rents will be significantly increased. At the recommendation of the Housing and Development administrator, the reports have been labeled "highly confidential" and publication is being withheld until after the election. On the basis of the report's findings and the recommendations of other analysts in the city government, Lindsay believes that the report's analyses are essentially correct, and plans to seek substantial changes in rent control—after the election.

Lindsay knows that to announce his intention prior to the election would cost many votes. He suspects that to acknowledge the existence of the report will raise serious doubts in many voters' minds about his support for rent control. He believes that Procaccino would be a disastrous mayor for New York City. He replies:

> I haven't seen this so-called report; there could well be such a report. The mayor sees thousands of reports from various persons, and it's the mayor's decision that counts in this whole matter of governing New York City, and my decisions have been constant, not only to be firm on rent control, which I am. I believe in it. I think we must have it.

Is Lindsay's statement justifiable?

Two hours after the debate, Lindsay and his staff are at campaign headquarters. A young aide says, The mayor's answer to the rent control question was ambiguous. We'd better put out a firmer denial. How about this?" He then proposes the following press release:

> Mayor Lindsay today branded as ridiculous the charge that he is soft on rent control. He said the city is not studying the watering down of controls, and if any recommendation for higher rents is made, he will reject it out of hand.

Is the aide's recommendation right or wrong?

5. Miller and Furloughs

It is early 1970. Jerome Miller has just taken office as head of Massachusetts' Department of Youth Services, the agency responsible for managing the state's programs for juvenile offenders. After 15 years of child-treatment experience, Miller—like many other progressives in his field—has come to believe that institutionalization is a disastrous policy, and that almost any environment outside the large state detention centers is better for the child and cheaper for the state. He believes the old, prison-like "reform schools" are brutal, oppressive institutions that teach little more than the finer points of crime; his ultimate goal is to shut them down entirely and replace them with a network of smaller scale, community-based halfway houses. But first he must prove to the legislature and the communities in which the houses will be located that the kids can be trusted.

Miller's first step toward deinstitutionalization is a program of weekend furloughs for confined teenage offenders. One hundred boys and girls go home on Friday afternoon, and 91 come back Monday morning. Miller is not alarmed, since this result conforms to his expectations, based on similar programs elsewhere, in which virtually all of the wanderers have returned within a week. But the press want to know what the "count" was immediately, and Miller fears that published reports of a nine percent AWOL rate will kill any chances for deinstitutionalization. He tells the press on Monday afternoon that all the furlough children were back on time. By Friday, the nine missing offenders have all returned.

Was Miller's statement to the press right or wrong?

6. Fiddling the Rules Committee Chairman

Elizabeth Jackson is a private citizen, head of an ad hoc lobbying group formed to support the Equal Rights Amendment in her state. It is December 1975. Her state has not yet ratified the ERA, but ratification is closer than it has ever been in the three years since Congress sent the amendment to the states.

(Background note: The ERA was passed by both houses of Congress in 1972. The congressional resolution provided that the amendment would become effective if ratified by the required three-fourths of the states (38) within seven years. By the end of 1973, 34 states had ratified the ERA. After a flurry of ratifications in the first two years, the battle for the ERA has come down to a grinding effort to win the few more states needed. Time seems to be on the side of the opponents. The women's movement no longer enjoys the media attention which helped win the initial passage of the ERA by projecting the image of a potent new political force. The ERA opponents seem to be getting stronger, and are able to use delaying tactics to their advantage as the 1979 deadline approaches.)

In Jackson's state, the ERA forces have had little success until this year. Although most legislators are unwilling to be recorded against the ERA, its opponents have bottled it up in committee in both houses, preventing any floor votes. Last election, the key opponent in the House retired, perhaps because he was unwilling to face the vigorous campaign of an opponent whom Jackson helped recruit. With him gone, and with the help of the majority leader, Jackson's group forced the bill out of committee, and the full House approved it. Now the end of the session is a day away, and the ERA languishes in the Senate Rules Committee.

The chairman of the Rules Committee, Senator Henderson, is a progressive force in the generally conservative Senate. Although he is personally ambivalent about the ERA, he has indicated to Jackson that it will reach the Senate floor. His cordiality and cooperative attitude have encouraged Jackson to be optimistic, but the end of the session is near, and the ERA still sits in Rules. Jackson now suspects that Henderson is holding the bill as a favor to his colleagues who would rather not vote on it.

Jackson is desperate to get the ERA approved this year. She knows that the national campaign against the ERA, led by Phyllis Schlafly, is raising funds to support a more intensive lobbying effort next year. Moreover, her key supporter in the House, the majority leader, is leaving to run for governor next year, and the Judiciary Committee chairman is running for Congress. Both of them helped to line up the necessary votes in the House, and without them next year, the prospects for the ERA look bleak. It looks to Jackson as if it's now or never.

She decided to change her tactics. She challenges Senator Henderson in his office. He's deliberately deceiving her, she charges, and she will make sure that he pays for it. He tells her that it is the Rules Committee members who are blocking the ERA, but she refuses to believe him. She tells him that her group is prepared to back Chris Carter, a young attorney active in local politics, who has agreed to run against Senator Henderson if he has sufficient funds and volunteers. She tells Senator Henderson that her group will contribute heavily to Carter unless ERA reaches the Senate floor.

In fact, she knows that her threat is pure fiction. While Carter has been rumored to be considering the race, she has not talked with him. The reason she has not is that she can see that her organization is running out of steam. They have no funds left, and fundraising lately has been hardly worth the effort. Volunteers are tiring of the struggle, and will probably disappear if they are not successful this time. Furthermore, she herself would find it difficult to oppose Senator Henderson because of his critical role in the passage of a wide variety of progressive legislation.

Is Jackson's lie right or wrong?

7. Breaking the Deadlock

Baker, the speaker of the House in the state of Washington, is faced with a deadlock between the House and the Senate over the contents of the biennial appropriations bill. The members of the House have generally accepted a set of optimistic predictions about revenues for the biennium, and have passed a budget containing cost of living increases for welfare recipients and increased funding for the state university system while preserving the status quo on eligibility requirements for some state welfare programs. The Senate has used a set of pessimistic revenue projections as a justification for tightening welfare eligibility requirements, keeping welfare payment rates constant, and making other cuts in the state budget. Both houses have accused each other of using the dispute over revenue projections as a smokescreen for real attempts to alter the spending priorities of the state to fit more liberal or more conservative values. A conference committee reported out a bill which split the difference on all key disputes, but that attempt at compromise was soundly defeated in both houses.

It is now 11 P.M. on the final day of the legislative session (the session is automatically adjourned at midnight because of a provision in the state constitution). Baker, his counterpart in the Senate, and the two Appropriations Committee chairmen are meeting in a conference committee. All of them are perfectly willing to accept the original compromise, but still think that neither house will back them. They decide to write a bill which is in fact the original compromise, but whose real terms are hidden from view by a series of technical amendments. Relying on the end of session chaos, Baker brings the bill before his caucus and then to the floor, and lies to the members about the net effects of various technical provisions. The bill passes the House. His Senate counterparts manage a similar sleight-of-hand, and the deadlock is broken.

Baker and his co-conspirators have deceived their members because they fear that if they do not, the result will be fiscal chaos. Is their action defensible?

8. Herman Fiddles Finnegan

Suppose that the acting director of the Bureau of Consular and Security Affairs in the Department of State, Philip Herman, is trying to substitute a permanent visa for foreign visitors to the US in place of the existing renewable visa. Only the US, among its major allies and trading partners, maintains such a restrictive policy, a legacy of McCarthyist fear of Communist infiltration and subversion, and Herman is attempting to eliminate this imbalance. To do so, he needs congressional approval. But the man he must convince is Representative Michael Finnegan, a fierce anti-Communist who heads the House Appropriations Subcommittee for the State Department. Finnegan is virulently opposed to any change in visa requirements that would make it possible for a single additional Communist to enter the country, no matter what benefits the US might derive from increased foreign visitation. In fact, he has blocked such efforts before. Without Finnegan's approval, there can be no change in the visa. Thus, Herman falsely tells Finnegan that the State Department is under heavy foreign pressure to abolish visas entirely, that unless the US liberalizes its visa regulations, other countries might retaliate by making it increasingly difficult for Americans to travel abroad, and that the best way to beat this pressure would be to adopt a permanent visa system, which would at least permit an initial check on suspect foreigners. Finnegan buys the story.

Is Herman's action right or wrong?

9. Covert Action in Chile (1)

It is early 1973. CIA Director Richard Helms has just been nominated by President Richard Nixon to be US Ambassador to Iran, but before he can take that post, he must be approved by the Senate. During his confirmation hearings before the Foreign Relations Committee, he is asked questions about alleged CIA covert activity in Chile.

In 1970, the CIA had spent over $8 million to prevent the election of Dr. Salvador Allende Gossens, a Marxist, as Chile's president. Despite the CIA money, Allende won the election by a small plurality. But since no candidate won a majority of the vote, the Chilean Congress was required to choose between the top two vote-getters in the general election. In the past, the Congress had always selected the leading candidate, and 1970 appeared to be no exception.

Shortly after the election, President Nixon informed Director Helms that an Allende regime would not be acceptable to the United States and instructed him to organize a military coup d'etat in Chile to prevent Allende's accession to the presidency. The CIA was to take this highly sensitive action without coordination with the Departments of State or Defense and without informing the US ambassador to Chile. Instead, the agency was to report, both for informational and approval purposes only to the president's assistant for national security affairs, Dr. Henry Kissinger, or his deputy.

Despite Helms' belief, expressed later, that the agency was "being asked to almost do the impossible," he attempted to carry out the president's order. In a flurry of activity immediately prior to the scheduled meeting of the Chilean Congress, the CIA made 21 contacts with key military and police officials in Chile. Those Chileans who were inclined to stage a coup were given assurances of strong support at the highest levels of the US government, both before and after a coup. Yet the coup never took place, and Dr. Allende took office. After the death in an abortive kidnap attempt of Chilean Army Commander-in-Chief General Rene Schneider, who opposed the coup, the plot was uncovered. CIA support for the conspirators was rumored, but the allegations were unconfirmed.

Now, in early 1973, with Allende still in power but facing increasing domestic opposition, Helms is asked about the CIA's alleged role in the 1970 coup attempt:

> *Senator Symington:* Did you try in the Central Intelligence Agency to overthrow the government of Chile?
>
> *Mr. Helms:* No, sir.
>
> *Senator Symington:* Did you have any money passed to the opponents of Allende?
>
> *Mr. Helms:* No, sir.
>
> *Senator Symington:* So the stories you were involved in that war are wrong?
>
> *Mr. Helms:* Yes, sir. I said to Senator Fulbright many months ago that if the Agency had really gotten in behind the other candidates and spent a lot of money and so forth the election might have come out differently.

Was Helms right or wrong?

10. Covert Action in Chile (2)

After the accession of Allende to power, CIA support of his opponents continued, albeit on a reduced scale. The stormy, three-year Allende presidency ended in September of 1973, when the Chilean military staged a coup in which he was killed. Although Thomas Karamessines, the CIA's deputy director for plans and head of the special Chile task force in 1970, later testified that "I am sure that the seeds that were laid in that effort in 1970 had their impact in 1973," no direct CIA involvement in the 1973 coup has ever been proven.

Only a few days after the coup, Henry Kissinger appeared before the Foreign Relations Committee, after being nominated to be secretary of state. In executive session, Kissinger was also asked about the CIA and Chile:

> *Senator McGee:* As you listen to some of the comments here this morning, there is a suggestion that the CIA has been deeply involved in Chilean affairs over a period of time in one way or another. This came out in the ITT hearings, for example. Was the CIA deeply involved at this time?
>
> *Mr. Kissinger:* The CIA had nothing to do with the coup, to the best of my knowledge and belief.

Evaluate Kissinger's statement.

			ETHICAL HYPOTHETICALS
R	W	1.	Analyst muffles uncertainties
R	W	2.	JFK, the "deal," and the denial
R	W	3.	Woodward lies to Deep Throat
R	W	4.	a) Lindsay in the debate b) the aide's proposed press release
R	W	5.	Miller and furloughs
R	W	6.	Deceiving the Rules Committee chairman
R	W	7.	Breaking the deadlock
R	W	8.	Herman fiddles Finnegan
R	W	9.	Covert action in Chile: Helms
R	W	10.	Covert action in Chile: Kissinger

Notes

1 *Hearings before the Committee on Foreign Relations*, United States Senate, 93rd Congress, First Session, On the Nomination of Richard Helms, Former Director of the CIA ... (Washington G.P.O., 1974), pp. 47–8.

2 This testimony was read into the *Congressional Record* (January 22, 1975) during further questions of Mr. Helms by the Senate Foreign Relations Committee.

3 *Report of the Senate Select Committee to Study Governmental Operations with Respect to Intelligence Activities—Covert Action in Chile 1963–1973—December 18, 1975,*—(Washington G.P.O., 1975), p. 20.

4 *Ibid.*, p.20.

5 *Ibid.*, p.24.

6 *Ibid.*, p.25.

7 Transcript of Meeting of Faculty Study Group, Cambridge, Mass. March 8, 1978, p. 10.

8 Richard Harris, "Reflections—Secrets", *The New Yorker* (April 10, 1978), p. 46.

9 Transcript of Faculty Study Group, p.25.

10 Harris, p.72.

11 "Between the Law and the Secrets", *New York Times* (November 2, 1977).

12 Anthony Lewis, "Mr. Helms and the Law" *New York Times* (November 3, 1977), p.35.

13 Harris, p.72.

CASE STUDY

Valerie is the director of institutional research for a large public university. One of the university's primary goals is to increase graduation rates, and it is her job to keep track of this. The state legislature has indicated that unless the university increases their graduation rate by 5 percent, they will lose funding, which would force the university to raise tuition. An increase in tuition would adversely affect, in particular, first-generation college students who traditionally have struggled to afford college tuition. After analyzing all of the data, Valerie realized that the overall graduation rate has increased by only 4 percent. However, that number is largely affected by first-generation college students, who have left the university at a higher rate. If that group were excluded from the data, the university would have reached their 5 percent goal. The university president asks to meet with her to discuss the results and pressures her to "massage the numbers" so that he can tell the state legislature that the university has met their goal. Valerie feels very uncomfortable with this request, because it won't accurately depict the overall graduation rate, but she also knows that the increase in tuition will likely reduce the number of first-generation college students who are able to attend the university. As a first-generation college student herself, she knows how important it is for these students to have the opportunity to pursue a college degree. What should she do? Should she report the accurate numbers or should she follow the president's request? Why? Is there something else she could do?

PART V

CORRUPTION IN GOVERNMENT

What's Going On Here?

CHAPTER 10

Corruption of Ethics

Domestic Bribery of Public Officials: Honest Services Fraud

SEE WHERE YOU STAND: 60 SECOND ETHICAL DILEMMA

Imagine that you are in the following situation and have one minute to make a decision about the most ethical course of action:

You work in the permitting department for a city, and you are an avid fan of the local baseball team. One day the liaison for the biggest construction company in the city comes in and asks you to help him file some permits. When you are done he says, "I see from the baseball on your desk that you are a fan of the George Washingtons. You have been so helpful today, and if you can continue to be this helpful, maybe I can get you some free tickets, since our firm has box seats." He isn't explicitly asking for something in return, and there isn't a policy overtly prohibiting you from accepting the tickets, but something doesn't feel right. What do you do?

INTRODUCTION TO CHAPTER

This first chapter in the corruption section examines one of the most commonly discussed corrupt practices: bribery. In particular, the author discusses various cases related to bribery under the honest services fraud statute. Although at first glance, bribery may seem like something that is clearly evident, it is often, as the courts have shown, much more difficult to clearly define. For example, what happens when that potential "bribe" comes in the form of campaign donations, which have seen greater protections since the Supreme Court's ruling in the *Citizens United* case? Although the punishment for bribery is much less severe than it was in ancient Persia (see this chapter's reading), public corruption still has real consequences for our democracy. If we no longer believe that public officials will do the right thing for all and will instead exchange individual favors for gifts (as is customary in many other governments), we will be faced with more than a legal dilemma—it could destabilize our democratic foundations. In many ways, as this author discusses, the legal arguments for charging someone for bribery under the honest services fraud statute has become much trickier. How explicit does the exchange have to be for it to be considered bribery? Does the person have to write it down or articulate it in a way that there is no other possible interpretation? Can there be some ambiguity? Although this reading is focused on the legal perspective, it raises important ethical questions about our expectations for public officials.

READING 11

Corruption of Ethics

DOMESTIC BRIBERY OF PUBLIC OFFICIALS: HONEST SERVICES FRAUD

By Orrin K. Ames III

INTRODUCTION

> There is a broad general consensus that governmental ethics are viewed as a pillar of democracy, and corrupt behavior can threaten democratic institutions.[1]

This article picks up where an excellent article titled *Can You Put a Price on Corruption? The Future of Honest Services Fraud,* co-authored by Lara L. Kessler, Ryan J. Hunt, and William Mawer, and published in this publication in 2012,[2] left off. The authors addressed the honest services mail fraud statute[3] and the United States Supreme Court's ruling in *Skilling v. United States*[4] in which the United States Supreme Court held that the honest services fraud statute would only apply where there had been actual bribery or a kickback. That ruling effectively put a stop to the efforts of U.S. Attorneys to utilize the honest services fraud statute to criminally prosecute traditional breaches of fiduciary duties in non-governmental, private business situations where the conduct involved undisclosed conflicts of interest.[5] Where the statute was the DOJ's primary weapon used to address both public corruption and private breaches of fiduciary duties in business settings,[6] with the *Skilling* ruling, its use in private fiduciary duty settings, absent traditional schemes to defraud, bribery, or kickbacks, was effectively diminished.[7]

Therefore, absent any corrective legislation by Congress,[8] for now, the focus under the honest services fraud statute must be on the types of questions traditionally raised in fraud cases, but with a specific focus on bribery and kickbacks in the public corruption context, both state and federal.[9] A primary question is how the courts will develop the concept of bribery and kickbacks in the context of the honest services fraud statute.[10]

The focus of the authors' article was on the effect of the *Skilling* ruling and how, and in what circumstances, the statute would be applied after that ruling. What the authors did not have an opportunity to address was the subsequent focus by the courts on the definition of bribery in public corruption settings, what that concept would mean in the new post-*Skilling* world, and how that concept would be adapted to the honest services fraud concept.[11] This article, therefore, builds on their excellent work and addresses those issues.

Post-Skilling Development of the Concept of Bribery

At the end of their analyses, the authors in the above article asked: " What Does the Ruling in *Skilling* Mean for the Future?"[12] Two recent decisions that have provided a partial answer by addressing bribery under the honest services fraud statute[13] in public corruption situations when First Amendment values are at stake, are the recent Sixth Circuit's decision in *United States v. Terry*,[14] and the District of Columbia Circuit's decision in *United States v. Ring*.[15] *Terry* Involved bribery in connection with campaign contributions. *Ring* involved bribery in connection with lobbying activities.[16] An earlier opinion involving the convictions of former Alabama Governor Don Siegelman and Richard Scrushy,[17] and a 2012 opinion from the United States District Court for the Middle District of Alabama, *United States v. McGregor*,[18] also provide the present context to help answer the authors' question. The *Siegelman* case involved bribery in a political issue campaign. The *McGregor* case involved bribery of public officials to get certain legislation passed. In the *McGregor* case, the thoughtful writing of Judge Myron Thompson on the issue of the meaning of bribery and the concept of a ***quid-pro-quo*** in the campaign contribution setting is extremely instructive.

While there were multiple issues in all of these cases, the issue with which this article deals is the courts' definition of bribery under the honest services fraud statute in a public corruption setting where First Amendment issues are at stake, the question of the whether there must be a *quid-pro-quo* proven under that statute and, if so, whether it must be stated or whether it is sufficient under if the *quid-pro-quo* is implicit. The Sixth and D.C. Circuits have now provided their answers to those questions by finding that an implicit *quid-pro-quo* is sufficient for culpability. Their answers continue the perspectives of the Eleventh Circuit in *Siegelman* and Judge Thompson's perspectives in *McGregor*.

Both the *Ring* and *Terry* courts addressed and drew on the 1991 United States Supreme Court decision in *McCormick v. United States*,[19] which was a decision dealing with the *Hobbs Act*,[20] for their perspectives on the contours of bribery.[21] The Hobbs Act addresses extortion in various forms, but, specifically extortion that does not necessarily involve physical coercion but involves extortion under color of one's official position.

McCormick, involved an allegation that Robert McCormick, who was then a member of the West Virginia House of Delegates, had wrongfully induced and received campaign contributions through the wrongful use of his official position. The facts showed that he had sponsored legislation that allowed foreign doctors to practice in West Virginia without passing the licensing exam. He mentioned to the foreign doctors' lobbyist that he had spent a lot of out of pocket money on his campaign and that he had heard nothing from the doctors. The lobbyist told him that he would talk with the doctors. Subsequently, cash payments from the doctors came in. He did not declare them as campaign contributions nor did he pay taxes on the payments.

The Supreme Court held that, under the Hobbs Act, "making campaign contributions can constitute criminal extortion only when made pursuant to an explicit quid pro quo agreement."[22] Therefore, two important concepts came out of *McCormick:* for a campaign contribution to be considered to have been *induced* by the power of a politician's office, there must be a *quid-pro-quo* i.e. an induced exchange of value; and, the *quid-pro-quo* had to be *explicit*. The issue that the *McCormick* decision left unanswered, however, was the meaning of the term *explicit*. There was no guidance on whether explicit meant expressed or explicit in the sense of an actual animating factor.

Terry was a campaign contribution case. It involved the bribery conviction of a Cuyahoga County (Ohio) Court of Common Pleas judge, Steven Terry, for agreeing to make, and making, certain rulings on summary judgment motions that were pending before him and that were favorable to an attorney, Joe O'Malley, who had sought the help of Frank Russo, the County Auditor. Russo, who was very powerful in Cleveland, Ohio politics, was also assisting Terry in Terry's re-election campaign and, therefore, campaign contributions were at issue.

As related by the Sixth Circuit in *Terry*, "[i]n ancient Persia, a judge who accepted a bribe was flayed alive and his successor was forced to sit on a chair made from the predecessor's skin."[23] At his trial, former Judge Terry did not face such an ultimate deterrent. Instead, after a five day trial, the jury convicted him on three out of five counts and the trial judge sentenced him to 63 months in prison. He can be thankful that he was not in ancient Persia!

He appealed and the issues that are relevant to this article were the contours of a bribe in a campaign contribution setting, as criminalized in the honest services fraud statute, what was necessary to avoid First Amendment issues and to make the linkage between an offer or an act of some type and an acceptance i.e. whether there had to be a *quid-pro-quo* and, if so, whether it had to be *expressed* in some way or whether it could it be inferred by a jury from all of the circumstances. The Sixth Circuit held in this campaign contribution case that a *quid-pro-quo* was necessary, that it had to be *explicit*, but that it did not have to be expressed.

The lawyer had approached Russo and asked him to get Terry to deny certain summary judgment motions that were pending before him. Russo assured the lawyer that Terry would do what was necessary. The court observed that "Russo promised to call Terry and make sure Terry did what he was 'supposed to do' with the cases."[24] The court observed that "Russo... expected that his political and financial patronage meant Terry " 'would do what [he] asked him to do.' "[25]

The F.B.I. was already investigating Russo and in subsequent telephone conversations between Russo and Terry that were intercepted by the FBI, it was clearly established that Russo made the request and Terry said that he would dismiss the motions. The court observed that in one of the conversations,"Russo told Terry to deny the motions... and Terry said he would."[26] Terry tried to get a magistrate judge to dismiss them, but that judge at least had the honor not to do it. He referred them back to Terry to handle and Terry did exactly what Russo had asked him to do.

Terry was indicted on conspiracy to commit mail fraud and honest services fraud; commission of mail fraud by granting the motions; and violations of honest services fraud by " 'accepting gifts, payments, and other things of value from Russo and others in exchange for favorable official action.' "[27] He was convicted on the conspiracy count and two of the three counts alleging commission of honest services fraud.

On appeal, Terry contended that, because the case involved a campaign contribution and that it was not a typical under-the-table type of payment, there should be two burdens of proof: one for politicians who are not getting campaign contributions; and one for those who are.[28] His position was based on the fact that, for honest services fraud, there must be a bribe and a *quid-pro-quo,* i.e the acceptance of something of value in exchange for official action.[29] His reasoning was that the receipt of a campaign contribution was not a *quid-pro-quo*, but an acceptance of a contribution and that to attribute a favorable official act to the concept of a *quid-pro-quo* when there had simply been a contribution would be an insufficient nexus to find a corrupt *quid-pro-quo*. Because bribery requires that a favorable act be causally linked with the receipt of something of value, Terry contended that the causal connection simply should not be made because, without more there would be a resulting infringement on the legitimate process of campaign contributions.[30]

The Sixth Circuit declined to make that burden of proof distinction and stated that the essence of what makes a *quid-pro-quo* criminal is *mens rea*. The court referred to it as "intent," but what the court held was that "the question is one of inferences taken from what the participants say, mean and do, all matters that juries are fully equipped to assess. '[M]otives and consequences, not formalities,' are the keys for determining whether a public official entered an agreement to accept a bribe, and the trier of fact is 'quite capable of deciding the intent with which words were spoken or actions taken as well as the reasonable construction given to them by the official and the payor.' "[31] In this context, the court quoted favorably from *Ring v. United States*,[32] that, intent " 'distinguishes criminal corruption from commonplace political and business activities.' "[33]

In contrast to the pure campaign contribution context of *Terry*, the D.C. Circuit's decision in *Ring*, which was decided before *Terry*, concerned lobbying and a massive investigation involving Jack Abramoff in which Ring was caught up.[34] The court described that investigation as "[exposing the dark underbelly of a profession that has long played an important role in American politics" and the case as probing "the boundary between legal lobbying and criminal conduct."[35]

In that context the court observed that while the "distinction between legal lobbying and criminal conduct may be subtle…it spells the difference between honest politics and criminal corruption."[36]

The facts showed that Ring's lobbying activities "included treating congressional and executive branch officials to dinners, drinks, travel, concerts, and sporting events."[37] Ring referred to these public officials as his " 'champions' "[38] and the evidence showed that they "often took actions that were favorable to Ring's clients."[39] The investigation revealed "meals, tickets, and travel [that] Ring provided to public officials were impermissibly linked to official acts that benefitted Ring and his clients."[40] As a result, the government indicted him on charges of violating the honest services fraud statute, payments of illegal gratuities, and conspiracy. The jury convicted Ring of some of the honest services fraud counts, the illegal gratuity count, and the conspiracy count.

Ring challenged the district court's instruction on the honest services fraud counts. He contended that an explicit *quid-pro-quo* was required and that the court's insruction had not made that clear. The D.C. Circuit stated that "[a]s relevant to the issue here, the government had to show that Ring gave gifts with an "'intent 'to influence' an official act' by way of a corrupt quid pro quo."[41] As in *Ring,* the concept of an *explicit quid-pro-quo* was acknowledged and, therefore, the question in *Terry* was whether the *quid-pro-quo* had to be stated or expressed in some way, or whether it could be implied by the actions and words of the participants and, therefore, inferred by a jury.

In the context of lobbying, gifts are given, but rarely with the stated and articulated understanding that a favorable act from the recipient is expected. Instead, the gifts are given and later the public official magically takes actions that benefit the lobbyist's client. This was the case in *Ring* and in much the same way as in *Terry* where the campaign contributions were being made and then *Terry* responded favorably when called upon by the briber without the briber ever referring to the contributions, *Ring's* lobbying targets did things favorable to Ring's clients.

The D.C. Circuit in *Ring recognized* that the Court in *McCormick* "expressly declined to decide whether the requirement [of an express and agreed to *quid-pro-quo*] 'exists in other contexts, such as when an elected official receives gifts, meals, travel expenses, or other items of value' "[42] and that the Court in *McCormick* did not clarify what it meant by "explicit."[43] U.S. District Judge Myron Thompson, in the *McGregor* case observed, as late as July, 2012, that "[t]he definition of 'explicit' remains hotly contested."[44]

With this issue left hanging, Ring made a rather appealing argument predicated on the First Amendment and, specifically, the right to petition government. He argued that lobbying was like contributing to political campaigns and that such activity implicated constitutionally protected conduct and, therefore, without elevating the standard of proof in such cases to the level of an "explicit quid pro quo agreement"[45] there would be an impingement on protected First Amendment activities. Ring's position, therefore, was that *explicit* meant *explicit* and that, in order to protect First Amendment values, such an element of a corrupt bribe should not be able to be inferred, but that the evidence had to show some outward expression of the agreement to avoid the chilling of First Amendment conduct.

While recognizing that the Supreme Court had not clarified that issue, the D.C. Circuit disagreed with Ring and made a statement that was not later picked up on by the *Terry* court. The D.C. Circuit said that an explicit *quid-pro-quo* instruction is not "required outside the campaign contribution text."[46] The D.C. Circuit, therefore, may have implicitly indicated that campaign financing cases might indeed be different and that it might be agreeing that, in addition to a Hobbs Act situation, in an honest services fraud case where campaign contributions are at issue, the requirement of an explicit *quid-pro-quo* might be appropriate.[47] While that statement is certainly *dictum,* it is a statement that was never addressed by the *Terry* court which was a campaign contribution case. Instead the *Terry* court cited *Ring* and the case of former Alabama Governor Don Siegelman[48] as cases that are representative of the struggle to determine the definition of *quid-pro-quo* in various contexts.[49]

The trial of former Governor Siegelman also involved Richard Scrushy who is the founder and former CEO of HealthSouth Corporation a major hospital corporation and home health care company that was started in Birmingham, Alabama, that grew state-wide, and that was a tremendous success until a major accounting fraud and corruption scandal brought the company down. As a result of that corruption and eventual bankruptcy, Scrushy and a number of other corporate officers were prosecuted by the federal government in a case which was the first case under Sarbanes-Oxley and the new certification requirements that not only did the CFOs of companies have to certify the companies' reports to the S.E.C., but so did the CEOs. The others who were prosecuted entered guilty pleas and struck deals with the DOJ. Only Scrushy went to trial in Birmingham, the home of HealthSouth, in what was to become a highly controversial trial on a number of levels. In the end, he was acquitted, but his troubles did not end there.

Scrushy eventually faced new charges when he was indicted by the federal authorities, along with former Alabama Governor Don Siegelman, for the appointment of Scrushy to the Alabama Certificate of Need Review Board (CON Board) that determined the number of healthcare facilities in the State. Decisions of that board affected HealthSouth's ability to grow and, therefore, it was important to Scrushy to be on the board again. He had already served on the Board under three previous governors of the State.

The charges on which Scrushy and Siegelman were convicted and that are relevant to this article are those involving honest services fraud. While there has been a tremendous amount of criticism of the Eleventh Circuit's upholding of the convictions on the honest service fraud counts,[50] a review of the testimony and evidence supporting the convictions postures perfectly the issue of what is an *explicit* agreement under the act, whether it has to be expressed in some way, and the role of a jury in making such a determination. Ultimately, the role of the inferential process by juries was sanctioned in *Scrushy* and later in *Ring* and *Terry* to find an *explicit* agreement.[51]

The facts showed that it was important to Scrushy to be on the CON Board because decisions made by that board affected whether HealthSouth would be able to grow. What transpired was essentially the same type of "agreement" that was never put in writing, that was never explicitly stated, but that produced reciprocal acts and results from which a jury was able to infer, under the honest services fraud statute, an *explicit quid-pro-quo* that was never *expressed*, but was nevertheless effective for both Siegelman and Scrushy to get the results that they wanted. As is true in many of these situations, intermediaries were used by both Siegelman and Scrushy to convey the making of reciprocal decisions and the taking of reciprocal acts that produced the results. It was the testimony of these intermediaries that resulted in the convictions.

Siegelman had recently been reelected and the primary campaign theme on which he had run was the establishment of a lottery in the State of Alabama.[52] After the election he created the Alabama Education Lottery Foundation (the Foundation) to raise money to campaign for voter approval of a ballot initiative to establish a state-wide lottery.[53] The Foundation eventually borrowed $730,789.29 from an Alabama bank to pay down the debt incurred by the Alabama Democrat Party for a voter campaign advocating the lottery. This debt was personally guaranteed by Siegelman. Scrushy had contributed to Siegelman's opponent. In that setting, Siegelman commented to Nick Bailey, one of Siegelman's closest associates, that Scrushy needed to contribute " 'at least $500,000 in order to 'make it right' with the Siegelman campaign.' "[54] Bailey also testified that Eric Hanson, and outside lobbyist for HealthSouth, had told him that "Scrushy wanted control of the CON Board."[55]

Mike Martin, the former CFO of HealthSouth testified that "having influence over the CON Board was important to Scrushy and HealthSouth because it determined the number of healthcare facilities in the state, thereby affecting HealthSouth's ability to grow."[56] He testified that "Scrushy told him that to 'have some influence or a spot on the CON Board,' they had to help Siegelman raise money for the lottery campaign. Scrushy said that if they do, '[they] would be assured a seat on the CON Board.' "[57] Martin then testified that they " 'were making a contribution ... in exchange for a spot on the CON Board.' "[58]

Bailey testified that Hanson, the lobbyist, " 'made it clear to him that if Mr. Scrushy gave the $500,000 to the lottery campaign that [they] would not let him down' with respect to the CON Board seat.'"[59] The evidence then showed that Scrushy gave instructions on how to make the payment in a secretive way, to include enlisting the assistance of their banker, who eventually refused to play any part in the transaction. Eventually, a way was found to make the payment in a way that masked it as a payment to the Siegelman campaign for the lottery.

Bailey testified to a meeting between Siegelman and Scrushy in Siegelman's office; Siegelman showed him the check; and Bailey asked, "[W]hat in the world is he [Scrushy] going to want for that?"[60] He testified that Siegelman replied, " 'the CON Board.' "[61] Bailey commented, " 'I wouldn't think that would be a problem, would it?"[62] At which point Siegelman replied, " 'I wouldn't think so.' "[63]

That meeting took place on July 14, 1999. Scrushy was appointed to the CON Board twelve days later. Bailey testified that Siegelman then went so far as to instruct him to contact the Board chair-designee and to tell her that he "wanted Scrushy to be the vice-chair of the CON Board."[64] Scrushy was then put in that position. Siegelman had told Bailey that he put Scrushy in that position " '[because [Scrushy] asked for it.' "[65]

The testimony showed that a second payment was made when Bailey and Siegelman went to the HealthSouth headquarters in Birmingham and Scrushy and Siegelman met privately in

Scrushy's office. That check was applied directly to the balance of money owed on the loan by the Foundation.

With these facts posturing the issue of an *explicit quid-pro-quo* in the context of Scrushy and Siegelman never having had a direct conversation (at least that the evidence was able to show) before the first payment was made, the Eleventh Circuit turned to *McCormick,* just as the courts in *Ring* and *Terry* did later to resolve the question of what was an *explicit quid-pro-quo* when there was no direct evidence of any conversational agreement, written agreement, or memoranda of any type confirming reciprocal understandings? It should also be noted that these payments by Scrushy were not for Siegelman's campaign for election or re-election; they were for an issue campaign i.e. the lottery that Siegelman supported.

As a result of the Supreme Court's decision in *McCormick,* the Eleventh Circuit accepted the requirement that, in order to be liable under the honest services fraud statute, there had to be an *explicit quid-pro-quo*. The question for the Eleventh Circuit, as it was later in *Terry* and *Ring,* was whether for something to be *explicit* it had to be manifested in some traditional way, such as in writing, an oral conversation that is overheard, or something that would provide more than circumstantial evidence of a common understanding and an agreement.

The Eleventh Circuit accepted the trial court's instruction that Scrushy and Siegelman had to "*agree*"[66] as part of the *quid-pro-quo* requirement, but Scrushy and Siegelman contended that such an instruction was still inadequate because the trial court should have instructed the jury that "not only must they find that Siegelman and Scrushy agreed to a *quid-pro-quo*, the CON Board seat for the donation, but that [the] agreement had to be *express*."[67] It was with this proposition that the Eleventh Circuit disagreed. The court said that *McCormick* had used the word *explicit,* but that that term "does not mean *express*."[68] That differentiation formed the *ratio decidendi* of the Eleventh Circuit's position and was, effectively, the basis of the courts' decisions later in *Terry and Ring*. With that differentiation, the court rejected Scrushy's and Siegelman's contention that "only 'proof of actual conversations by [them]' [would] do."[69]

The court rejected the positions taken by Scrushy and Siegelman in their briefs that "only *express* words of promise overheard by third parties or by some means of electronic surveillance [would] do.[70] The Eleventh Circuit described the standard being advocated by them as "stringent"[71] and said that *McCormick* did not require that. The court said that, in order to meet the *explicit* test, there was "no reqirement that [the] agreement be memorialized in writing, or even, as defendants suggest, be overheard by a third party."[72] The court said that "the agreement must be *explicit,* but there is no requirement that it be *express*."[73] Giving recognition to the role of circumstantial evidence and jury decision-making, the court held that an explicit agreement may be "'implied from [the official's] words and actions'"[74] and evidence of bribery "may be supported by 'inferences drawn from relevant and competent circumstantial evidence.'"[75]

Before *Terry* and *Ring*, United States District Judge Myron Thompson in the Middle District of Alabama presided over one of the most recent, highly publicized cases in Alabama. The allegations were against gambling facility operators, lobbyists, lawmakers, and legislative staff. The allegations were that the defendants conspired to buy and sell votes of Alabama lawmakers to ensure the passage of a bill that would authorize a constitutional referendum on whether to legalize electronic bingo in Alabama. The allegations included charges of federal-programs bribery, extortion, honest services mail and wire fraud, obstruction of justice, and conspiracy to commit federal programs bribery. In the end, the defendants were acquitted, but Judge Thompson considered the bribery issues to be so important that he wrote a special opinion[76] after the conclusion of the trial in which he set out his jury instructions and traced the *quid-pro-quo* issues through the *McCormick, Evans,*[77] and *Siegelman* cases. Judge Thompson's thoughtful and thorough analysis mirrored what were the subsequent perspectives in *Terry* and *Ring.*

Judge Thompson concluded that a *quid-pro-quo* was necessary, but he also observed that, in campaign contribution cases, because of the First Amendment, there had developed an elevated burden of persuasion. While this concept, *per se*, was not articulated in *Terry* or *Ring,* it was effectively used by the courts in those cases because of their perspectives on the need for *explicit quid-pro-quo* instructions. It is the requirement, in these types of public corruption cases, that there be an *explicit* understanding and agreement for the exchange of something of value and that Judge Thompson described as an elevated burden persuasion. On the issue of what *explicit* meant, he cited Justice Kennedy's admonition in *Evans* that *quid-pro-quos* did not have to be stated in *expressed* terms because that would not be a realistic perspective given how such bribery activities actually take place.[78] Judge Thompson, using Justice Kennedy's perspectives, stated that "a quid pro quo need not be expressly stated orally or put in writing. Rather an explicit quid pro quo could be inferred from vague words and conduct."[79]

Describing what he viewed to be the current state of the law, as of July 24, 2012, the date of his writing, he said that many of the cases had tried to conflate the concept of a *quid-pro-quo* with an agreement, but admonished that "[f]ederal corruption laws are not limited to completed agreements to exchange a vote for a campaign contribution...[and that his instructions] distinguished between a quid pro quo *agreement* and a quid pro quo *promise* or *solicitation.*"[80] He thus incorporated the *quid-pro-quo* concept into consummated agreements, solicitations, and promises. He further observed that with a consummated agreement, both parties can be liable; with a promise, only the person offering to make the payment may be liable; and for a solicitation, only the public official might be liable.[81] He did not address the law of attempts in formulating this perspective.

While Judge Thompson's perspectives predated *Terry* and *Ring,* they form a consistent and developing perspective on the concept of *quid-pro-quo* in bribery jurisprudence and the struggles that the courts had post-*Skilling* with how to fashion a body of bribery law that conformed to the underlying values present in the honest services fraud statute and the conduct that that statute is designed to reach. What is common to all of these perspectives is that the *quid-pro-quo* is the inducing and animating factor underlying bribery. Added into that basic concept, in public corruption cases where First Amendment issues may be implicated is what Judge Thompson referred to as an elevated burden of persuasion as a requirement that the agreement be an *explicit* underlying reality understood and agreed to by both parties.[82] The requirement that the agreement and the understanding be *explicit* balances the First Amendment concerns in campaign contribution, issue contribution, and lobbying settings. The fact that such agreements need not be expressed in writing or orally does not diminish the First Amendment protections, it only affects the way that such *explicit* agreements can be proven by the inferential process from the parties' actions, words, and conduct. Such *explicit* understandings are still the *animating* realities of culpable bribery in these political settings.

The recognition that *explicit* does not mean *express* and that bribery-type evidence can be shown by circumstantial evidence from which juries are perfectly capable of drawing rational inferences, formed the heart of the Eleventh Circuit's position in *Siegelman* and, later, the positions of the courts in *Terry* and *Ring*. This is a realistic position that satisfies Justice Kennedy's concern that, "otherwise, the law's effect could be frustrated by knowing winks and nods.'"[83] This reconciliation of the concepts of *explicit* and *express* seems to offer the best compromise to effectively reach bribery in the public corruption setting, which is inherently secretive but which is an issue that juries, with proper instructions, are capable of handling, using their common sense and the inferential process, and protecting First Amendment values at the same time.

Conclusion

The Supreme Court's decision in *Skilling* confining the honest services fraud statute to bribery and graft gutted the statute's continuing use by federal prosecutors to reach breaches of fiduciary duties in the private setting where there was a conflict of interest. It, therefore, removed an arrow in the quiver of prosecutors' ability to address breaches of fiduciary duties in private businesses and, thereby, removed one means to enforce ethical conduct in the private business sector.[84] Whether Congress responds and amends the statute to return its capacity to be used in that area remains to be seen.

In the meantime, even with the resolution of the definition of bribery in public corruption settings such as occurred in *Siegelman, McGregor, Terry,* and *Ring,* because of the language of the statute, there will be an inevitable continuing common law-type of refinement of honest services law, to include bribery and kickbacks, by the federal circuits.[85] This process will take place out of necessity in spite of strong objections to such a process in the area of criminal law.[86]

Notes

1 Hon. Pamela Mathy, *Honest Services Fraud After Skilling,* 42 ST. MARY'S L.J. 645, 715 (2011).

2 Lara L. Kessler, Ryan J. Hunt, William Mawer, *Can You Put a Price on Corruption? The Future of Honest Services Fraud,* 4 SO J. BUS. AND ETHICS 112 (2012).

3 18 *U.S.C* §§1341, 1346.

4 130 S.Ct. 2869 (2010).

5 *See generally* Mathy, *supra* note 1 at 700-01; Lori A. McMillan, *Honest Services Update: Directors' Liability Concerns After Skilling and Black,* 18 TEX. WESELYAN L.REV. 149 (2011); Elizabeth R. Sheyn, *Criminalizing the Denial of Honest Services After Skilling,* 2011 WISC. L.REV. 27, 65.

6 McMillan, *supra* note 5 at 156. *See also* Lisa Kern Griffin, *The Federal Common Law Crime of Corruption,* 89 N.C.REV. 1815 (2011).

7 *See* Mathy, *supra* note 1 at 700. *But cf.* Joan K. Krause, *Skilling and the Pursuit of Health Care Fraud,* 66 U. MIAMI L.REV. 363, 364 (2012) ("[W]hile Skilling is widely considered to have narrowed the scope of honest services fraud overall, it may turn out to have the paradoxical effect of inviting additional prosecutions of physicians and others in the health care industry" because of activities of bribery and kickbacks that "have particular salience in health care.").

8 *See* Susan Kavanagh, *DOJ Urges Congress to Repair the Honest Services Fraud Statute,* 17 FED. ETHICS RPT. 9 (Oct. 2010) (addressing comments by then Assistant Attorney General Lanny Breuer).

9 *See* Alex Stein, *Corrupt Intentions: Bribery, Unlawful Gratuity, and Honest Services Fraud,* 75 LAW & CONTEMP. PROBS. 61 (2012) (bribery and related offenses addressed from an economics perspective). Honest services fraud is sometimes referred to as "'fiduciary fraud.'"); Krause, *supra* note 7. Therefore, fiduciary relationships between the public and public officials are still an underpinning concept. See *Skilling,* 130 S.Ct. at 2930-31 (public and public officials example); United States v. Milovanovic, 678 F.3d 713, 721-22, 728-29 (9th Cir. 2012); United States v. Tanabe, 2012 WL 5868968 * 4 (N.D. Cal. Nov. 19, 2012) ("The fiduciary duty required is not limited to the classic definition of the term but also extends to defendants who assume a comparable duty of loyalty, trust, or confidence with the victim."); United States v. Langford, 647 F.3d 1309, 1320 (11th Cir. 2011) (refernces to the "fiduciary duty of the intangible right of honest services."); United States v. deVegter, 198 F.3d 1324, 1328 (11th Cir. 1999) ("Public officials inherently owe a fiduciary duty to the public to make governmental decisions in the public's best interest... When official action is corrupted by secret bribes or kickbacks, the essence of the political contract is violated."). *See also* Geraldine Szott Moohr, *Mail Fraud and the Intangible Rights Doctrine: Someone to Watch Over Us,* 31 HARV. J. ON LEGIS. 153, 163 (1994) (pointing out that, as contrasted with traditional fraud, fiduciary fraud may not involve any misleading of a third party from whom the fiduciary receives a benefit.).

10 Mathy, *supra* note 1 at 691 ("[W]e do not know how the courts will define 'bribes' and 'kickbacks' ....").

11 Mathy, *supra* note 1 at 707-08 ("With respect to post-Skiiling honest services prosecutions alleging a scheme involving bribes or kickbacks, the definition of "bribery" and "kickbacks" may not be as straightforward as one might initially conclude."); Note, Jared B. Cohen, *The Commonwealth's Right to "Honest Services": Prosecuting Public Corruption in Massachusetts,* 93 B.U.L.REV 201, 213 (2013) (" 'bribes' and 'kidkbacks' are not fully self-defining terms which eliminate the problem of interpretation. After Skilling, it still remains for the federal courts to conduct the fact intensive, context-specific inquiries necessary to determine just what kinds of schemes qualify.").

12 Kessler, *supra* note 2 at 119.

13 For characteristics of bribery, *see* Carl Pacini, *The Foreign Corrupt Practices Act: Taking a Bite Out of Bribery in International Business Transactions,* 17 FORDHAM J. CORP. & FIN. L. 545, 548–551 (2012). One characteristic described is that bribery is "a crime of calculation [in which] public officials weigh expected benefits from corrupt behavior against the punishment imposed by society if they get caught. The transaction costs of illegal exchanges are important for maintaining secrecy."). For an interesting article that discusses the adverse costs of bribery on a business, *see* Philip M. Nichols, *The Business Case for Complying With Bribery Laws,* 49 AM. BUS. L.J. 325 (2012).

14 707 F.3d 607 (6th Cir. 2013), *reh'g and reh'g en banc denied (*April 29, 2013).

15 706 F.3d 460 (D.C. Cir. 2013), *reh'g en banc denied* (March 21, 2013), petition for *Cert.* filed, 82 USLW 3004 (June 17, 2013).

16 It is suggested that, as part of a company's compliance and ethics program, and in keeping with a board's fiduciary duty of oversight, monitoring of lobbying activities should be considered as part of risk assessment and management. Having a corporation's name associated with a lobbyist who is caught up in a scandal like the Abramoff scandal, would severly damage a company's good will and, in addition, the company might initially be a target of any criminal investigation arising out of the lobbying issues. An "effective" compliance and ethics program will help in the event that prosecutors turn their sights on the organization.

17 Siegelman v. United States, 640 F.3d 1159 (11th Cir. 2011), *cert denied* 132 S.Ct. 2711 (2012).

18 879 F.Supp.2d 1308 (M.D. Ala. 2012).

19 500 U.S. 257 (1991).

20 18 *U.S.C* §7206(1).

21 For a recognition that the courts will look to other cases and statutes, *see,* United States v. Scruggs, 714 F.3d 258, 266 (5th Cir. 2013) ("In *Skilling,* the Court did not crystalize what constitutes a 'paradigmatic bribe,' but it did observe that the 'prohibition on bribes and kickbacks draws content' from case law and federal statutes.")(citation omitted).

22 *Ring,* 706 F.3d at 465 citing *McCormick,* 500 U.S. at 271–274.

23 *Terry,* 707 F.3d at 612 citing HERODOTUS, THE HISTORIES 5:25 (A.D. Godley, trans. Harvard University Press 1920).

24 *Terry,* 707 F.3d at 610.

25 *Id.*

26 *Id.*

27 *Id.*

28 *Id.* at 613–14.

29 *Id.*at 612.

30 *See Scruggs,* 714 F.3d at 268 (overbreath argument made and the court responded: "We see no real likelihood that §1346 will chill a significant amount of protected political speech, if any…."); United States v. Nelson, 712 F.3d 498 (11th Cir. 2013) (vagueness argument rejected).

31 *Terry,* 707 F.3d at 613 (citations omitted).

32 706 F.3d 460 (D.C. Cir. 2013).

33 *Terry,* 707 F.3d at 613 citing *Ring,* 706 F.3d at 468.

34 *See Convictions in the Abramoff Corruption Probe,* http://foxnews.com/us/2012/04/21/convictions-in-abramoff-corruption-probe/ (list of people, including Ring, caught up in the probe). Jack Abramoff now has his own talk radio program. *See* Lloyd Grave, *Jack Abramoff on His New Talk Radio Show, Lobbying Reform & More,* http://thedailybeast.com/articles/2012/07/16/jack-abramoff-on-his-new-talk-radio/.

35 *Ring,* 706 F.3d at 463.

36 *Id.* at 464.

37 *Id.* at 464.

38 *Id.*

39 *Id.*

40 *Id.*

41 *Id.* at 465.

42 *Ring,* 706 F.3d at 465 citing *McCormick,* 500 U.S. at 274 n. 10.

43 *Ring,* 706 F.3d at 466.

44 *McGregor,* 879 F.Supp.2d at 314.

45 *Ring,* 706 F.3d at 465–66.

46 *Id.* at 466.

47 "But even assuming as much, we believe that campaign contributions can be distinguished from other things of value." *Id.*

48 United States v. Siegelman, 640 F.3d 1159, 1171 (11th Cir. 2011), *cert denied* 132 S.Ct. 2711 (2012).

49 *Terry,* 707 F.3d at 612–13.

50 *See* Anthony J. Gaugham, *The Case for Limiting Federal Criminal Jurisdiction Over State and Local Campaign Contributions,* 65 ARK. L.REV. 587, 605–610 (2012) and sources cited therein describing the disagreements as "withering criticisms" and reviewing the criticisms of the trial court's ruling and the ruling of the Eleventh Circuit.

51 Regarding the inferential process, *see* Orrin K. Ames III, *Summary Judgments in Alabama: The Role of Inferences in Meeting a Party's Burdens,* 27 AM. J. TRIAL ADV. 329 (2003) and sources cited therein.

52 The establishment of a state lottery was eventually rejected by the voters of Alabama.

53 *Siegelman,* 640 F.3d at 1165.

54 *Id.* at 1166.

55 *Id.*

56 *Id.*

57 *Id.*

58 *Id.*

59 *Id.*

60 *Id.* at 1167.

61 *Id.*

62 *Id.*

63 *Id.*

64 *Id.*

65 *Id.*

66 *Id.* at 1170.

67 *Id.* at 1171.

68 *Id.*

69 *Id.*

70 *Id.*

71 *Id.*

72 *Id.*

73 *Id.*

74 *Id.* at 1172.

75 *Id.*(citation omitted).

76 United States v. McGregor, 879 F.Supp.2d 1308 (M.D. Ala. 2012).

77 Evans v. United States, 504 U.S. 255 (1992).

78 *Evans,* 504 U.S. at 274 ("The official and the payor need not state the quid pro quo in express terms, for otherwise the law's effect could be frustrated by knowing winks and nods.").

79 *McGregor,* 879 F.Supp.2d at 1316.

80 *Id.* at 1317. *See also* Stuart P. Green, Matthew B. Kugler, *Public Perceptions of White Collar Crime Culpability: Bribery, Perjury, and Fraud,* 75 LAW & CONTEMP. PROBS. 33, 39–40 (2012) (addressing the distinctions).

81 *McGregor,* 879 F.Supp.2d at 1317–18.

82 *See generally* Green, *supra* note 80 at 40 ("[A]s traditionally understood, bribery consists of a bilateral agreement or quid pro quo in which the bribee solicits or accepts something of value from the briber in exchange for the bribee's acting, or agreeing to act, on the briber's behalf. This exchange requires a meeting of the minds, with the bribee agreeing to 'be influenced' in the performance of an official act.").

83 *Evans,* 504 U.S. at 274.

84 *See* Anita Cava, Brian M. Stewart, *Quid Pro Quo Corruption is "So Yesterday": Restoring Honest Services Fraud After Skilling and Black,* 12 U.C. DAVIS BUS. L.J. 1 (2011).

85 *See* Cohen, *supra* note 11 at 203; Griffin *supra* note 6 at 1846–47 ("[P]ublic corruption prosecutions have engaged courts in teasing out case by case the principles and standards that define harmful influences...The statute uses only twenty-eight words and leaves it to the courts to supply limiting principles and monitor extensions, and at the same time, it vests substantial discretion in prosecutors to test the boundaries of the law...Carving out cases that merit prosecution is thus a classic common law undertaking. Common law interpretation is incremental and potentially inconsistent, but it is also patient and flexible enough to operationalize subtle limiting principles like harm.").

86 *See* Sorich v. United States, 555U.S. 1204, 129 S.Ct. 1308, 1310 (2009) (J. Scalia dissenting from a denial of *certiorari*) ("[I]t is simply not fair to prosecute someone for a crime that has not been defined until the judicial decision that sends him to jail.").

CASE STUDY

In 2014, Robert McDonnell, the former governor of Virginia, was convicted of corruption for receiving more than $175,000 in gifts in exchange for using his office to help support Mr. Williams' fledgling diet supplement company. Although the meetings that were set up by Governor McDonnell didn't have the intended impact on the company, the lower courts felt that it met the quid pro quo bribery requirement. The Supreme Court overturned the decision, writing that the behavior in this case, arranging meetings, was not an "official act" that would meet the standard for bribery.[1] Although the legal debate has now been resolved, the ethical questions remain. The gifts (assuming there was no quid pro quo) did not violate Virginia law, and public officials do frequently help their constituents. However, is accepting these types of extravagant gifts from constituents, even without an explicit expectation, ethical? How do you determine whether or not you are acting in your official capacity? Or whether there really is an expectation for something in return?

---

1 Liptak, Adam. "Supreme Court Vacates Ex-Virginia Governor's Graft Conviction." *The New York Times*, June 27, 2016.

CHAPTER 11

The Dirty-Hands Theory of Command

SEE WHERE YOU STAND: 60 SECOND ETHICAL DILEMMA

Imagine that you are in the following situation and have one minute to make a decision about the most ethical course of action:

You are a police officer who has just captured a suspect who planted bombs that will detonate within the next 30 minutes in a major metropolitan city, leading to thousands of deaths. The suspect refuses to talk to you, so your boss suggests torture (which would be illegal), because he claims it is the only way to get the necessary information to prevent this catastrophic situation. What would you do?

INTRODUCTION TO CHAPTER

Is it ever okay to use immoral means to achieve moral ends? That is the central question the author addresses in this chapter. Is there any moral difference between the United States causing civilian casualties in the pursuit of terrorists and terrorists purposely killing civilians? The intents behind the actions are very different (i.e., the US tries to avoid civilian casualties, while the terrorists are trying to hurt civilians), but in both scenarios, innocent people are being harmed. What role does intent play in determining whether or not something is moral? The author in this chapter cites a variety of philosophers in asking some very difficult questions.

Are certain people predisposed to be more or less comfortable with having "dirty hands"? What role does guilt play? Does it matter whether or not the person who committed the immoral act feels guilty? Are people (or countries) that have acted immorally capable of changing and becoming moral? The author also discusses Immanuel Kant's publicity principle and the extent to which openness is required for an action in the public sector to be considered moral. Transparency in the public sector has long been considered important, but how tenuous is the connection between publicity and morality? Does an action need to be public to be moral? These are tough questions, and unfortunately there are no easy answers, but they will continue to help you build your framework to determine what is or is not moral.

READING 12

The Dirty-Hands Theory of Command

By *Sidney Axinn*

If we take our subject seriously, the theory of leadership known as "dirty hands" must be considered. Without this theory, a discussion of military morality would seem unreal. Briefly, the theory holds that in order to govern an institution, one must sometimes do things that are immoral. To act properly as a mayor of a city, a chief of a police department, a head of a large corporation, or a commander of an engaged military unit, one must have morally **dirty hands**. Further, this theory insists, we do not want leaders who are so concerned with their own personal morality that they will not do "what is necessary" to solve the problem or win the battle. A commander who is not willing to get his or her hands dirty is not going to be successful. We have an inept leader if we have a person so morally fastidious that he or she will not break the law when that is the only way to success.

The phrase *dirty hands* may have been taken from Jean Paul Sartre's play of that name (*Les Mains Sales*), but the idea is much older. One classic source is Niccolô Machiavelli's *The Prince,* published after his death in 1532:

> Experience shows that princes in our times who have done great things *have cared little for honesty.* ... It is not necessary for a prince to have the good qualities mentioned above, but **it** is necessary to seem to have them. I would say this: to have them and use them *all the time is dangerous,* but seeming to have them is useful. He should seem to be pious, faithful, humane, honest, religious, and to be so. But he should have his mind so prepared that when occasion requires, he is able to change to

> the opposite. ... *It is often necessary to act contrary to faith, charity, humanity, and religion in order to maintain the state.* ... If possible, he ought not, as I have said before, turn away from what is good, *but he should be able to do evil if necessary* (emphasis mine).[1]

In Machiavelli's view, it is "dangerous" to have as prince and commander an individual who has more respect for honesty, morality, and military honor than he has for the future of the state. Is Machiavelli right? Can an effective commander be a "goody-goody"—always going by the book, always obeying the laws of war? Some authors think that the problem is not solvable, that there is no answer to it.

Illustrations of dirty-hands situations are found both in and out of military history. Whenever we are tempted to use an immoral means to reach a desirable goal, we have the problem. The serious version faces us when the goal absolutely *must* be gained, and the *only* way to reach that goal is morally unacceptable. Carl Klockars calls it a "Dirty-Harry case."

Dirty Harry

Dirty Harry is the term Carl B. Klockars uses in his study of the above problem in police work.[2] He takes that name from the title of a 1971 Warner Brothers film in which a police inspector tortures a psychopathic killer in order to force the killer to tell where he has confined a young child. The child had been buried with enough oxygen to keep her alive for a few hours. The psychopath is the only source of information on the location of the child, and apparently torture is the single way to make him talk. Dirty Harry is the police inspector who applies the torture. The effectiveness of the means is irrelevant to the moral issue. In this particular film, although the killer reveals the child's whereabouts, the child is already dead when help arrives and the killer is set free because Inspector Harry's way of getting the information is not admissible in court. Even if Harry's use of torture did save the life of the child or if it had resulted in the conviction of the psychopath, we would still have the moral question.

The Dirty Harry case is one example of this moral issue as it applies to police work. Unfortunately, dirty-hands questions are not unique to international warfare either. While these cases are quite clear in military and police work, they can occur in more diffuse forms in trying to reach almost any goal. Of course, the obvious military parallel to the Dirty Harry case is the matter of torturing newly captured prisoners to get information. To make the parallel complete, the situation should be one in which the information *absolutely must* be obtained and which *only* torture of the prisoner can produce. (Chapter 10 considers torture in more detail.)

In his well-known and widely discussed book, *Just and Unjust Wars,*[3] Michael Walzer introduces the dirty-hands problem by saying, "I have left the hardest question for last,"[4] and then: "The available answers are all likely to make us uneasy." In "The Dirty Harry Problem," Klockars calls the problem "insoluble."[5] According to these commentators, a robust cheerfulness or confidence in one's judgment is hardly enough: These problems may be unsolvable. One wonders just what is so impossible here?

Simply put, a dirty-hands problem is a case in which only immoral or forbidden *means* can reach a necessary *goal*. This calls for separate attention to means and to ends or goals. Consider the range of styles in which we might respond.

Four Styles

Universal Fairness

From the assumptions of this view, no one can be used merely and totally as a means to the goals of others. So, torture of prisoners is wrong, and no goal can be so important as to justify an immoral means. Take the extreme case: Either torture a particular prisoner or the war will certainly be lost! According to universal fairness, that war should be lost. (There is more to be considered here, but it will wait until we have discussed the other three styles.)

Social Utility

The social utility attitude would consider the matter in terms of its overall result. It would insist that the means are questionable but only immoral *when looked at in isolation from the major goals of the activity.* The majority of persons concerned will benefit greatly from torture of the prisoner, as they must win the war. The torture, therefore, is justified.

Individualism

Suppose the commanding officer considers whether it is to his or her personal advantage to take the risk of being caught and court-martialed for torture of the POW. The advantage to him might be a successful mission—a successful conclusion to the war—and the great satisfaction of having personally contributed to that national goal. If the torture can be done quickly and covered up, the personal advantages may be appealing. The risks include the chance that, even with the torture, the war might be lost and that he or she will be tried by the enemy for the violation. From this standpoint, the individual may use any means if it produces a personal advantage.

Religious Styles

While there is more than one religious style, these often have in common the view that the commands or goals of God or the gods are sacred. Sacred goals must be fought for, and these goals are so absolutely important and desirable that there are no restrictions on the means to be used. In a religious war, if torture of a POW is necessary to achieve God's purposes, so be it. As mentioned earlier, this is a narrow view of religion: The variety of ideas of God and varieties of religion are certainly not well represented by this comment, taking the "commands or goals of God" as the only interpretation for any religion.

After this quick review of apparent alternatives, where are we? There are three positions that may countenance dirty hands, and one, universal fairness, that categorically rejects such means. We now turn to two prominent authors who find themselves defending, with certain qualifications, the use of dirty hands: English philosopher Bernard Williams and American political scientist Michael Walzer.

The So-called Moral Value of Guilt

In one study of dirty hands, Bernard Williams puts heavy reliance on the notion that there are different "sorts of persons."[6] He directs his comments on dirty hands to the activities of politicians, but his conclusions bear on the general problem: "There are actions which remain morally disagreeable even when politically justified." If they are politically "justified," Williams wants to have them done, but he is not willing to make rules about them or to trust just anyone to carry out these justified but immoral (he prefers the term *disagreeable*) acts. He wants us to put in positions of power "only those who are reluctant or disinclined to do the morally disagreeable when it is really necessary." If we pick this sort of person, we may expect or hope that he or she will not also have dirty hands "when it is not necessary." It is easy to grasp at least a part of Williams's point. Habits are notoriously hard to break, and the habit of getting dirty hands can obviously be a problem. What solution does he offer? Williams has the notion that there are different "sorts" of persons and that some are "reluctant" to behave immorally. These persons, when they do behave immorally, suffer a "genuine disquiet" (p. 63).

Williams's reliance on the "sort" of person who suffers "genuine disquiet" is quite close to a conclusion that Michael Walzer reaches.[7] Walzer discusses the case of Arthur Harris, the commander of the British Bomber Command in World War II who directed the forces that carried out the British terror bombing of German cities. Walzer takes it that Churchill was as guilty of dirty hands as was Harris. However, while Churchill never gave that description of the bombing of German civilians, never called himself and Harris guilty of dirty hands, he did do (actually, did not do) something that Walzer finds significant. After the war, the British Fighter Command (Tactical Air Force) received great public honors, including a plaque in Westminster Abbey with the names of those who died defending Britain. No such honors, however, were paid to Bomber Command (Strategic Air Force), although it had suffered greater losses, and their commander, Arthur Harris, received no public honors either. Why? Walzer thinks that it is because Churchill and the British public were guilty of dirty hands in the bombing of civilians and that they recognized their guilt. Walzer holds that this British *guilt* is a significant moral matter.

Just what is the value of that British guilt? Walzer says that when "collective survival" is at stake, the leaders must be utilitarian and must choose the social utility pattern. Afterward, however, they should feel guilty: "And they can only prove their honor by accepting responsibility for those decisions and by living out the agony."[8] Strange honor. Walzer's people who live out the agony and Williams's people who suffer genuine disquiet are much the same. Are there such people? If so, what special moral value would they have for us in this problem?

Consider these two cases:

1. Someone stabs you in the back, and as you fall to your death, you realize that *the killer feels guilty.*
2. Someone stabs you in the back, and as you fall to your death, you realize that *the killer does not feel guilty.*

Is there a serious difference between the two? Is the killer in case 1 a more moral or better person because he or she feels guilt? Is he or she less likely to do it again? Does the existence of guilt have any value for the victim, the killer, or the world? We turn to each of these questions below. Walzer tells us that without guilt there is less agony and less honor. (Personally, I hold guilt to be a specious notion and find both Williams and Walzer taken in by an almost empty idea.)

Whether a person who feels guilt is less likely to repeat the behavior is unclear and certainly unproved. People get used to their feelings, discover that they can live with their guilt, and may even come to enjoy it in a way. It would take a lot of evidence to make a case for the view that guilt protects us from repeating an act, and it is probably impossible to get such evidence. One use of the term *guilt* can be noted in the following parole situation.

Suppose a prisoner in a civilian prison is called before a parole board. The board has the power to reduce the sentence and perhaps to grant an immediate release on parole. The prisoner is asked, "Are you sorry about the crime that you committed?" If he or she shows no remorse, repentance, or guilt, the board will not be inclined toward leniency. So, the prisoner expresses "profound guilt" by insisting that because of constant feelings of guilt and of sympathy for the victim and the victim's family, he or she has not had a solid night's sleep for all the years in prison. How can the parole board decide whether the prisoner does feel guilty or merely says so? Equally, can the prisoner, him- or herself, know which is the fact?

Guilt is a well-known term that has been used for centuries, but it still may be an empty word with no real content.[9] Presumably, we learn to express guilt and to recognize the appropriate situations in which to express it, but this social learning may take place without any such thing as an actual feeling of guilt.

Regret over mistakes is a more general category. Certainly we make mistakes that we are sorry about, but where guilt means regretting a moral error, the truth is far from obvious. We may regret being caught, a different matter from regret for moral decay. Some people say that they can distinguish between regret over being caught and guilt over a personal moral indiscretion, but it is hard to find their arguments convincing. Neither Walzer nor Williams has given us a usable basis for dealing with the problem of dirty hands.

If we turn from the question of the morality of the individual to the morality of the community, we may find a helpful viewpoint. Start with a general statement of the problem from Walzer: "A nation fighting a just war, when it is desperate and survival itself is at risk, must use unscrupulous or morally ignorant soldiers; and as soon as their usefulness is past, it must disown them."[10]

This parallels the conclusion that Klockars reached in his analysis of the Dirty Harry problem. Klockars insists that the police must sometimes break the law in apprehending those who break the law. His advice is that we allow police to break the law themselves and gain the benefits of their dirty hands, but then he urges "the punishment of police who resort to dirty means to achieve some unquestionably good and morally compelling end."[11]

Both Walzer and Klockars hold that we must acquiesce, and even approve and sometimes order, our agents' use of dirty hands. After reaching our goals by such means, we must then punish or disown those who have carried out our requirements! Why this reversal? Why punish those who essentially carry out our orders? Because that punishment shows both us and the world that we know we are guilty!

We return to one of the questions above: Is there any useful difference between an immoral action that is and one that is not followed or accompanied by so-called guilt, as in the case of the stabbing? With respect to an individual, as suggested by the parole board example, we can never trust a statement of guilt. Without needing any confidence in the intention, we can, however, be aware of behavior.

In the case of a social group such as a nation, an expression of guilt accompanied by appropriate actions may have significant consequences. Appropriate actions might be compensation to victims and punishment of those who ordered and carried out the dirty deed. Such a group expression of guilt constitutes a parallel to the religious idea of becoming a new person, of making a radical change in the ultimate moral basis of one's motives. Can a nation become a new nation? Can a nation behave badly and then become morally new? Japan and the two Germanys after World War II are perhaps examples of efforts to do this. The Germans have exhibited supporting behavior by making substantial financial compensation to Jewish victims. While the idea is not completely imaginary, history is not cluttered with examples of national moral rejuvenation. Still, if expressions of guilt are predictions of desirable behavior, we need not be completely suspicious of the existence of guilt.

Collective Morality

The question of **collective morality** is somewhat novel. It refers to the morality of the nation itself and not to the morality of its individual citizens. The nation here is thought of as a collective entity, not a distributive one with its members being considered one at a time. It is this entity that Jean-Jacques Rousseau called "this public person" and "a moral and collective body."[12] If, as the nominalists put it, there is no such entity as the nation itself, then it can hardly have moral properties. However, even a nominalist view of reality can allow that there is an entity such as a nation, provided that it is given a definition in terms of actual individuals. Such a definition might be that a nation is a thing composed of all the citizens living at certain times and under certain legal systems and, perhaps, all the territory within certain bounds. Just as all the furniture in a room can be thought of as one thing, although made up of separate pieces, a nation can be considered one thing, although made up of separate individuals. In this sense, a nation can name something that certainly does exist, and one may consider that nation's behavior and make judgments about that behavior.

If a nation changes its legal system, changes its main political officials, and makes serious restitution for damages, we might call it an essentially new nation. If an expression of guilt for dirty hands led to those changes or to some movement toward those changes, the expression of guilt would have pragmatic meaning. If nothing happens as a result of the expression of guilt, that guilt must count as empty.

A Kantian Solution to the Problem of Dirty Hands

Even if we do not find a perfect solution, we can get some assistance with our problem in the work of Immanuel Kant. While writing on a different but related matter (the question of the possibility of humanity reaching a state of permanent peace), Kant analyzes the relations between politics and morality.[13] This question is close to the dirty-hands issue because *politics* refers to the machinery used to reach desirable goals and *morality,* for Kant, refers to the duty to follow rules that can be universalized. This view of morality is the universal fairness position that we take to be the basis of the war conventions.

Kant contrasts *a political moralist* to a *moral politician*. The first, the political moralist, shapes morality to fit political ends. The second, the moral politician, makes his or her political activities fit within moral limits. In our case, we must contrast a *military moralist,* who would restrict morality to military bounds, to a *moral militarist,* who would restrict military activity to moral limits. The former subordinates principles to ends, the latter ends to principles. Kant respects only the one who keeps principles intact, taking moral principles to be absolute—that is, the moral militarist. The title of this book follows from Kant's distinction.

What advice would Kant have for those who must weigh the alternatives in the dirty-hands problem? He offers two rules. These are derived from the idea that, as Kant puts it, "Every claim of right must have [the] capacity for publicity."[14] If it can't be made public, it can't be right. Let us dwell a moment on this before we apply it to dirty hands.

The Hague requirement implies that there be a declaration of war before the first act of war. A public declaration of war, publicly worn uniforms, and careful attention to the requirements of military honor are all connected with this assumption about the test of publicity. However, the details of a planned attack or other action need not be made public in advance; that's not required by Kant's principle. A declaration of war is a public announcement of the sort of action that will be taken, not a promise to publish all plans in advance, but all actions, including military actions, must have, as quoted above, the *capacity for publicity.* Kant puts the heart of the matter in two principles—one negative and one affirmative.

The Principles of Publicity

> *"All actions that affect the rights of other men are wrong if their maxim [rule] is not consistent with publicity."*
>
> —Immanuel Kant, "Perpetual Peace"

The maxim or rule must be immoral if it "cannot be *openly divulged* without at the same time defeating my own intention, i.e., must be kept *secret* for it to succeed, or if I cannot *publicly acknowledge* it without thereby inevitably arousing everyone's opposition."[15] Note that it is the rule or maxim of the action, not the action itself, that must be able to stand publicity. The line between assassinations and legitimate military actions is drawn on this principle. Assassination rules must be kept secret in order to succeed; military rules need not be.

As an example, Kant discusses the case of a people who are oppressed by a tyrant. Can they use rebellion to overthrow him? A powerful ruler can openly say that he will punish by death the leader of any rebellion; a small group of rebels without wide support would have to keep their maxim secret. Conclusion: Under such circumstances, a rebellion is not justified.

In a second example, Kant takes the case of a nation that has made a certain promise to another nation but later finds that its own "well-being is at stake" unless it is released from that promise. To break its promise would be to follow a rule or maxim like this: If an agreement is difficult or disagreeable, this nation will simply break it. Ah, Kant insists, if this maxim were known, other nations would not take seriously the word or promises of such a nation. Conclusion: Such a maxim would be self-defeating because it would be destroyed by publicity. This result shows that a maxim is wrong.

Kant gives other examples of the negative principle, but these should do for the moment. He then points out that the negative principle alone is not enough for a decision. When a proposed action fails the test of this principle, it is wrong; however, all proposals that pass the test may not be acceptable. Kant mentions that a ruler who has "decisively supreme power, has no need to keep his maxims secret." Therefore, Kant offers *the affirmative principle*: "All maxims [rules] that *require* publicity (in order not to fail of their end) agree with both politics and morality."[16]

To require publicity in order to work is something different from merely being able to stand publicity. If a maxim (rule, law) requires publicity to be effective, then the public is not going to be suspicious of the question about which rule is being used. The political goal—of having the public satisfied with the conditions under which it lives—is more likely to be attained when the public is aware of the rules of the system than when these rules are kept secret.

Can these two principles solve the dirty-hands problem? Start with the Dirty Harry question. Can Inspector Harry Callahan's maxim pass both the negative and affirmative tests? He would state his maxim as: "When the life of one member of the community is at stake, I will take away the rights of the suspected criminal." The community would hardly accept such a maxim because of the enormous danger to themselves in a rule that allowed the loss of their right to be free of torture. Under Harry's maxim, a citizen's being "suspected" but not convicted of a crime would be enough to allow the police to use torture. Conclusion: The publicity principles deny Harry his right to torture to get the information. When you go by the book, it must be an open book—open to the public.

The formal proof that Dirty Harry was dirty is not really surprising. That's how he got his name. The question of this chapter still remains: If we know that an action is wrong, that it is obviously immoral taken by itself, may we still use it to reach an absolutely desirable goal? Harry is quite aware of the restrictions against police brutality and against the use of torture by the police; however, he chooses the risk of this violation over the risk of the loss of the child's life. The child also has a right—the right to police protection when threatened by a psychotic killer.

This balance of risks, this way of preferring one risk to the other, is Harry's style. We can easily understand the other way of balancing those risks, another style, but we cannot find one style always more desirable than the other. We can, however, make a different judgment. We can raise the question of the general results of one style or the other over time, and we may find that in the long run there are general advantages to a mixture of styles. To the question "Was Harry right?", we must say that he was not. The conflict of rights between the child and the suspect leaves us with no way of preserving all rights. However, suppose that the question is presented to us as "Would we be delighted to have found that his choice saved the life of the child?" Our answer must be "Yes, indeed." If we give contradictory answers to the same question, we are incoherent. If we give different answers to different questions, the matter is far from the same. We can say "No" to the first and "Yes" to the second.

If we ask one question, we must criticize Harry. If we ask another, we are enthusiastic over Harry's objective. Which question *should* we ask? Which way should we balance the risks of error? That question is equivalent to asking if there is one perfect style. To that, we can respond as follows: Any style that is morally acceptable must lie within the boundaries of the two principles of publicity. If the maxims of the moral actor can satisfy both the negative and affirmative tests for publicity, those maxims are acceptable. If Harry or his department could make his maxim public and if the maxim needs publicity in order to work, it would be moral. If one granted the argument that, after such publicity, psychopathic killing would not occur, Harry and his department could go public and be heroes. With a case that strong, Harry would not be dirty.

Application to the Terror Bombing of Germany

With this in mind, let us return to the dirty-hands question involved in the terror bombing of Germany. Suppose that Commander Harris and Prime Minister Churchill had made their maxim public. Would the British public have accepted, even in World War II, this rule: "To win this war, to crush the morale of the Nazis and thereby speed their defeat, we will bomb civilian populations in German cities"? Even if the British had, there is the matter of world opinion. To publicize this maxim would have been to accept the idea that civilians are legitimate targets. No government seems quite ready to take responsibility or blame for such an enormous change in military morality.

We have not yet considered the affirmative principle in connection with the terror bombing of German cities. Did the Harris/Churchill rule *require* publicity in order to be effective? If the objective of terror bombing had been to make clear to the victims just who is responsible for the terror, then the bombing would have worked only if it had been known to its targets. Accepting this argument, both negative and positive principles of publicity might have permitted the bombing, had the British been willing to face the consequences of allowing publicity for their rule. However, the high moral position of the nations at war against Nazism was inconsistent with terror bombing of innocent civilians. Conclusion: The bombing was not justified.

Again we have a choice of pertinent, significant questions. Is the essential question: "Is it right to bomb the German civilians?" Or, does the moral issue turn on the question: "Is this bombing of civilians going to end the war more quickly than any other method?" We can give different answers to the two questions. To the matter of bombing innocent civilians, we must say "No"; however, to the question of our desire for an early end of the war, we may say "Yes." The answer to the second question is bought at the cost of the first.

Does our desire to end a war justify committing war crimes, having dirty hands? No. A major purpose of the war conventions is to deny exactly that; however, without justifying the crimes, even while clearly condemning them, we can still point to the actual consequences of those crimes. We can note, with honesty, just what the crimes have led to without agreeing that the crimes were desirable or praiseworthy. (That the bombing of German cities crushed morale is far from obvious. The opposite effect may have occurred.)

The Reign of Terror

Kant himself followed the pattern above in his views of the French Revolution. He did not justify the Reign of Terror, which included the barbaric use of the guillotine on about twenty-five hundred people, but he did note the feeling of pleasure, close to enthusiasm, that he and others had from the news of the overthrow of the monarchy and the moves to republican government.[17] Did he feel guilty about the Terror? We must answer the two questions involved separately. He condemned it and those whose acts it was; he regretted it, but this regret did not mean that he could not celebrate the gains brought about by the French Revolution and even its period of Terror. This was no cover-up of the crimes. He wrote that the Revolution "may be so *filled with misery and atrocities* that no right-thinking man would ever decide to make the same experiment again at such a price, even if he could hope to carry it out successfully at the second attempt" (emphasis mine). He calls an atrocity an atrocity; the French revolutionaries had dirty hands. His next sentence considers a separate question: "But I maintain that this revolution has aroused in the hearts and desires of all spectators who are not themselves caught up in it a *sympathy* which borders almost on enthusiasm."[18]

The Fallacy of Many Questions

It is commonplace in logic to mention the fallacy of many questions. Consider the classic example, "Have you stopped beating your wife?" This question presupposes a prior question, "Have you started beating your wife?", and an affirmative answer to that. The fallacy consists in treating two or more questions as if they were but a single issue to which one answer would be adequate. Some of the questions raised about dirty hands are cases of the fallacy of many questions. Examples might be the question, "How do you justify the terror bombing of Germany?", and the question, "Don't you justify ending the war as quickly as possible?" Before answering either one of these, we would want to separate the questions involved and distinguish between our view of the means and our view of the results.

Can a commander (consciously?) choose to use dirty hands to accomplish his or her mission? As argued above, the two publicity principles are the required test. Hands are not dirty, however, if the maxim of their action passes the publicity tests. What if the maxim fails the tests; what if publicity is not acceptable or required?

Awareness of the sturdy fallacy of many questions can help separate the pieces of the problem, but that awareness does not tell us how to deal with those individual pieces. Must we countenance dirty hands? Must we justify them in some cases? Despite the various threads of the issue considered above, the answer should be "No."

What, then, is the attitude toward those who have done the work, who have dirty hands? They must be punished for the crimes, of course. It is not enough to think that they will suffer "guilt" and that such suffering is adequate punishment. It is merely a romantic myth to assume that those with dirty hands are "living out the agony," as Walzer put it. Such a maxim would run like this: "Hire people to commit war crimes and then disown them and hope that they feel guilty and live in agony afterward." We could not publicize such a maxim because it would justify almost every war crime. If we were strong enough to get away with it, we would not need it; with less strength, we would be afraid of becoming the maxim's victims. Formally, that maxim fails both publicity principles: We would be afraid to have it known, and it does not require publicity to reach its goal.

Does this leave us with the hypocrisy of Walzer's sad conclusion "that a nation fighting a just war, when it is desperate and survival itself is at risk, must use unscrupulous or morally ignorant soldiers; and as soon as their usefulness is past, it must disown them"?[19] Merely to punish those who have done our dirty work, at our command, is certainly not adequate. We must consider two variations of the problem.

In one set of cases, the war crimes are not absolutely necessary to winning the war. Then, if we hold that crime should not pay, we must insist that war crimes should not pay; therefore, those who are responsible for war crimes are to be punished and the victims compensated (where compensation is possible). This principle must also apply to those who employ and direct the physical perpetrators of the crimes. The politicians and the citizens who are responsible for and benefit from the crimes must not be allowed to pretend innocence. They can be punished and can pay compensation.

In another set of cases, let us assume that war crimes are *absolutely necessary* to winning a war. Can we ever suppose that war crimes and only war crimes can do it? It must be extremely hard to establish such a necessity, and, even with *necessity,* even if the war cannot be won without the crime, that may not be *sufficient.* Wars are notoriously hard to predict; they take surprising turns. To know that one or more war crimes are *both necessary and sufficient* to win a war would take a greater ability to predict the future than anyone can claim. However, even if we had such unavailable knowledge, we have concluded that unless both publicity principles are satisfied, dirty hands still cannot be justified. There are hands so dirty that we should not use them to win a war. There are wars that should not be fought and wars that should not be won. The moral hope, of course, is to fight only those that should be won.

There are three possible conclusions to a war: It may be won, it may be lost, and it may end in a stalemate of one sort or another. The United States has not won all of its wars, but it has not lost any to an invading force. A stalemate in Korea or a withdrawal in Vietnam is far from a loss to an invader. The style of response to the dirty-hands choice may well differ in the three different kinds of threat. Reluctance to use dirty hands to win or to reach a stalemate might not be reluctance in face of a risk of loss or perhaps of surrender to an invader. Despite the anticipation of a different attitude in a different situation, despite the moral panic to be expected from the threat of losing a war, *dirty hands* is simply a new name for an old pattern. The old name was *war crimes,* and an honorable military cannot choose them under either name.

In the next chapter we must consider how to apply these views of dirty hands to the questions involved in torture.

Notes

1 Karl F. Thompson, trans., in Karl F Thompson, *Classics of Western Thought: Middle Ages, Renaissance, and Reformation,* 3rd ed. (New York: Harcourt Brace Jovanovich, 1980), pp. 312–313.

2 Carl B. Klockars, "The Dirty Harry Problem," in *Moral issues in Police Work,* ed. Frederick A. Elliston and Michael Feldberg (Totowa, N.J.: Rowman and Allanheld, 1985), pp. 55–71.

3 Michael Walzer, *Just and Unjust Wars: A Moral Argument with Historical Illustrations* (New York: Basic Books, 1977).

4 *Ibid.,* p. 323. Walzer had given the problem an extended analysis in his "Political Action: The Problem of Dirty Hands," *Philosophy and Public Affairs* 2 (1973): 160–180.

5 Klockars, "The Dirty Harry Problem," p. 55.

6 Bernard Williams, "Politics and Moral Character," in his *Moral Luck* (Cambridge: Cambridge University Press, 1981), pp. 54–70. All the Williams references in this section are to this chapter.

7 Walzer, *Just and Unjust Wars,* pp. 323–326.

8 *Ibid.,* p. 326.

9 A historian of ideas, George Boas, has noted, "It is always the emotional coefficient of ideas that retains its potency after an idea has lost its descriptive meaning," in his article, "Vox Populi," in *Dictionary of the History of Ideas,* ed. Philip P. Wiener (New York: Charles Scribner's Sons, 1973), vol. 4, p. 500. Perhaps there are also ideas that have a significant emotional sense without ever having a descriptive meaning. The idea of guilt may have had just that history, or even less tangible than that, it may be a name for an emotion that does not exist. Without subscribing to complete "emotivism" in ethical theory, we can agree that at least certain terms are merely emotive but that, among those terms, at least some may be names for emotions that do not exist. This last is the category to which guilt is most safely assigned. (I am told that this view is idiosyncratic.)

10 Walzer, *Just and Unjust Wars,* p. 325.

11 Klockars, "The Dirty Harry Problem," p. 70.

12 Jean-Jacques Rousseau, *The Social Contract;* the quotations are from *Classics of Western Thought, The Modern World,* ed. Charles Hirschfeld and Edgar E. Knoebel, 3rd ed. (New York: Harcourt Brace Jovanovich, 1980), p. 194.

13 Immanuel Kant, "To Perpetual Peace, A Philosophical Sketch," trans. Ted Humphrey, in Immanuel Kant, *Perpetual Peace and Other Essays* (Indianapolis: Hackett Publishing, 1983), pp. 107–143. As in most scholarly work on Kant, this edition gives the Berlin edition page numbers in the margins, and I do so here in brackets, for the Kant references in this section.

14 Kant, "Perpetual Peace," [381].

15 *Ibid.*

16 *Ibid.,* [386].

17 See Sidney Axinn, "Kant, Authority, and the French Revolution," *Journal of the History of Ideas* 32, no. 3 (1971): 423–432. Kant's view referred to in the text may be found in translation by F. B. Nisbet, in his "The Contest of the Faculties," in *Kant's Political Writings,* ed. Hans Reiss (Cambridge: Cambridge University Press, 1970), p. 182.

18 *Kant's Political Writings,* p. 182.

19 Walzer, *Just and Unjust Wars,* p. 325.

Bibliography

Axinn, Sidney. "Kant, Authority, and the French Revolution." *Journal of the History of Ideas* 32, no. 3(1971): 423–432.

Elliston, Frederick A., and Michael Feldberg, eds. *Moral Issues in Police Work.* Totowa, N.J.: Rowman and Allanheld, 1985.

Kant, Immanuel. *Kant's Political Writings.* Edited by Hans Reiss. Cambridge: Cambridge University Press, 1970.

Kant, Immanuel. *Perpetual Peace and Other Essays.* Edited by Ted Humphrey. Indianapolis: Hackett Publishing, 1983.

Walzer, Michael. *Just and Unjust Wars: A Moral Argument with Historical Illustrations.* New York: Basic Books, 1977.

Walzer, Michael. "Political Action: The Problem of Dirty Hands." *Philosophy and Public Affairs* 2(1973): 160–180.

Williams, Bernard. *Moral Luck,* Cambridge: Cambridge University Press, 1981.

CASE STUDY

Miguel works as an assistant to the police chief of a major metropolitan city. The police department has been under scrutiny after an investigation of an officer's inappropriate behavior was made public. The police chief has been meeting with police officers in small groups to talk about the department's culture, the rules, and what can be done to ensure this does not happen again. Miguel has received a public records request for information about these meetings. He knows that the conversations were sensitive in nature, and although the police chief's meetings seem to have been effective (in ensuring the officers understand appropriate and inappropriate behavior), the derogatory language he used may harm the department's reputation even more. The state's law requires him to provide available information, so he could (1) provide just the calendar information about how often the meetings occurred and other readily available administrative details, or he could (2) try to track down additional notes from the meetings. What should he do? Should all of the information that he can possibly find be made public, regardless of whether or not it will impact the department's reputation? At what point will he have fulfilled the request and "done his job"? What ethical questions does he need to consider?

PART VI

ETHICS AND PUBLIC POLICY

Understanding the Ethical Dimensions of Decision Making

CHAPTER 12

Ethics for Policy Analysts

SEE WHERE YOU STAND: 60 SECOND ETHICAL DILEMMA

Imagine that you are in the following situation and have one minute to make a decision about the most ethical course of action:

You work in a public agency that requires you to officially declare any gifts over 20 dollars that you receive. One day, a recruiter for another organization asks if they can take you to lunch. You go to the lunch and he picks up the tab ($20.50 for your lunch), but you realize you aren't interested in the job. The dollar value is barely over the requirement, and you worry that if you do declare it, your boss will consider you disloyal for considering another position, which could harm the positive effect you are having on the organization. What do you do?

INTRODUCTION TO CHAPTER

In this penultimate chapter, the authors employ an economics perspective to public policy, specifically discussing just or ethical distributions and redistributions of resources in a society. Referencing many of the ethical theories discussed throughout the book, the reading in this chapter examines ethical claims from different political perspectives. Distributive justice is examined from conservative, liberal, and libertarian perspectives. As you read this chapter, think about the distributions of goods and services from public agencies in your community.

Which ones align with which political perspectives discussed in the chapter? Is there variation between your community and a community in which someone else may live? Are some goods and services delivered in a more utilitarian way while others are provided in a more libertarian way? Why do you think this is the case?

READING 13

Ethics for Policy Analysts

By William K. Bellinger

> If liberty and equality ... are chiefly to be found in democracy, they will be best attained when all persons alike share in the government to the utmost.[1]
>
> (Aristotle)

> Our task as humans is to find the few principles that will calm the infinite anguish of free souls.[2]
>
> (Albert Camus)

> All animals are equal but some animals are more equal than others.[3]
>
> (George Orwell)

While economics is often thought of as the study of market value, ethics can be thought of as the study of moral value. Ethics is the study of the meaning of right versus wrong or moral versus immoral actions, and the application of these concepts to everyday life. In Western thought, ethics dates back at least to the ancient Greeks, particularly Plato and Aristotle. General ethical principles operate at the personal and institutional levels and are, or should be, an important part of our lives as well as our policies.

One important challenge in studying ethics arises from its many conflicting ethical theories. In modern ethics these theories range in time of origin from Plato and Aristotle through the present day and in ideology from highly conservative to revolutionary. Ethics may arise from religious or secular sources, and all major religions have one or more related codes of ethics. Because there are so many views of right and wrong, informed ethical choice is often very difficult.

Another challenge for the student of ethics arises from the need to think about the meaning of right and wrong with an open mind. This is difficult because as children many of us are taught about right and wrong in a rather authoritarian or paternalistic manner that doesn't allow much room for thought. A final challenge is that, like statistics, values and value judgments can be misused or misinterpreted, and must be considered cautiously.

Your Turn 13.1: What are your views on each of the following questions? Think about how you would explain or support your views. Are you satisfied with the quality of your arguments? If possible, discuss them with friends or classmates.

a. Does an individual have a right to engage in self-destructive behavior, and does government have the right to prevent him or her from doing so?
b. Does an affluent society have the responsibility to provide an adequate minimum level of income for those who cannot support themselves? For those who choose not to support themselves?
c. Is it ethically necessary to provide the highest technically possible level of safety in transportation, factories, and homes, regardless of the cost to consumers, taxpayers, or workers?
d. Should income equality be an important goal of tax-and-spending policies? Should the rich pay a higher percentage of their income in taxes than the poor?

Ethical Goals

While the field of ethics includes a wide range of ideologies, arguments, and ways of writing, there are a few common goals for society which guide the writings of most of the great moral philosophers. Three of these ethical goals, in no particular order, are basic human rights, freedom, and equality.

Basic Human Rights

Philosophers sometimes establish ethical principles based on a set of minimum human rights. Essential questions about human rights include these three:

1. What are rights?
2. Which rights are basic?
3. What is the basis in argument for these rights?

Each will be discussed briefly.

In this context a **right** is a power or privilege to which one is entitled. If one has rights, then others have a corresponding duty to act in accordance with that person's rights. For example, if a person has a right to own possessions (property rights), we have a duty not to steal those possessions. If a person has a right to life, we have a duty not to kill her. In policy terms, rights tend to represent a set of minimum standards for an acceptable human existence, and the concept of equal rights means that we have a responsibility not to violate the basic rights of anyone.

But what items should we include in our list of human rights? Different answers to this question arise from different sources. One set of rights is found in John Locke's theory of the state of nature from which society arises:

> The state of nature has a law of nature to govern it, which ... teaches that, being all equal and independent, no one ought to harm another in his life, health, liberty, or possessions.
>
> (Locke 1955: 5–6)

There is a corresponding set of responsibilities based on these rights. According to Locke, these are to not "harm another" in his rights. In other words, one should not take another's life, deliberately injure or sicken another, restrict their liberty or take their possessions.

The policy role of basic rights and liberties is to establish what Henry Shue (1980) calls a "moral minimum—the lower limits on tolerable human conduct, individual and institutional" (p. ix). At a minimum, these basic human rights require us to not actively deprive another of his life, health, liberty or property or, more generally, to not harm other humans. An argument for why we choose to honor the rights of others comes from Plato:

> ... to do wrong is, in itself, a desirable thing; on the other hand, it is not at all desirable to suffer wrong, and the harm to the sufferer outweighs the advantage to the doer. Consequently, when men have had a taste of both, those who have not the power to seize the advantage and escape the harm decide that they would be better off if they made a compact neither to do wrong nor to suffer it.
>
> (Jones *et al.* 1969: 26)

Doing wrong in this context means stealing from or otherwise exploiting another person for one's own gain. As advantageous as such actions may seem to the perpetrator, they clearly harm the victim. Since in an amoral society any of us might be victims, it is in our best interest to accept social norms which reject victimizing others. Within the Judeo-Christian tradition an even more familiar statement of the responsibilities consistent with these rights is found in some of the Ten Commandments, most notably "thou shall not kill" and "thou shall not steal."

In a modern and more affluent context, however, some argue that the rights to life and health require society to provide sufficient resources to maintain the life and health of those who might not be capable of doing so on their own (Shue 1980: 22-4). Shue's argument that we are morally required to support the destitute expands Locke's view of our responsibilities to the poor and is widely accepted in modern policy, in part because the greater affluence of modern developed countries makes such aid less of a burden on others. In conclusion, adherence to the principle of basic human rights requires us not to harm other person's rights, and perhaps to provide sufficient aid to those whose basic human rights are being inadequately preserved.

Freedom

Freedom is an important component of basic human rights, yet is subject to many different interpretations. In the most common ethical definition, freedom means the absence of limits or constraints on an individual's actions. As Locke states:

> To understand political power aright, and derive it from its original, we must consider what state all men are naturally in, and that is a state of perfect freedom to order their actions ... as they think fit, within the bounds of the law of nature, without asking leave, or depending upon the will of any other man.
>
> (Locke 1955: 4)

In a policy context, freedom can also be usefully thought of as freedom of choice, as in the freedom to choose any job, political party, religion, intoxicating substance, or point of view.

Of particular importance in a policy context is the distinction that is sometimes drawn between the phrases **freedom to** ... and **freedom from** ..., as in the freedom to do something and the freedom from a harmful or unjust situation. The most notable example of "freedom from" as a separate concept comes from Marxists who often emphasize freedom from oppression, exploitation, or alienation (Lukes 1985: Ch. 5). Often, however, these phrases do not conflict. One may be free to vote or free from barriers to voting.

Freedom as a basic human right is not the same thing as political freedom or democracy. The freedom to choose between two or more oppressive political parties would not impress most defenders of individual liberty. However, freedom to act as we wish has always been understood to be limited in a civilized society. Perhaps the most common policy question relating to liberty involves the degree to which government should limit our freedom in order to protect others from harm. Ethical theories that emphasize the evils of inequality, exploitation, or sin tend to see an intrusive government as a necessary means of controlling these evils. Theories which emphasize freedom and individual choice tend to see government control as harmful, and individual vice as the lesser of two evils.

Another long-standing issue involving the limits of liberty is whether an individual should have the freedom to act in a self-destructive way. Most modern libertarians argue that no limits should be placed on individual behavior unless it involves direct and significant harm to others, but even among the greatest philosophers of freedom there is disagreement over this issue. John Locke, for instance, states that "though man in that state [of nature] has an uncontrollable liberty to dispose of his person or possessions, yet he has not the liberty to destroy himself " (1955: 5). On the other side of the issue, Robert Nozick states that, "My non-paternalistic position holds that someone may choose (or permit another) to do to himself anything, unless he has acquired an obligation to some third party not to do or allow it" (Nozick 1974: 58). The question of whether society is morally required to place controls on deviant or self-destructive individual behavior is one of many legitimately debatable ethical issues.

Equality

Ethics also involves determining how to distribute the rights, incomes, legal status, and other aspects of society which we deem to be important. This dimension of ethics is often referred to as distributional justice. Equality is the most common norm in ethics for determining how various rights and resources in society should be distributed. The dominance of equality in ethics is suggested by Amartya Sen:

> ... a common characteristic of virtually all the approaches to the ethics of social arrangements that have stood the test of time is to want equality of something—something that has an important place in the particular theory. Not only do income-egalitarians ... demand equal incomes, and welfare-egalitarians ask for equal welfare levels, but also classical utilitarians insist on equal weights on the utilities of all, and pure libertarians demand equality with respect to an entire class of rights and liberties. They are all "egalitarians" in some essential way.
>
> (Sen 1992: ix)

The fundamental issue raised by Sen's quote involves the multitude of goals to which equality may be applied. The implications of Sen's observation are profound indeed, for it calls into question the common debate over the roles of equality and liberty and its implications for the size and role of government. Those who favor equality of freedoms and individual rights tend to favor minimal government since those in positions of authority or power are likely to have greater individual and legal rights than others. Those who are most concerned with equal incomes and living standards tend to favor stronger government as the most efficient means of redistributing income and protecting minimum standards of living. For example, a crucial element in the ongoing debate over affirmative action policies in U.S. higher education is the ethical debate over equal opportunity versus equal outcomes. Notice that equality is the stated goal of both sides of this debate, but the interpretation of the goal is very different.

While equality is among the most general theoretical standards for judging the ethics of public policy, other distributional goals exist. Maximizing a goodness is also consistent with many ethical theories, and meeting minimum standards of behavior is also important for some policy issues. This list of basic philosophical principles is limited to a selection of goals related to public policy, specifically basic human rights, liberty, and equality, but others exist, particularly those relating to individual behavior. Honesty, courage, purity, and generosity are examples of important ethical goals that are more personal in nature.

The next section of this chapter will provide an overview of three ethical theories representing a wide range of ethical goals and policy implications. The primary purposes of this discussion are to illustrate the diversity and sophistication of ethical theory and to establish a minimal theoretical base for considering the ethical challenges that arise in public policy. The theories chosen are secular in nature, though religious ethics are equally broad in their implications for public policy and individual behavior. For example, Christian views on policy may range from highly conservative (Falwell *et al.* 1981) to radical (Miranda 1974; Wallis 1984). The three theories discussed below are either recent or have significant recent support, and range from strongly supportive of equality, including the equality of incomes, to libertarian and opposed to the involuntary redistribution of income. The three theories are utilitarianism and the theories of John Rawls and Robert Nozick.

Utilitarianism

Utilitarianism is the branch of ethics most closely associated with economics and benefit–cost analysis. Utilitarianism began with the writing of Jeremy Bentham in the early nineteenth century. Other utilitarians writing in the 1800s include John Stuart Mill and Henry Sidgwick. Modern writers associated with utilitarianism include J.J.C. Smart, Amartya Sen, and Partha Dasgupta. Brief discussions of utilitarian ethics usually begin with the famous utilitarian goal, **the greatest good for the greatest number**. The most basic questions that come to mind when analyzing this phrase are: **(1) What do we mean by good**, and **(2) What is the greatest number?**

Utilitarianism defines the good in a very general and relative sense. As Bentham defines the term:

> By utility is meant that property in any object, whereby it tends to produce benefit, advantage, pleasure, good, or happiness ..., or to prevent the happening of mischief, pain, evil, or unhappiness to the party whose interest is considered.
>
> (Jones *et al.* 1969: 308)

Two aspects of this quote are particularly significant. First, utility involves an unusually broad definition of the good, including items such as pleasure which in some contexts might be considered immoral or sinful. According to this definition, something that is useful to a person is good because it adds utility, and something which is pleasantly intoxicating to the same person is also good for the same reason.

Secondly, each person's utility is determined by his or her own tastes. Laws and social norms may influence a person's utility by imposing feelings of guilt, social pressure, or actual punishment on those actions which violate social rules, but the basic judgment about personal utility still rests with the individual. In this sense utilitarianism is relatively weak in its ability to provide moral judgments about individual behavior. On the other hand, it is unusually capable of avoiding paternalistic or authoritarian judgments about what is good and bad in a given situation. This tension between individual pleasure and social norms has led to varying interpretations of utilitarianism, which will be discussed later.

Now let us consider the meaning of the term "greatest number." According to Jeremy Bentham, the greatest number represents the total number of individuals in a given community:

> The community is a fictitious body, composed of the individual persons who are constituting ... its members. The interest of the community then is ... the sum of the interests of the several members who compose it.
>
> (Jones *et al.* 1969: 308)

Interestingly, there is little support in utilitarianism for the usual limits placed on the size or inclusiveness of a community. Sidgwick, among others, defines the ultimate goal of utilitarianism as "*universal* happiness" (1962: 413). There is little basis in utilitarianism for limiting our analysis to citizens of a particular nation, ethnic group or religion, or even of a particular species.

> Are we to extend our concern to all the beings capable of pleasure and pain whose feelings are affected by our conduct? Or are we to confine our view to human happiness? The former view is the one adopted by Bentham and Mill, and (I believe) by the Utilitarian school generally.
>
> (Sidgwick 1962: 414)

Clearly, utilitarianism requires us to consider the well-being of the citizens of all nations as equally important. Nationalism is inconsistent with utilitarianism. Also, utilitarian thinking may require that the well-being of non-human species be considered when setting policy. When considering environmental or international policy, the greatest number is a very large number indeed!

Perhaps we should consider a more structured interpretation of the meaning of utilitarian ethics. Sen and Williams (1982) offer three basic principles for utilitarian theory. These principles are listed and defined below:

1. **Welfarism** implies that individual utility, or welfare, is the basis for assigning an ethical value for the utilitarian. Therefore the value of an action is based on the net benefits to those affected by the action, as opposed to its consistency with some overarching

principle. Furthermore, the benefits and costs of income redistribution are based on the utility gained or lost, rather than on the actual dollar amount transferred.

2 **Sum-ranking** means that society should determine the overall net benefits of a policy to society by adding the utilities of all affected individuals. It further means that all individual utilities should be weighted equally.

3 **Consequentialism** means that policy choices should be made with regard to the consequences (ends) of the policy, rather than the means by which the ends are achieved.
(Sen and Williams 1982: 3–4)

The first two principles, welfarism and sum-ranking, are unique to utilitarianism, while consequentialism is true of some important alternative ethical theories.

Extreme Versus Restricted Utilitarianism

Scholars largely agree that under some interpretations, utilitarianism can be inconsistent with the observance of human rights and even with the basic meaning of ethics itself. If one allows the net gains in society's total utility to determine policy, no matter how badly one individual is hurt in the process, individual rights are clearly at risk. Because of these tensions between utilitarianism and basic human rights, as well as discomfort with the role of hedonism in Bentham's analysis, utilitarianism has been interpreted in a more limited way by most of the utilitarians who followed him. John Stuart Mill, Henry Sidgwick, and Amartya Sen, among others, might be best characterized as **restricted utilitarians,** after the terminology of J.J.C. Smart (1956), while Bentham's theory would be categorized as **extreme utilitarianism**.

Restricted utilitarianism uses the logic of utilitarianism at a general level in order to establish a set of guiding principles for society. Each of these principles is judged according to its ability to achieve the greatest good for the greatest number, or equivalently the greatest net good for society as a whole, according to the principles of welfarism, the rank-sum rule, and consequentialism. If a rule provides the greatest level of pleasure minus pain for society, it should be adopted. Once a rule is adopted, however, each individual should act according to the rule whether or not it is in his or her best interest. On the other hand, in **extreme utilitarianism** an individual may judge each action according to its utility independent of any general rules. If rules exist under extreme utilitarianism, they are not absolutely binding on the individual. Smart describes the difference between extreme and restricted utilitarianism as follows:

> A more modest form of utilitarianism ... [holds] that moral rules are more than rules of thumb. In general the rightness of an action is *not* to be tested by evaluating its consequences but only by considering whether or not it falls under a certain rule. Whether the **rule** is to be considered an acceptable moral rule is, however, to be decided by considering the consequences

> of adopting the rule. Broadly, then, actions are to be tested by rules and rules by consequences.
>
> (Smart 1969: 625–6)

The actual rules which are likely to pass such a test vary with the author, but usually bear a close relationship to basic human and legal rights. For example, John Stuart Mill suggests six rules of justice which promote the greater good. These are (1) not depriving people of their legal rights, (2) of their basic human rights, or (3) of things they deserve. Also, one must (4) not break promises and agreements, (5) show unjust favoritism toward some over others, or (6) treat people unequally (Mill 1957: 54–7). Writing from a libertarian perspective, Hayek uses utilitarian logic to argue that liberty should be the primary goal of government:

> Our faith in freedom does not rest on the foreseeable results in particular circumstances but on the belief that it will, on balance, release more forces for the good than for the bad.
>
> (Hayek 1960: 31)

Restricted utilitarianism therefore can be used to establish rules which defend basic human rights by weighing the societal benefits and costs of those rules.

An example of how extreme and restricted utilitarianism might differ regarding a policy issue is the death penalty. An extreme utilitarian would be willing to support the death penalty if the benefits of execution to society in terms of satisfaction, future safety, or cost outweigh the disutility to the individual who is executed. A follower of Mill or Locke might question the death penalty due to its violation of the condemned person's right to life.

Weaknesses of Utilitarianism

Because of utilitarianism's role as the philosophical cornerstone of benefit–cost analysis, some mention should be made of the many criticisms of the theory. In spite of its widespread use and wide range of policy applications, utilitarianism is not an ideal means of analyzing many moral issues. A selection of critical arguments will be arranged as they relate to consequentialism, the rank-sum rule, and welfarism.

As stated earlier, consequentialism says that a policy is just if its results are just, or that the ends justify the means. Because of its consequentialism, extreme utilitarianism offers a relatively poor defense of human rights. If a policy results in net gains to society, it is of relatively little importance to extreme utilitarians whether some people's rights are violated in the process. Similarly, it matters little whether a redistribution of income is accomplished through voluntary charity, or by government policy, or by theft. A consequentialist theory will see little difference between aiding the poor through the Salvation Army, Robin Hood's merry men, or government, though their methods differ considerably.

When one adds the rank-sum rule to consequentialism, the logic of extreme utilitarianism permits even tragic consequences for the few to be outweighed by modest improvements in well-being for the many. The basic logic of the rank-sum rule suggests that a policy is acceptable whenever the added utility to the winners outweighs lost utility for the losers, even if the losers suffer a loss of basic human rights. For example, extreme utilitarian thought might say that a group of starving persons would be morally right to sacrifice and consume one member in order for others to survive. Many other theories would disagree.

Furthermore, some argue that utilitarianism is inconsistent with the goal of income equality or with the transfer of income to the poor. Because the utility of the rich and poor are equally weighted through the rank-sum rule, gains to the poor through income transfers would be offset by losses to the rich. This argument isn't necessarily true, however, as long as the utility the poor gain from the income transfer is greater than the utility lost by the rich. If the economic principle of diminishing marginal utility applies to income, the utility benefits of an income transfer to the poor are likely to outweigh the utility losses by the rich, unless there is significant waste caused by the transfer program. The tendency of non-economists to confuse income and utility is the likely source of this critique of utilitarianism. However, benefit–cost analysis generally weighs individual monetary gains and losses equally, and is therefore more subject to this critique than the utilitarian principles on which it is based.

Welfarism is also the basis for much criticism. Bentham's emphasis on pleasure as the basis for well-being is rejected by many moral philosophers, including restricted utilitarians. Most religions consider the pursuit of some pleasures to be immoral. For example, extreme utilitarianism suggests that if a person's pleasure from heavy drinking outweighs the pain caused to him and others, then drinking is morally justified. The same logic applies to any intoxicating substance. Similarly, because utility is based on each individual's preferences, utilitarian thought includes a large degree of moral relativism. One is reminded of such 1960s expressions as "if it feels good, do it." Individual morality is generally considered a reasonable goal for society, and extreme utilitarianism offers a relatively weak basis for such moral judgments.

Furthermore, despite Bentham's effort to measure utility through a detailed categorization of types and degrees of pleasure and pain, utility is usually not measurable. If one cannot measure the utility gains and losses of an action, one also cannot add or subtract them. Unless indirect means of measuring utility are used, this problem has the potential to destroy the usefulness of the rank-sum rule. Fortunately for utilitarianism and for policy analysis, economists have developed indirect measures of utility that allow the theory to be applied in a more explicit way than many alternative theories. However, these methods are inexact and controversial, and present a challenge for utilitarian theory.

In conclusion, utilitarianism is the closest thing to a paradigm for analyzing the ethics of public policy, but it is subject to relatively serious flaws and limitations. Compared to most ethical theories, utilitarianism tends to be more concerned with efficiency and its potential to increase the overall wealth of a society. It also emphasizes individual tastes and choice more than most ethical theories. Ironically, utilitarianism might be the strongest ethical theory in situations where ethics is least important. In other words, utilitarianism may be most useful for analyzing policies if lives are not threatened and the least well-off in society are not seriously harmed.

John Rawls and the Difference Principle

The next two theories arise from single individuals, John Rawls and Robert Nozick, both of whom published their most influential works in the 1970s. The first of these works is *A Theory of Justice* by John Rawls (1971). The major characteristic of Rawls' theory is its strong emphasis on equality of incomes, wealth, political rights, and other outcomes, along with its dominant concern for the least well-off in society. Rawls' strong defense of equality makes his theory relatively consistent with a liberal political ideology and a highly egalitarian approach to social policy.

The Original Position

Rawls develops his theoretical approach through an abstract model that is somewhat related to Locke's theory of the social contract. The primary difference between the assumptions of Rawls and Locke is that Rawls' analysis of the formation of the social contract begins with a set of abstract assumptions, rather than as a set of (debatable) fundamental truths about the state of nature. Rawls' goal is to create a situation where thought can be applied to the question of distributional justice without the corrupting combination of self-interest and social differences. Rawls calls this abstract situation the **original position**. As Rawls describes it,

> The original position ... is a state of affairs in which the parties are equally represented as moral persons and the outcome is not conditioned by arbitrary contingencies or the relative balance of social forces.
>
> (p. 120)

This original position assumes that all parties have equal rights and equal access to the decision-making process, so that any decision made by the group while in the original position is fair (pp. 128–9).

The most important assumption regarding the original position is the information each person lacks. All persons in the original position are assumed to be ignorant about their own status in society, income level, natural ability, and any groups or coalitions to which they belong. Any individual may be powerful or dependent, rich or poor, part of an influential group or alone, but in the original position nobody will be aware of these indicators of privilege or power. This lack of awareness of one's social, political, or economic standing is called the **"veil of ignorance."**

This veil of ignorance serves a very important purpose in determining how the group will decide its principles of justice. As Rawls states, "No one knows his situation in society nor his natural assets, and therefore no one is in a position to tailor principles to his advantage" (1971: 139). In other words, people behind the veil of ignorance are not in a position to bargain for political, social, or economic advantages for themselves or others in a similar situation because they don't know their situation. Therefore, those in the original position will have no alternative except to choose society's laws and norms in a truly impartial manner.

The Difference Principle

Rawls suggests that those in an original position will choose total equality as a starting point for their society:

> Since it is not reasonable for him to expect more than an equal share in the division of social goods, and since it is not rational for him to agree to less, the sensible thing for him to do is to acknowledge as the first principle of justice one requiring an equal distribution. ...Thus, the parties start with a principle establishing equal liberty for all, including equality of opportunity, as well as an equal distribution of income and wealth.
>
> (pp. 150–1)

However, equality of income need not persist if individuals display different skills and levels of effort in their work. In such a case, allowing the most productive to earn and keep extra income may help to increase the overall productivity of society. A wealthier society then has the potential to increase the well-being of those who are least well off. This brings us to Rawls' primary contribution to the concept of distributive justice, the difference principle:

> **[The difference principle:]** All social primary goods—liberty and opportunity, income and wealth, and the bases of self-respect—are to be distributed equally unless an unequal distribution of any or all of these goods is to the advantage of the least favored.
>
> (1971: 303)

The most fundamental and controversial part of the difference principle is its complete focus on the least well-off person. Only when the least well-off person benefits from inequality is that inequality justifiable, according to Rawls. The difference principle is also expressed in more mathematical terms as a **maxi-min** solution to the problem of social justice, where maxi-min is an abbreviation for **maximizing the minimum,** or maximizing the well-being of the least well-off person. This aspect of Rawls' theory is discussed in the final section of this chapter.

Your Turn 13.2: Assume that you are one of three people in a very small society, and that your group is under the veil of ignorance. You may choose any of the following three distributions of income. Which income distribution do you choose? Which distribution is consistent with the difference principle? If your preferred choice differs from that of the difference principle, discuss why. If not, defend the difference principle against any challenges.

	DISTRIBUTION 1	DISTRIBUTION 2	DISTRIBUTION 3
PERSON 1	$15,000	$14,000	$13,000
PERSON 2	$15,000	$20,000	$1,000,000,000
PERSON 3	$15,000	$20,000	$1,000,000,000

Distribution 1 gives everyone $15,000, distribution 2 gives each person a 2/3 chance of earning $20,000 and a 1/3 chance of earning $14,000, and distribution 3 gives each person a 2/3 chance of becoming a billionaire and a 1/3 chance of earning $13,000.

Rawls is not concerned with income distribution alone. Liberty, equality, and productivity are all goals in Rawls' theory of justice. Within this brief list of primary goods, Rawls establishes definite priorities regarding their relative importance. The first priority within the difference principle is assigned to liberty, which means that liberty cannot be restricted in pursuit of any other goal except liberty itself. Furthermore, any restriction on liberty must meet two conditions: "(a) a less extensive liberty must strengthen the total system of liberty shared by all; and (b) a less than equal liberty must be acceptable to those with the lesser liberty." (Rawls 1971: 302) Once these conditions for liberty are established and maintained, then society can consider the goals of equality and efficiency. Here also, Rawls argues that equality should have a clear priority over efficiency, and that equality should be compromised only if the least well-off benefits.

The difference principle implies that once liberty is fairly distributed, the financial well-being of the least well-off person is of primary importance to society. Clearly this view imposes a greater pressure for equality than utilitarianism, which weighs the utility of the poorest persons equally with that of others. Indeed, Rawls is among the most egalitarian of all well-known philosophers.

Robert Nozick and the Ethics of the Minimalist State

Both utilitarians and John Rawls can be classified as consequentialists, meaning that the justice of an outcome is more fundamental to their theories than the process by which that outcome is achieved. Many libertarian conservatives find this apparent lack of concern with the method of redistribution to be unjust. For those individuals, the ethical theory of Robert Nozick stands as a beacon. Nozick's ethical theory emphasizes the process by which society evolves from the state of nature into a civil and affluent society and how this evolution affects the status of individuals. Nozick's approach begins with a state of nature similar to John Locke's in which perfect liberty and equality exist. Two issues that arise as society evolves from this natural state are the evolution of government and of social inequality.

Mutual Protection and the Minimal State

In Nozick's theory government evolves as a solution to the dangers that exist in a pure state of nature. Conflict between individuals may arise in a state of nature, and without the rule of law the resolution of disagreements is likely to involve violence. If agreements are made between individuals, in the absence of law enforcement of those agreements may also involve violence. In order to reduce this threat of force individuals form organizations for mutual protection. Extended families, clans, or tribes are early forms of these organizations. These organizations offer a means of resolving disputes among members as well as protection against violence from non-members. However, if several such organizations exist conflict is not eliminated and battles are likely. Therefore, merger of these organizations is the most peaceful alternative. When a single mutual protection society has been formed within a region, it can be called a government.

In this story the most unique feature of government is its monopoly on the use of force, since all members agree to give up the use of force against other members when they join the mutual aid societies. Also, the most basic tasks of government are the enforcement of law and the protection of order. This is Nozick's view of the minimal state, one that provides a system of law and order through its monopoly on the use of force.

Just Acquisition and Just Transfer

Other policy implications of Nozick's theory arise from his description of the process by which inequality develops, and the degree to which government should control this inequality. First, Nozick rejects the usual meaning of the term distribution in a society with a minimal government:

> There is no *central* distribution, no person or group entitled to control all the resources, jointly deciding how they are to be doled out. What each person gets, he gets from others who give to him in exchange for something, or as a gift. In a free society ... new holdings arise out of the voluntary exchanges and actions of persons.
>
> (Nozick 1974: 149–50)

Rather than worry about the degree of inequality of wealth or income, Nozick proposes that we should concern ourselves with how wealth or income is acquired: "A distribution is just if it arises from another just distribution by legitimate means" (p. 150). As this sentence suggests, the most fundamental dimension of Nozick's theory of distribution involves determining which **means** of acquiring income or wealth are ethical and which are not.

Starting from Locke's state of nature, where no individual or group owns any land or resources, wealth may be acquired in two steps. The first step is the initial acquisition of wealth or property. The second is the transfer of wealth or property from one person to another. Either of these steps may be accomplished by just or unjust means. Property may be claimed initially by individuals or groups for ownership through **just acquisition** if certain criteria are met. Locke argued that an individual can justly claim unowned property if she mixes her labor with the resources of the land (Locke 1955: 22). For example, picking an apple from a common tree allows an individual to claim ownership of the apple. However, the right to claim ownership of land and resources also has ethical limits. First, one person's labor may not be owned by another. Slavery is unjust in Nozick's theory. More generally, Nozick suggests that if the property is not spoiled, if adequate property remains for others, and if the property is used productively, the acquisition of unowned property is just.

The second method for acquisition is the transfer of income or wealth from one person to another. Transfers are considered just by Nozick if they are made through voluntary and informed exchange between the two parties. If a person offers a service which many people are freely willing to pay for, then there is no ethical limit on that person's earned income. His best-known example of this principle, which I will update a bit, involves a basketball star. Michael Jordan, formerly of the Chicago Bulls, is widely considered to be the best basketball player who ever lived. Let's assume that Mr. Jordan signed a contract that required $5 of each ticket purchased to go to him. Customers know this, and with the purchase of each ticket drop their $5 for Mr. Jordan in a separate slot. If 4 million fans each pay $5 of the ticket price to Michael, he would earn a hefty salary of $20,000,000. If firms hired him to represent their products or star in their cartoons, he would gain additional income. Since this endorsement process involves voluntary and informed exchange, it is fair within the Nozick framework.

The fairness of government redistribution can also be considered through Nozick's argument. According to Nozick, appropriating a large part of Jordan's income through the tax system in order to bring it into line with some preconceived pattern of income distribution would be quite unfair. To Nozick, the compulsory payment of taxes is a form of forced labor because it claims the fruits of one's labor without her agreement. The same logic suggests that no individual should be forced to contribute to the payment of a minimum level of income for the poor, although voluntary contributions to charity are encouraged. The claiming of money by government through the threat of force is not consistent with Nozick's principle of a just transfer.

Moral Side Constraints

A third concept which is often ignored in brief summaries of Nozick's work is the principle of moral side constraints. **Moral side constraints** refer to limits on what individuals, groups, or institutions may do in pursuing their ethical or other goals. These constraints need not be the same as the goals themselves. As an example, Nozick states that basic rights could be viewed as side constraints. In Nozick's theory, side constraints are crucial to understanding the difference between just and unjust acquisitions of property or transfers of income.

Side constraints differ from moral goals in potentially important ways. A constraint creates an absolute limit on certain unjust actions. For example, the goal of protecting human rights might allow the state to violate the rights of a few violent criminals in order to eliminate their ability to violate the rights of others. However, a constraint which precludes any violation of human rights would not permit the state to violate the rights of criminals. Society's means for dealing with criminals would be limited to those which did not violate their fundamental rights. On the other hand, once the basic rights constraint is met, there is no further obligation for individuals or government to pursue the issue. If an affluent society adopts a social policy which says that society should maximize its total welfare subject to the constraint that it provide basic nutrition to all individuals, the provision of food for the least well off is all that would be required. One interesting application of side constraints is the strong case Nozick makes for extending these side constraints to non-humans. Nozick makes a convincing case for the non-exploitation of animals, including vegetarianism, based on his side constraints involving basic rights (1974: 35–42).

In conclusion, moral side constraints play an important role in Nozick's theory. However, constraints may also be utilized to prevent unjust results that might be permitted under any other ethical theory. Side constraints represent a useful supplement for any theory whose goals offer inadequate moral guidance in a particular policy area.

A Graphical Representation of Income Redistribution and Ethical Theory

Graphical analysis of the tradeoff between income equality and efficiency can aid in our understanding of the degree to which various theories support income redistribution. This section begins by presenting a simple two-dimensional model within which income distribution can take place. The basic principles of utilitarianism, John Rawls, and Robert Nozick will then be presented in graphical terms, and the degree of income redistribution prescribed by each theory will be analyzed.

The Utility Possibilities Frontier

Generally the first graph one sees in introductory economics is the production possibilities frontier, which displays the combinations of two goods a society can produce given limited resources and technology. The utility possibilities frontier (UPF) is very similar in appearance to the production possibilities frontier. The UPF connects all possible combinations of total utility that may be achieved by two individuals given fixed resources and technology. Let's begin with a simple model of society with several simplifying assumptions. The model assumes that there are two people, Ritchie Rich and Paul Poorly, who have identical preferences. The model also assumes that only Ritchie is productive while Paul produces nothing. We also assume that Ritchie and Paul do not care about each other, meaning that neither receives utility from the other's well-being. Given these assumptions, without a government-mandated transfer of income

Ritchie will receive a utility level U_1 on the horizontal axis in Figures 13.1 and 13.2, and Paul will receive no utility and presumably starve.

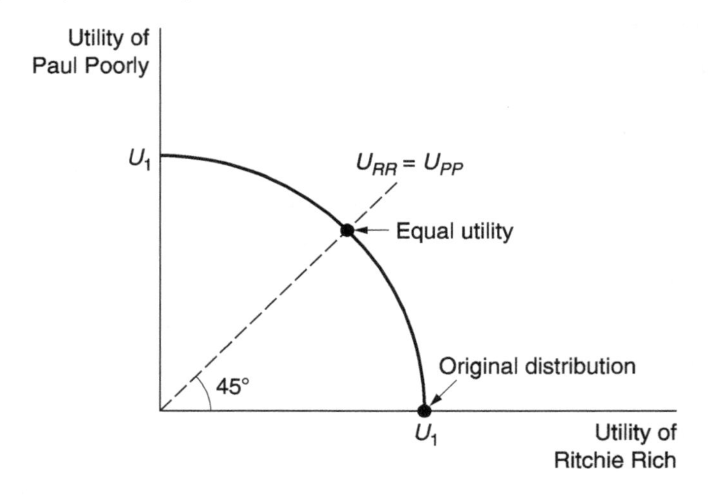

Figure 13.1 Utility possibilities frontier with neutral transfers.

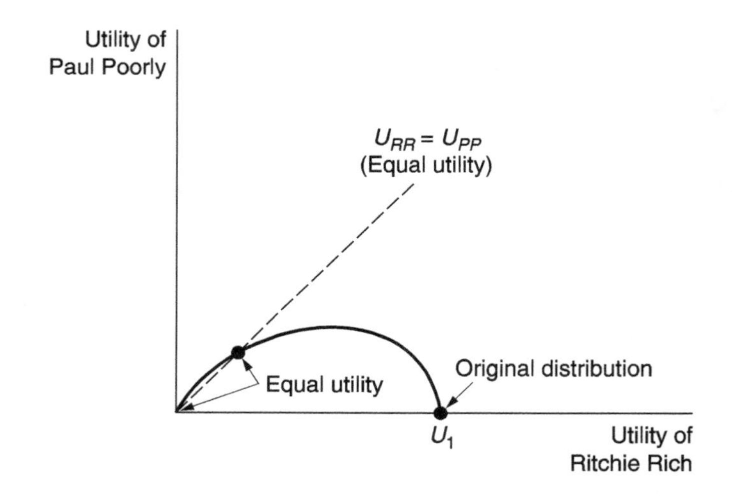

Figure 13.2 Utility possibilities frontier with non-neutral transfers.

The slope of a UPF curve equals the change in Paul's utility divided by the change in Ritchie's utility ($-U_P/U_R$). Figures 13.1 and 13.2 are based on different assumptions about the productivity effects of an income transfer. Figure 13.1 assumes that the transfer of income from Ritchie to Paul does not affect anyone's behavior, including Ritchie's. Therefore, even if the government took all of Ritchie's income he would continue to produce the original amount of goods. Therefore, it would be possible to achieve a utility level for Paul of U_1 on the vertical axis, which is identical to Ritchie's original utility level, by giving all of Ritchie's income to Paul. More generally, the UPF will be symmetric on either side of the 45-degree line representing equal utility. Transfers of income that don't affect behavior are called neutral transfers.

Definition: A neutral transfer is a transfer of income which does not alter either party's behavior.

Figure 13.2 is based on the assumption that an income transfer from Ritchie to Paul will reduce Ritchie's productivity due to a reduction in his motivation and ability to work. Also, in Figure 13.2 the utility possibilities frontier touches the dashed line indicating equal utilities twice, once at zero utility for both, and once at a somewhat higher point. This higher point occurs if one assumes that in a situation of total equality Paul will still produce enough to provide a positive level of income for himself and for Paul, because the alternative (zero utility for both) would not be pleasant for Ritchie. A transfer that affects behavior is called a non-neutral transfer.

Definition: A non-neutral transfer alters at least one party's behavior. In this example a non-neutral transfer reduces Ritchie's productivity.

Utility frontier models with neutral and non-neutral transfers provide a two-fold test of various ethical theories as they relate to income distribution. The neutral transfer model tests whether a theory favors total equality if there is no corresponding loss of productivity. The non-neutral transfer model allows us to compare the degree of redistribution favored by various theories when redistribution causes a loss of output and income. The utilitarian approach, the Rawlsian difference principle, and two interpretations of Nozick's libertarian theory will be compared through this two-fold test.

It might be worth reviewing briefly why the utility possibilities curve bows outward in the neutral transfer case. First, the role of income in this story should be made explicit. In Figure 13.3, the solid line displays all possible distributions of income (not utility) assuming that all transfers are neutral and the total income available to the two individuals is fixed. This income possibilities curve with neutral transfers shows that one dollar more for Paul means one dollar less for Ritchie. This linear **income** possibilities curve is consistent with the bowed UPF in Figure 13.1 because of a crucial economics concept, **the law of diminishing marginal utility.** The law of diminishing marginal utility states that as more units of a good are consumed, less additional (marginal) utility will be gained from consuming another unit. In our example, at the original income distribution Paul has no income. Therefore, the first few dollars Paul receives from Ritchie will provide a great deal of added utility because of Paul's high marginal utility for the food or other goods he can buy with those dollars. On the other hand, Ritchie starts out with a great deal of money, so the utility he loses when the first few dollars are taken away will be small since the marginal utility of the last few goods he could purchase with that money will be low. Therefore, if the two men have equal tastes, transferring a dollar from Ritchie to Paul will add more to Paul's total utility than it takes away from Ritchie's. Therefore, redistributing some income from the rich to the poor is likely to add to society's utility if tastes are approximately equal.

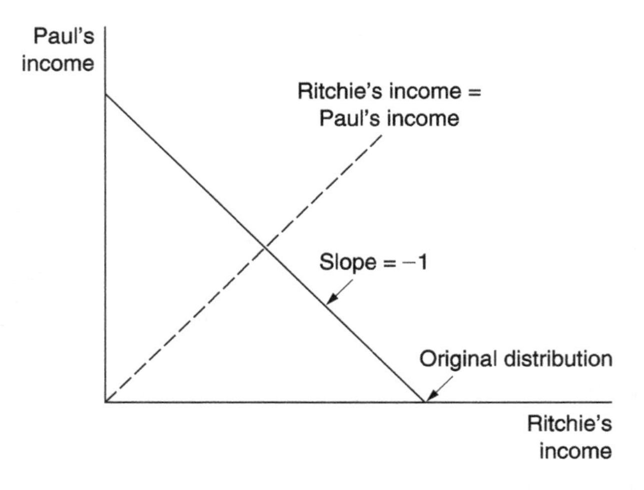

Figure 13.3 Income possibilities with neutral transfers.

In order to compare the ideal degree of redistribution under these different philosophical principles, we need a tool that identifies an explicit redistribution goal for each ethical theory. This principle is easily incorporated in a mathematical model called the social welfare function. Generally defined, the social welfare function defines the well-being of society as some function of the utilities of its members. However, the weight given to the well-being of different individuals varies across different ethical theories. Each will be identified in the analysis to follow.

Utilitarian Redistribution

The most fundamental utilitarian principle is summarized in the phrase "the greatest good for the greatest number." This phrase means that society is best off when it maximizes the sum of the utilities of all individuals when each individual's utility is equally weighted. If U_R and U_P represent the utilities of Ritchie and Paul, respectively, then the utilitarian social welfare function will appear as follows:

$$SWF_{Utilitarian} = U_R + U_P \tag{13.1}$$

or, equivalently, that

$$U_P = SWF_{Utilitarian} - U_R \tag{13.2}$$

The first equation defines the utilitarian social welfare function, while the second identifies the same function in a form that can be interpreted graphically as social indifference curves. **Social indifference curves** identify all possible combinations of utilities that provide an equal level of social welfare for society. The slope for a utilitarian social indifference curve is equal to a negative one, as seen by the minus sign in the second equation.

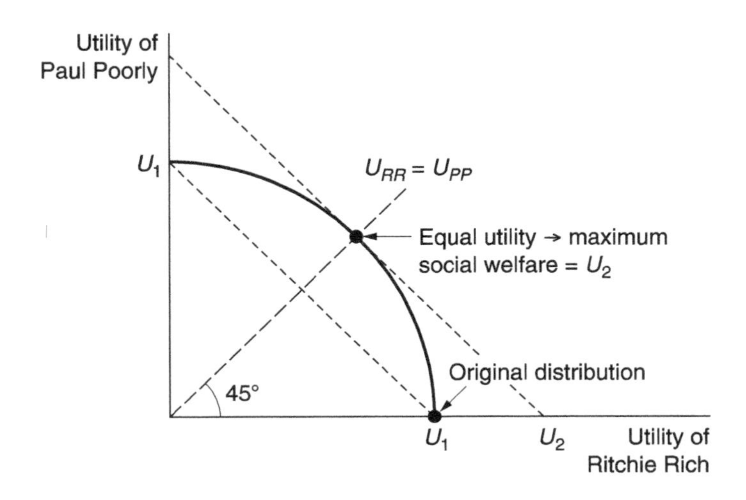

Figure 13.4 Utilitarian optimal transfer with neutral transfers.

The first graphical test of our ethical theories involves the just distribution given neutral transfers. Figure 13.4 shows that if transfers are neutral and people have equal tastes, the highest level of utilitarian social welfare is achieved where utility levels and incomes are totally equal.

> **A proposed definition:** An ethical theory may be categorized as **income-egalitarian** if it favors total equality of incomes in the presence of neutral and costless transfers.

Under this definition, utilitarianism would be categorized as an income-egalitarian ethical theory.

A graph with non-neutral transfers such as Figure 13.5 allows us to judge the optimal amount of income redistribution when there is a tradeoff between equality and efficiency. In the case of utilitarianism, the ideal amount of redistribution would leave Ritchie with utility level U_{R2} on the horizontal axis and Paul with level U_{P2} on the vertical axis. Compared to the Rawlsian case to follow, this graphical analysis of a non-neutral transfer suggests that utilitarian theory prescribes some redistribution but leaves a relatively large degree of inequality.

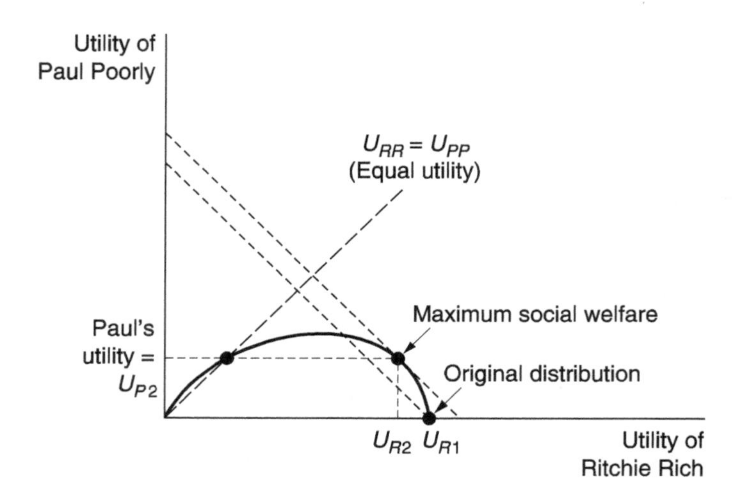

Figure 13.5 Utilitarian optimal transfer with non-neutral transfers.

Utilitarianism offers the following general rule for income redistribution in the neutral and non-neutral transfer cases.

> **The utilitarian redistribution rule:** Redistribute income as long as the marginal utility of the income gained is greater than the marginal utility of the income lost.

The greatest challenge in applying this principle is the generally impossible task of measuring and comparing the utilities of two different persons. Therefore, in practice, the utilitarian approach is not likely to provide exact guidance for redistribution policy. However, it is important to know that utilitarian principles favor some redistribution under non-neutral circumstances, and favor total equality under ideal circumstances.

Rawlsian Redistribution

The essential principle for a formal Rawlsian model of redistribution is the **difference principle**. To repeat, Rawls (1971: 62) states the difference principle as follows:

> All social values ... are to be distributed equally unless an unequal distribution of any, or all, of these values is to everyone's advantage.

The difference principle is also labeled the **maxi-min** principle, which states that the goal of society is to maximize the well-being of the least well-off person. In our example, if a state of total equality results in a large decrease in Ritchie's productivity, then both Ritchie and Paul may be better off if a degree of inequality is allowed to exist. However, if productivity is unaffected by redistribution, as in the case of neutral transfers, Rawls' difference principle would prescribe total income equality.

Mathematically, the difference principle implies that social welfare depends only on the well-being of the least well-off person. In terms of a formula, **the Rawlsian social welfare function** is defined as follows:

$$SWF_{Rawls} = \min[U_{Ritchie}, U_{Paul}], \quad (13.3)$$

where **min** is short for minimum, and society's goal is to maximize this function given its limited resources. In terms of numbers, if Ritchie's utility is 10 and Paul's is 5, society's social welfare equals 5. If Ritchie's utility is 1,000,000 and Paul's is 5, then society's welfare still equals 5. Only the well-being of the poorest person matters under Rawls' theory when measuring social welfare.

Graphically, this function produces social indifference curves which are L-shaped. In Figure 13.6 the dashed 45-degree line defines all points of equal utility for Ritchie and Paul. Everywhere to the right of the 45-degree line Ritchie has a higher level of utility than Paul, and therefore only Paul's utility (the lower of the two) will count in the Rawlsian social welfare function. For example, at point C in Figure 13.6 Paul has the lowest utility, so the Rawlsian social welfare function at that point equals $\min[U_{Ritchie}, U_{Paul}] = U_{Paul}$. From point C, any increase Paul receives will increase the well-being of the least well-off person and therefore society's social utility. However, from point C added income for Ritchie leaves social welfare unchanged. Another important implication of the difference principle can be seen in the level of social welfare achieved at the original income distribution (point A). According to Rawls, this point represents a social welfare of zero, because the least well-off person (Paul) has zero utility.

We can consider the redistributional implications of the Rawlsian difference principle by viewing Figure 13.7. In this graph both the neutral and non-neutral transfer UPFs are included. In the case of neutral transfers complete equality is the preferred result and welfare level 4 is the highest of any possible distribution. However, the non-neutral case does not necessarily lead to total equality. Consider points A and B on the non-neutral utility possibilities curve. Point A represents total equality, but point B provides greater utility for both Paul and Ritchie. Therefore, since the least well-off party benefits from the inequality at point B, it is the preferred point according to the difference principle.

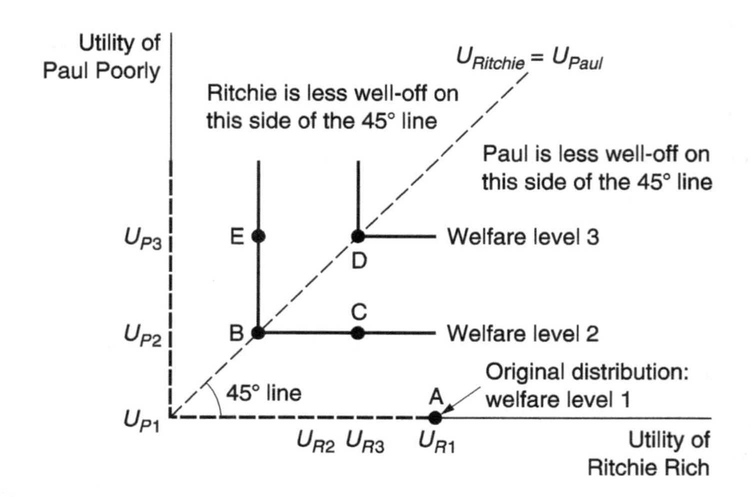

Figure 13.6 Rawlsian social indifference curves.

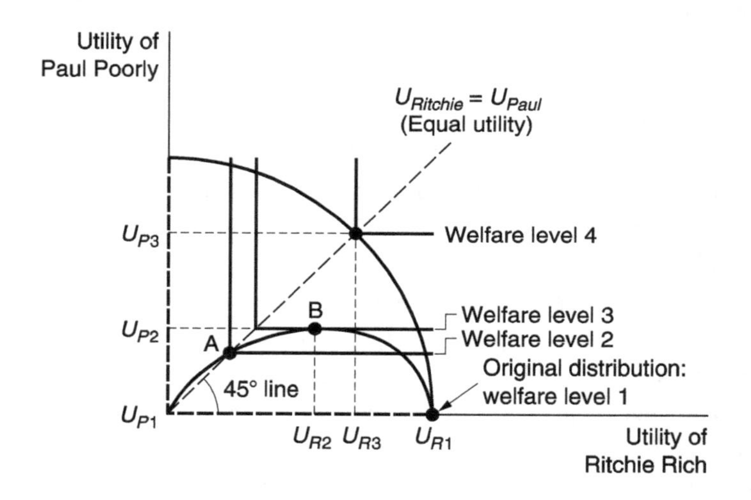

Figure 13.7 Rawlsian optimal transfers.

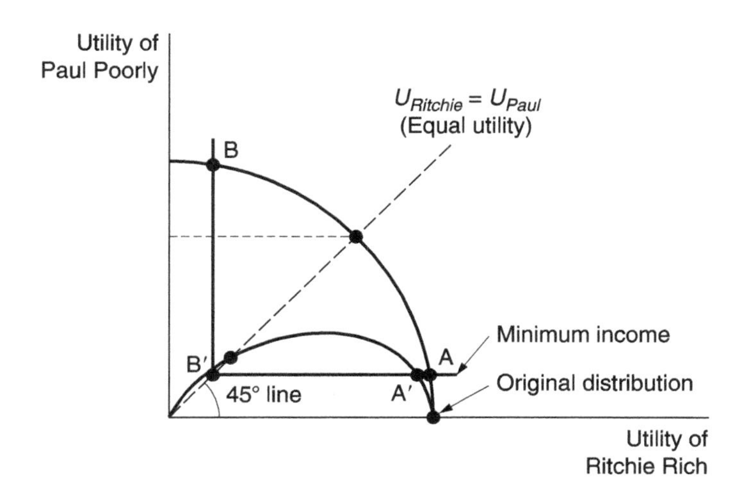

Figure 13.8 Zero Transfers and a minimum income level.

Nozick: Zero Transfers Versus a Minimum Income

As noted earlier, Nozick argues that minimal government should not require individuals to pay taxes in order to transfer income to the least well-off in society. According to a strict application of Nozick's theory, the original distribution in our model is moral if Ritchie's income was achieved by just means. On the other hand, if we allow a minimum income level for all as a basic right or moral side constraint, then society would accept as moral any distribution that provided at least that minimum income level for each person. In Figure 13.8 both neutral and non-neutral UPFs are presented, and a hypothetical minimum income level for both individuals is represented by the social indifference curve labeled "Minimum income." If neutral transfers exist, a required minimum income implies that Paul should receive at least enough income to get to point A and Ritchie must achieve at least point B. Any point between A and B meets the minimum income constraint for both people and is therefore just. Similarly, with non-neutral transfers Paul must receive income consistent with point A′ and Ritchie is guaranteed at least B′. One major challenge in this policy is to determine the minimum income level. The minimum moral requirement under a basic rights theory is that it must be at least enough to ensure survival, although affluent societies may adopt a somewhat higher standard. However, Nozick's basic principle of just distribution does not require a governmentally imposed minimum level of redistribution.

According to this graphical analysis, different ethical theories suggest very different answers to the issue of how much equality or income redistribution is consistent with a just society. The utilitarian approach prescribes a totally equal income distribution in the case of neutral transfers and equal tastes, but a relatively unequal distribution in the non-neutral case. Rawls' difference principle also prescribes total equality in the neutral transfer case, but its primary concern with the least well-off person allows for far less inequality, and far more efficiency loss, than the utilitarian approach if transfers are non-neutral. Nozick's basic theory does not require any income transfer to Paul unless it is voluntary. If the basic human right to survival is added as a moral side constraint, redistribution must be sufficient to allow Paul to survive. Since Paul's survival does not depend on the degree of lost productivity from Ritchie, the minimum amount of income Paul receives is the same in the neutral and non-neutral cases. The rather extreme graphical difference between the Rawls and Nozick models mirrors the substantial differences in their theories.

Conclusion

These few examples from ethical theory may help to illustrate the importance of ethics in formulating and administering public policy. They also serve to point out the difficulty in applying different ethical theories to specific situations. The greatest possible total happiness, the greatest possible equality, the greatest possible achievement of basic human rights, and the greatest possible adherence to a fair process are very different goals for society, and inevitably lead to conflicting policy judgments.

> **Your Turn 2.3:** If you had to choose, would you identify yourself as most in agreement with utilitarians, Rawls, or Nozick? In groups, discuss the reasons for your preferences. If people have different choices, discuss how the group might resolve these differences through reasoning. Don't be disappointed if you cannot resolve your differences.

Because of the diversity of ethical theory, we face a challenge in applying ethics to policy decisions. One way to apply ethics to policy is to choose a particular ethical perspective which most generally satisfies your ideology or sense of justice and apply it in every possible situation to which it relates. However, if our brief tour through ethical thought results only in a new language for defending your previous beliefs or self-interest, then our tour hasn't been as productive as it should have been. Ethics is most effective when it leads to the universal application of norms which, for many, involve a degree of personal sacrifice for the social good.

However, even if your choice is primarily based on ideology, understanding more about ethics may deepen your understanding of the logic and limitations of your particular ethical and ideological preferences, and also introduce a healthy degree of open-mindedness to your policy positions. It is also necessary to understand that adopting a particular moral theory does not make one morally superior to someone with a different moral compass. The dedicated critical thinker can find logical weaknesses and fundamental questions in any theory, including one's particular favorite. Therefore, a degree of tolerance is required when discussing ethical issues with people who hold different viewpoints.

Finally, and most importantly, moral claims may be counterproductive in policy debates if they are used as an excuse for not thinking seriously about an issue or listening carefully to other viewpoints. Intolerance and ignorance of detail are often justified through moral claims, and this common misuse of ethics can lead to poor societal outcomes. Finally, the passion with which one defends a particular view shouldn't be allowed to mask weaknesses in her position or lead to an exaggerated view of her ethical standing. People who speak with great passion and certainty about what is right and wrong are at least as likely to be incorrect or unclear as those who speak cautiously. All of these cautions are useful in guiding your defense or critique of any ethical viewpoint, but should not prevent you from adopting a world view with which you are comfortable.

Rather than defining oneself in terms of a dominant ethical viewpoint, one might apply different ethical approaches in different situations through a careful weighing of the moral questions raised by a particular policy issue. For example, Rawls' difference principle seems relatively inconsistent with the moral dimension of decisions involving present and future generations,[4] extreme utilitarianism seems inconsistent with questions of basic human rights, and Nozick's theory seems disconnected from issues involving the very poor. On the other hand, each theory also has its strengths, as we have seen.

A third method of utilizing ethics in formulating policy is to adopt a set of moral standards as side constraints on policy, and then leave policy makers free to pursue other ethical, economic, or political goals. For example, one might choose policies which best combine political and economic goals subject to the constraint that basic human and legal rights not be violated. Retaining only enough ethical thought to maintain minimum moral standards seems to place ethics in a secondary position compared to political and economic factors, and some readers will prefer to adopt a view that sets the goal of justice as their highest priority. However, those rights which are accepted as constraints would be fundamental to the design of policy in either case.

Notes

1 Aristotle, *Politics*, Book 4, Part 4 (http://classics.mit.edu/Aristotle/politics.4.four.html).

2 Camus, *Lyrical and Critical Essays*. Available at the Philosophical Society, Bon Mot Archive 10 (http://www.philosophicalsociety.com/bonmot10.htm).

3 George Orwell, *Animal Farm* (Harcourt Brace Jovanovich, 1946), Ch. 10.

4 Rawls realizes this limitation of the difference principle, and proposes a completely different approach to the fair treatment of future versus current generations, known as the just savings principle (Rawls 1971: 285–9).

Bibliography

Rawls, John, *A Theory of Justice* (Cambridge, MA: Harvard University Press, 1971).

Your Turn solutions

Chapter 12

Your Turn 13.2: The maxi-min principle would lead to the choice of distribution number one, where the lowest level of income is $15,000. The inequality which exists in the second and third distributions does not improve the income level of person number one, and therefore would violate the difference principle.

Other Your Turn questions in Chapter 12 are discussion questions.

CASE STUDY

Peyton works in the outreach office of a large city. One of his responsibilities is to decide which organizations the city will partner with to offer low-cost or free after-school activities for low-income children. He has looked through all of the proposals and narrowed it down to two organizations. One of the organizations is well established and would be able to use the money right away, but they aren't located very close to some of the most challenging neighborhoods (who would benefit from these programs the most). The other organization has just been created, so they don't have the structure in place to be able to use the funding immediately, but they are located closer to the neighborhoods that would most benefit from these programs and therefore may be more effective in the long run. The requirements for the funding stipulate that this particular allocation must go to only one organization; Peyton cannot split it between both of them. What should he do? Which organization should receive the money? Why?

CHAPTER 13

Public Reporting of School Performance

Ethical Issues

SEE WHERE YOU STAND: 60 SECOND ETHICAL DILEMMA

Imagine that you are in the following situation and have one minute to make a decision about the most ethical course of action:

You are driving to a meeting with a coworker in one of your organization's vehicles. You arrive an hour early, so your coworker suggests driving around to do some shopping. The rules state that you must use the vehicle only for work-related events. Your coworker's suggestion would involve driving only a few miles in the same area, so it's not clear if it would really be a violation, and spending time bonding with your coworker may be helpful in your low-morale department, but you aren't sure it's ethical. What do you do?

INTRODUCTION TO CHAPTER

This final chapter discusses how to make ethical decisions when data (in this case, data about educational performance) can be interpreted multiple ways. What values should guide you? How do you decide how to present data when stakeholders have different ideas about what is best to present? The author discusses the importance of transparency and accountability, hallmarks of public service. How does the demand for transparency and accountability change the way public servants make decisions? Does it make public-sector employees more ethical? Does it create unintended consequences that could be problematic? This article applies two opposing ethical frameworks to this issue, which by now you should be familiar with: the deontological approach and the consequentialist (utilitarian) approach. Consider which approach seems most ethical in this situation. Why? Does the approach you've chosen seem generally more ethical to you, or is it situation-specific?

Public Reporting of School Performance

Ethical Issues

By Peter Godard

Education data professionals devote a substantial amount of their time to collecting, summarizing and reporting school performance data. Federal and state laws prescribe much of the work required, and most of us in the profession work hard to ensure fairness and accuracy in the implementation of those laws. Nonetheless, we often find ourselves in a difficult position as we try to reconcile divergent stakeholder perspectives on the ethics of reporting these data. We are presented with an ethical dilemma: Where statutes and policies allow room for interpretation, what set of values should guide implementation?

One common ethical perspective we encounter is that government entities—including school districts and state departments of education—should operate in a manner that is open and **transparent** to citizens. Education stakeholders who highly value this ethical perspective often emphasize that public sector employees should be **accountable** for acting in the public interest. They also stress that the public has a right to know about the finances, operations and outcomes of publicly-funded activities. These stakeholders argue that all data collected about student and school performance should be made readily available to the public. This perspective is sometimes accompanied by the belief that transparency of government operations and results will both strengthen the democratic process and empower members of the public to take action to improve the system.

Education data professionals also commonly encounter an alternative ethical perspective that, at times, conflicts with the values of transparency and accountability. Education stakeholders who take this alternative perspective argue that ethical decisions about publicly reporting education data should be made to maximize

Peter Godard, "Public Reporting of School Performance: Ethical Issues," *International Forum of Teaching and Studies*, pp. 47-59.

positive impact for students. From this perspective, these stakeholders often contend that public reporting of school performance data should be more nuanced and restricted.

A reasonable person could adopt either of these perspectives or favor one ethical perspective in certain situations but not others. Yet, the current education policy environment requires that multiple ethical perspectives be considered in order to best assure the success of systems-level projects like public data reporting. This sometimes puts education data professionals in the challenging position of answering a difficult question: what action should we take when thoughtful, well-intentioned stakeholders disagree? Another helpful way to frame this question is: how can we best work together when we value different things?

This article provides guidance for education data professionals in exploring these questions. In the first sections, the article contains background and context on the topic of school performance reporting. The article then includes an exploration of two formal ethical frameworks and their application to the dilemmas education data professionals face in publicly reporting data. These frameworks are the deontological and the consequentialist, and they mirror the two perspectives described above. The article also contains a case study from my own experience and a summary of implications for professional practice.

Education Data as a Tool for Transparent Government

Openness and transparency in governance have a long history in the United States. As early as 1822, President James Madison wrote, "A popular Government, without popular information ... is but a Prologue to a Farce or a Tragedy ... A people who mean to be their own Governors must arm themselves with the power which knowledge gives" (Madison, 1999, p. 790). At the federal level, the Freedom of Information (**FOIA**) Act (1966), grounded in the principle that Madison described, guarantees public access to government records and data (Piotrowski, 2007, p. 2). All fifty states and the District of Columbia have also enacted open records acts (Reporters Committee for Freedom of the Press, 2011, p. 1).

With the advent of the internet, many government entities have taken steps to provide access to data through means that members of Congress could not have envisioned when they enacted FOIA. For example, in 2009, President Obama issued a memorandum to the heads of all federal agencies to announce an Open Government Directive that would leverage technology tools to, "create an unprecedented level of openness in government" (Obama, 2009, p. 1). Following the release of this memorandum and a subsequent directive from the Office of Management and Budget (Orzag, 1999), the federal government made great strides in digital open governance through the creation of an open data portal (http://www.data.gov), a transparency dashboard (http://www.whitehouse.gov/open/around), and a site for accountability and performance management (http://www.performance.gov). Many state and local governments have also worked to develop digital open government tools. In Illinois, for example, the executive branch has created an open data portal (http://data.illinois.gov), and the Governor has issued an executive order to establish an open operating standard (Quinn, 2012).

This call for transparency and accountability is certainly nothing new for schools and other K-12 education entities. In fact, the entry of the open data movement into the education sector layers new issues on an already complicated history. For more than a century, state governments have publicly reported information about public school quality and performance. In Illinois, for example, State Superintendent of Public Instruction Francis Blair implemented a formal process of school review and recognition as early as 1907. Through on-site reviews of factors ranging from the orderliness of the classroom library to the level of sanitation at a school's well or cistern, schools could earn either a standard diploma of quality or a gold doorplate indicating that the school had earned 'superior' status (Blair, 1912, p. 9–13).

As technology has reduced the cost of collecting and reporting data, state and local governments have supplemented compliance reporting in the vein of these diplomas and doorplates with reports on student outcomes like standardized test results and graduation rates. The No Child Left Behind (NCLB) Act (2001) accelerated this shift by creating a federal requirement for annual state and district report cards that include test score proficiency, student subgroup proficiency, and test score improvement trends. Within the last five years, as the U.S. Department of Education has granted waivers to NCLB, many states have expanded their public reporting to include additional data such as student academic growth, postsecondary readiness and achievement gap closure (Mikulecky & Christie, 2014). Using Illinois again as an example, the Illinois School Report Card Act (2012) requires public reporting of nearly forty data elements including kindergarten readiness, advanced course taking in high school, college enrollment for high school graduates, and remediation required for those students who enroll in college.

Throughout this history, many have advocated for public reporting on school performance based on the utility of the information for improving schools. Education leaders and advocates alike have suggested that, when a community knows about a school's strengths and weaknesses, its members are more likely to take actions to better the school. Illinois Superintendent of Public Instruction Francis Blair (1914), for example, wrote that the publication of school ratings was undertaken, "in order that a campaign for the improvement of ... schools might be energetically and intelligently carried on" (p. 5). A century later, Illinois Superintendent of Education Christopher Koch highlighted the same theme when he announced the release of the new electronic Illinois School Report Card on illinoisreportcard.com:

"The data we're releasing today ... provide a better picture of student and school growth than ever before. We're no longer providing just a snapshot of student performance but offering something more akin to a video of ongoing progress toward ensuring that every public school student in Illinois is prepared to succeed in college and careers" (Illinois State Board of Education, 2013).

At the time of the release, Robin Steans (2013), executive director of the education policy lobbying organization Advance Illinois, also wrote, "the State School Report Card gives parents actionable information—news they can use, and news that lays the foundation for conversation, community engagement, and informed planning around school improvement."

Outside the education field, others have argued, without regard to the potential for school improvement, that openness and transparency in government is a moral imperative in our liberal democratic society. Researcher Jerry Brito, for example, suggests, "Each time government data is freed, citizens gain useful access to valuable information that rightly belongs to them. But perhaps more importantly, government is forced to deal with the new reality of a networked world in which the people demand free online access to public information" (Brito, 2013, p. 241). Advocates like Brito leave no room to consider the possible consequences of reporting data. They argue that government transparency is critical at any cost so that our system of government can continue to function as it was designed. Perhaps the most controversial exemplar of this view point is Edward Snowden, the National Security Agency (NSA) contractor who compiled and leaked documents demonstrating the types of information the NSA was collecting on U.S. citizens (Gellman, Solanti & Tate, 2014). Although Snowden's actions were likely illegal, he is hailed by some as a national hero for making the government's spying on U.S. citizens known. Although the issues inherent in publicly reporting education data are generally much less controversial, the same ethical principle used by Snowden's defenders can be applied.

Transparency's Unintended Consequences

The reasoning described in the section above has become the dominant narrative about the public reporting of school performance both because it is espoused by most in positions of power and also because most public education data reporting has been codified in both federal and state law. Certainly, the desire to improve public schools and the moral imperative for transparent government are commendable ideals. However, there are compelling alternative views on the ethics of this issue that are also worth consideration. Advocates for these views suggest that the public reporting of school performance data needs to more limited to achieve the best results for students.

One claim of this ilk is that school performance rating and reporting systems reduce the quality and breadth of students' educational experiences by incentivizing 'teaching to the test.' For example, a study conducted by the Center for Education Policy showed that, following the passage of NCLB, 62 percent of school districts have increased time spent on content areas covered by state tests and that 42 percent of districts cut time from one or more other subjects or activities (e.g., social sciences, science, art, music, recess) to accommodate the focus on English Language Arts and math (McMurrer, 2007). From this, some conclude that attempts to quantify and report student learning may have the perverse consequence of limiting learning opportunities for those students.

A second alternative view worthy of consideration is that public rating and reporting of school performance unfairly puts the full onus of responsibility for improvement on those that work in the school system when, in fact, inadequate resources and out-of-school factors better explain poor student outcomes. This, some argue, focuses attention and energy toward individual responsibility when attention to social and economic context would be more beneficial. For example, Diane Ravich, a historian of education, traces the advent of the school accountability movement to the report *Equality of Educational Opportunity*, known as the Coleman report for its lead author, sociologist James Coleman (1966). Following the publication of this report, Ravitch suggests that: "although professional educators continued to believe that any inadequacies in the schools could be resolved by additional resources—policy makers, public officials, community activists and parents started to conclude that many of the problems were structural consequences of the bureaucratic (read: professional) system of public education and could only be addressed by market competition or structural changes" (Ravitch, 2002, p. 12).

This perspective was further developed and institutionalized during the Reagan administration with the publication of *A Nation at Risk* (U.S. Department of Education, National Commission on Excellence in Education 1983), and codified in law with the passage of NCLB (2001). In the shadow of these expensive and largely ineffective NCLB accountability policies, Ravitch (2012) counters:

"[The view that public schools are failing] is utter nonsense ... Low performance, contrary to the [beliefs of those in the] current pseudo-reform movement, is not caused by unions ... or teachers, [it] is caused by the toxic combination of poverty and segregation. One vision [for the future of education] is the carrot and stick philosophy of school reform. This philosophy is rooted in the belief that teachers, administrators and students need to be threatened and rewarded in order to raise test scores ... What you should know is that this approach has failed: it has failed again, and again, and again ... This [philosophy] is not school reform, it is the status quo ... it is official state and federal policy across this country. The other vision for school reform rests on a different perspective, and it begins with the simple question: what kind of school do you want for your own child? Most parents want small classes, a safe campus, experienced teachers, stability, a full curriculum, science labs, history, civics, foreign languages, and arts classes. Aren't these the reasons that parents move to the suburbs and pay for elite private schools? Don't you think that poor families want exactly the same things for their children?"

Ravitch suggests that the public reporting of data through school report cards and accountability systems is misguided. She argues that students would be better served by revising or eliminating the legal requirement for school accountability. Her analysis is affirmed and contextualized by Stan Karp (2004), an educator and activist, when he writes: "NCLB imposes a mandate on schools that is put to no other institution in society: wipe out inequalities while the factors that help produce them stay in place...If this sounds unfair and absurd, that's because it is. Imagine a federal law that declared that 100 percent of all citizens must have adequate healthcare in twelve years or sanctions will be imposed on doctors and hospitals. Or all crime must be eliminated in twelve years or the local police department will face privatization" (p.54, 60).

The bottom line for those who agree with Karp and Ravitch is that decisions about the public reporting of data should be based on what is best for students, and from their perspective NCLB-style accountability reporting is not what is best for students.

A third alternative view worthy of consideration is that the public rating and reporting of school performance data can be harmful to students' self-esteem and ultimate success. This perspective is well argued by political scientist Jeanne Theoharis (2009) who writes: "it has become common sense to bemoan the declining value of education within urban Black and Latino communities, to assume a priori that students who value education succeed in school and those with poor values drop out. This misinformed discussion about values not only takes the responsibility for schools away from the society that creates them and places it solely on students and their parents but distorts the regard for education in the African American and Latino communities" (p. 90).

Through student interviews and case-study analysis, Theoharis demonstrates that students attending under-resourced urban schools are expected to be responsible for attending school, completing assignments and planning for college while the school districts they attend are not equally accountable for providing adequate classes, materials and facilities. She highlights the stories of students who feel anxious and demoralized by standardized tests. Although these tests—and their public reporting—may have been designed to highlight systemic failure, the students she interviewed unfairly perceive them as a mirror of their own personal failings.

The multiple perspectives represented in this section and the preceding section demonstrates the complexity of the ethical dilemmas surrounding the public reporting of school performance data. Any one of these perspectives seems reasonable in isolation. Yet, balancing the perspectives to make ethical professional decisions about what action to take in reporting data is difficult. In the following sections, I have analyzed these perspectives in the context of formal ethical frameworks to provide further insight into the underlying assumptions and values behind each one.

Deontological Framework Defined

Deontology makes a good starting place for the ethical analysis in this article not only because it is relatively simple compared to other ethical frameworks but also because deontological thinking proceeds from the intuitive ethical question: how are we supposed to behave? Ethicists in the deontological tradition are most concerned with principles of what action is right or just even when that action may be difficult or even harmful. The term deontology, which has Greek roots, means the study of duty or the study of what one ought to do (Freeman, 2001). Deontological ethics are also sometimes called virtue ethics because of their focus is what is right or virtuous (Hursthouse, 2012). Using an example already described, those who believe Edward Snowden acted ethically in exposing NSA documents generally build their arguments on a deontological foundation. They would argue that the U.S. government should always be open and transparent even when doing so may act against the best interests of national security with grave consequences at stake.

Perhaps the most familiar modern philosopher of ethics in the deontological tradition is Immanuel Kant. In the late eighteenth century, Kant (2012) developed a secular duty-based system of ethics grounded not in religious tradition, but human reason. Kant's ethical framework—the categorical imperative—consists of three maxims. In describing his first maxim, Kant writes, "Act only according to that maxim whereby you can at the same time will that it should become a universal law without contradiction." In other words, Kant believes an ethical or moral proposition must not be contextual to a particular person or situation; it must be universal. Kant explains his second maxim by stating, "Act in such a way that you treat humanity, whether in your own person or in the person of any other, never merely as a means to an end but always at the same time as an end." By this statement, Kant means that an ethical action must affirm the humanity of the actor and the individuals affected by the action; the action may not treat either party merely as a means to an end. Synthesizing both of these ideas into a universal deontological law, Kant declares a third maxim: "Therefore, every rational being must so act as if he were through his maxim always a legislating member in the universal kingdom of ends." He avows that ethical behavior's aim is compliance with universal, non-contextual moral law that affirms the humanity of all affected.

More recent formulations of deontological ethics have been outlined by W.D. Ross (1930), H.A. Pritchard (1949), and John Rawls (1971). Ross is best known as a translator and commentator on Aristotlean moral philosophy. However, his original work was also influential in the development of modern ethics. His philosophy differed from Kant's in that it pointed to multiple irreducible—and sometimes conflicting—moral duties rather than a universal source of moral obligation. He further asserted that, "the moral convictions of thoughtful and well-educated people are the data of ethics" (Ross, 1930, p. 41). Similarly, Pritchard argued that truths of how we ought to act stand on their own without regard to their consequences. John Rawls' influential theory of justice builds on these earlier ethical frameworks and specifically contends that an ethical distribution of social goods such as liberty, opportunity and wealth should be equal unless an unequal distribution of these goods is to the advantage of the least favored.

Deontological Framework Applied

Data experts facing ethical dilemmas related to the public reporting of data would be wise to familiarize themselves with *The Forum Guide to Data Ethics* (2010) ("Forum Guide"). The Forum Guide was developed by the National Forum on Education Statistics, a national consortium of education data professionals organized by the U.S. Department of Education. The Forum Guide adopts a deontological approach to formulating an ethical system for those who work with education data. It defines ethics as either, "(1) a set of principles of proper conduct," or "(2) the rules or standards governing the conduct of a person or the members of a profession" (p. 1). The Forum

Guide presents a code of ethics written for a broad range of professionals who work with student data: from classroom teachers, to database administrators, to policy-makers. It documents nine ethical core principles related to professional work with education data. The authors call their core principles cannons, and they are listed in Table 14.1 below. Notably, the authors recommend not only that data professionals make themselves familiar with these cannons, but that they engage in ongoing dialogue with stakeholders and other professionals in order to maximize the usefulness of the ethical framework.

Table 14.1 Eight Cannons from The Forum Guide to Data Ethics (p. 7)

INTEGRITY
1. Demonstrate honesty, integrity, and professionalism at all times.
2. Appreciate that, while data represent attributes of real people, they do not describe the whole person.
3. Be aware of applicable statutes, regulations, practices, and ethical standards governing data collection and reporting.
4. Report information accurately and without bias.
5. Be accountable, and hold others accountable, for ethical use of data.
DATA QUALITY
6. Promote data quality by adhering to best practices and operating standards
7. Provide all relevant data, definitions, and documentation to promote comprehensive understanding and accurate analysis when releasing information.
SECURITY
8. Treat data systems as valuable organizational assets.
9. Safeguard sensitive data to guarantee privacy and confidentiality.

These standards of professional ethics seek to provide universal guidelines for right and wrong in working with education data. Several of the cannons relate specifically to the public reporting of school performance data. For example, in describing Cannon one, which calls for integrity and professionalism at all times, the guide states that experts, "behave 'professionally' when they accurately report data ... no matter the consequences" (p. 9). Further, Cannon three implores data experts to be aware of applicable statutes and regulations. The Forum Guide notes, "The temptation to break the rules arises now and again. And ignorance of a legal requirement does not cancel the ethical obligation to meet it" (p. 13). From this deontological perspective, professionals are obliged to publicly report mandated statistics no matters the impact of this action on the educational system or its stakeholders.

The Forum Guide also includes several cannons that may, at times, stand in conflict with the cannons exhorting data professionals to follow the letter of the law regardless of the consequences. These include cannon two, which implores data experts to appreciate that, while data may represent attributes of real people, they do not fully describe those people; Cannon four, which recommends reporting accurately and without bias; and Cannon seven, which recommends providing all relevant data, definitions and documentation to promote comprehensive understanding and accurate analysis when releasing this information. These three cannons help reduce the likelihood that stakeholders may be harmed by misinterpretation of the data. For example, acting with the awareness that data about a person can never fully describe that person may guide a data expert to contextualize a report in a way that partially addresses the issues raised by Diane Ravitch and Jeanne Theoaris and described in the background section of this article. Concrete examples of results derived from the application of these cannons can be seen in the contextual factors provided for each metric displayed on the State of Illinois' online report card (http://www.illinoisreportcard.com) and the thoughtful analysis included in the data stories on the State of Rhode Island's data hub (http://ridatahub.org/datastories/).

A second deontological perspective on the ethical dilemma of publicly reporting school performance comes from advocates for an open and transparent government. The Reporters Committee for the Freedom of the Press ("Reporters Committee") is an exemplar of this perspective. This organization provides legal representation to members of the press with the mission to, "protect the right to gather and distribute news ... and to preserve the principles of free speech and unfettered press, as guaranteed by the First Amendment of the U.S. Constitution" (Reporters Committee on the Freedom of the Press, n.d.). The organization recommends that reporters operate within their own code of professional ethics (Reporters Committee on the Freedom of the Press, 2012), but also asserts that government has an absolute duty to operate transparently. Because they value fairness and accuracy, many education data professionals feel uneasy when they are put in the position of completing a Freedom of Information Act request for data that are incomplete or erroneous. Those who adopt the ethical perspective supported by the Reporters Committee believe this action simply fulfills an ethical duty. Their belief, grounded in deontological ethical reasoning, is that reporters have a right to obtain and write about data the government has gathered, even when the data are erroneous.

It is important to note that many advocates for government transparency do not adopt the absolutist deontological perspective of the Reporters Committee. They recognize the limitations of government data, but they value the positive benefits that transparency can have for improving results by informing the public. The non-profit organization greatschools.org, for example, works to provide easy access to public school performance for parents so that they can make better educational choices for their children. The ethical beliefs of advocates like these are not grounded in deontological ethical reasoning, but consequentialist thinking, the subject of the next section of this article.

Consequentialist Framework Defined

By applying the consequentialist ethical framework, data experts can understand the ethical tensions inherent in the public reporting of school performance quite differently. Rather than seeking an external code of ethics like the *The Forum Guide to Data Ethics* (2010), an ethicist from a consequentialist background would guide data experts to act ethically by considering the outcome, or consequences, of their actions. From this perspective, data should be publicly reported not when an external ethical standard requires it, but rather when reporting data is the action with the most beneficial outcome. Put another way, the ethical choice is the one that maximizes benefits, or utility, for the most people. Act-utilitarian reasoning is the form of consequentialist thinking underlying the analysis at hand. Act-utilitarianism holds, in addition to the views just described, that, "happiness, pleasure, well-being, utility or some combination of these are the only factors that ... make for the goodness of consequences" (Slote, 2001, p.1). This form of ethics distinguishes itself from other forms of consequentialism by ignoring such possible goods as unappreciated beauty, the fairness of the distribution of positive and negative consequences, and the possession of truth or honor (Slote, 2001).

The theory of act-utilitarianism has evolved into its current form over several centuries, and it has ancient roots in multiple ethical traditions (Lyons, 2001). Jeremy Bentham published the first thorough description of a utilitarian ethical system in 1789. In Bentham's (1961) formulation of the theory, he posits, "Nature has placed mankind under the governance of two sovereign masters, *pain* and *pleasure*. It is for them alone to point out what we ought to do" (p. 17). On this foundation, Bentham builds his principle of utility which, "approves or disapproves of every action whatsoever, according to the tendency which it appears to have to augment or diminish the happiness of the party whose interest is in question" (p. 17). Shifting his focus from the individual to the community, Bentham postulates, "The community is a fictitious *body*, composed of the individual persons who are its ... *members*. The interest of the community then is ... the sum of the interests of the several members who compose it" (p. 18). He goes on to suggest that an action of government, being merely a special type of act, may be considered ethical when, "the tendency which it has to augment the happiness of the community is greater than any which it has to diminish it" (p. 18). His work proceeds to describe in detail a utilitarian ethic and its application to public policy and government administration.

Many other authors have written about and offered refinements to the utilitarian ethical framework since the publication of Bentham's work. A few of the more significant contributors include John Stuart Mill (1961), Henry Sidgwick (2011), and G.E. Moore (1907). Smart (1973) has synthesized the areas of agreement and divergence among these and other utilitarian thinkers and introduced the following definition of the framework: "[Act-utilitarianism is] a system of ethics which is free from traditional and theological associations ... Act-utilitarianism is the view that the rightness or wrongness of an action depends only on the total goodness or badness of its consequences, i.e., on the effect of the action on the welfare of all human beings (or perhaps all sentient beings)" (p. 4).

Smart differentiates the act-utilitarian system of ethics from rule-utilitarian systems which guide ethical decision making not by the outcome of actions but by rules based on the probability of outcomes. Smart also describes a key discriminator among act-utilitarian thinkers related to the evaluation of consequences: the hedonistic variant (Bentham, 1961) evaluates consequences entirely on the intensity and duration of pleasure; the non-hedonistic variant (Mill, 1961) also considers in the evaluation of consequences the nature of the pleasure (e.g., pleasure in creativity over sadistic pleasure). Finally, Smart notes, "Another type of ultimate disagreement between utilitarians, whether hedonisitic or ideal, can arise over whether we should try to maximize the *average* happiness of a human being … or whether we should try to maximize the *total* happiness" (p. 27).

Consequentialist Framework Applied

This long period of development in the field of philosophy has created an ethical system that is very useful in the fields of public policy and educational leadership. According to David Lyons (2001), the utilitarian tradition, "has frequently served as the ideological basis for political, economic, and social reforms" (p. 1). This history makes consequentialist ethics generally, and act-utilitarianism specifically, particularly worthy of consideration in matters of public policy related to reporting on school performance.

Several of the ethical arguments outlined in the background sections of this article conform to an act-utilitarian ethic. For example, the argument that overemphasis on public reporting and accountability may lead schools to focus too heavily on the subjects included on accountability assessments is grounded in a utilitarian perspective. Proponents of this argument believe that reducing the emphasis on public reporting and accountability will ultimately have the greatest utility for students. Similarly, Diane Ravitch's perspective on the issue of school performance reporting is also grounded in utilitarian ethics. She argues that policies requiring performance reporting and school accountability have not benefited students because they are putting the onus for change on the wrong people. She suggests that modifying the methodology for reporting on school performance and the consequences of this reporting for schools and teachers would lead to the best outcome for students. Jeanne Theoharis' perspective on reducing the harm to students from testing that is damaging to their self-esteem is also grounded in this utilitarian tradition of maximizing utility.

Each of these individuals values results for students over a deontological ethical standard like government transparency or legal compliance, even though they have not specifically described their thinking in utilitarian terms. Implicitly, each author has employed cost-benefit analysis, a form of decision support familiar to most policy analysts. Decisions related to school performance reporting do not lend themselves easily to formal, econometric cost-benefit analysis. However, Table 14.2 below summarizes some of the possible benefits and costs that data professionals may consider when ethical dilemmas about public reporting of school performance arise. This framework is a useful exercise for making decisions related to performance reporting as it may provide additional insight beyond that revealed through application of tools like the Forum Guide described previously.

Table 14.2 Costs & Benefits of Public Reporting of Education Data

COSTS	BENEFITS
–Incentivize neglect of subjects and learning activities that don't contribute directly to measureable performance (e.g., art, social studies, health) –Place emphasis on the role of the individual in getting better results while neglecting larger social responsibility to provide adequate resources –Degrade self-image of students held accountable without adequate support –Create potentially difficult working conditions for educators and corrode professional community –Create an incentive structure aligned only to academic outcomes, to the exclusion of building curiosity, love of learning, social skills, or emotional intelligence	–Provide parents and community members 'consumer information' to make choices about where to live and what schools to choose –Provide parents and community members information to advocate for resources or changes to school operations –Empower parents and community members with information to fully engage as well-informed partners in school improvement –Create accountability for actions of public employees –Foster democratic process by increasing openness and transparency

The categories in Table 14.2 demonstrate what benefits and costs exist. It may seem a logical next step to quantify and aggregate them to support decision making. In fact, this type of analysis is highly valued in rational-bureaucratic organizations like state departments of education and school districts. However, even the earliest studies of these types of organizations (Weber, 1946) note the limits and pitfalls of such highly rational decision-making. It is critical for education data professionals to understand that the value of each of these costs and benefits likely varies depending on what role in the educational system the evaluator of the costs and benefits plays. The bureaucratically valued benefit maximizing decision may not appear to maximize benefits from all perspectives.

Ralph Ellis (1998) has addressed this shortcoming in his work on ethics and public policy analysis. He notes several technical problems with the approach. He writes, "some approaches to policy analysis ... give the initial impression of a completely empirical and mathematical discipline whose purpose is to determine more efficient means toward certain social goals" (p. 3). However, he suggests, "extremely quantitative approaches ... often ignore ... the ways in which science may lend itself to ideologically- and value-driven interpretations which pass themselves off to the public as 'objective facts'" (p. 4). An example of this phenomenon is the use of school performance data to select schools for closure or extreme intervention like replacing the leaders and staff. To many stakeholders, it may seem like an objective fact that schools with the lowest percent of students meeting academic standards are the *worst* schools, especially when the data are reported by experts in positions of power. Yet, this conclusion is laden with value judgments, including the belief that academic proficiency in reading and math is the primary goal of schooling, that the quality of education in a school is measurable by reading and math proficiency alone, and that student academic proficiency rather than student academic growth is the best measure of academic outcomes.

Ellis also points out that even with the best evidence it is often difficult to know which among a set of possible actions provides the greatest benefit. This difficulty, he suggests, is caused not only by methodological issues but also by differences in values and priorities among stakeholders. Ellis sums up the objective of his work when he writes,"the goal ... is to make utility, justice, and procedural legitimacy commensurable with each other in a coherent and practically accessible way" (p. 5). His book *Just Results* is very useful for practitioners who seek a form of decision analysis that address the limitations of traditional cost-benefit analysis grounded in act-utilitarianism.

CASE STUDY: PUBLICLY REPORTING RESULTS FROM THE ILLINOIS SURVEY OF LEARNING CONDITIONS

The foregoing analysis covers a wide field of education policy and ethical issues. A concrete example may guide data professionals in determining how to apply this analysis to their own practice settings. The case study below provides such an example; it is based on my own experience in the field. In 2013, i was responsible for leading a team of education data professionals at the Illinois state board of education in summarizing and reporting the results of a survey administered to students and teachers about their schools. A recently enacted state law had required development, administration, and public reporting on a survey of learning conditions. Consequently, we procured and administered a survey through which we collected data from more than 70 percent of both students and teachers across the state. As principals and superintendents reviewed our preliminary data, they were interested in the responses students and teachers gave to the questions we asked. However, they also raised concerns about publicly reporting the statistical measures built from those questions, even though—from a purely statistical perspective—the calculation of the measures was sound.

For my team of education data professionals, these events created an ethical dilemma. We felt obligated to report data that had been collected and analyzed with public funds using a survey that had already proven to be a powerful tool for school improvement in several school districts. We also felt obligated to respect the professional opinions of the educators who advocated for suppressing the statistical measures because, in their judgment, the release would have a negative impact on school communities and student outcomes.

We ultimately decided—within the bounds of the state law—to report only the raw data from the survey for the first year of administration, leaving reporting of the statistical measures for the following year. We worried that this would make it more difficult for the average citizen to interpret the survey results. However, we believed the decision was ultimately in the best interest of students. By taking the additional year, we reasoned that we could take the time needed to build understanding of and acceptance for the survey tool. We planned to spend the year conducting additional research on the survey's items and its use in school districts and working closely with superintendents and principals to address the concerns they had raised. We hypothesized that these steps would, in turn, increase the likelihood that school communities would use the data to identify and act on areas for improvement. In an interview with the Chicago tribune, I stated, "we want to have the same level of confidence in these data as we do in other data [we already report]. We have decided to proceed with caution." In an editorial, the Chicago tribune (2013, Oct. 21) responded to the state board of education's decision by writing, "come on. We all paid for this information. Don't hide it. Share it." In this case, my team at the state board of education made an ethical decision based on a utilitarian analysis, and the tribune editors disagreed from a deontological basis.

In the year that followed, we hired an external evaluator to collect and report district perspectives on the use of the data for improving schools. Our evaluator, the Illinois Education Research Council, analyzed data from surveys of principals and superintendents about their perception of our survey of learning conditions and their use of the data. The evaluator also conducted case study interviews with superintendents, principals and teachers in 15 school districts across the state. The report issued by the evaluator highlighted the need to build trust in these data through both changes to the administration and training of school personnel (Klostermann et al, 2014). The report also highlighted promising practices undertaken by some of the school districts interviewed. One district, for example, used the data to identify weaknesses in transitioning students into their freshman year of high school. As a result of their analysis of the data, district staff implemented a successful transition program for their students.

During that year, we also convened groups of teachers, superintendents and principals to engage in conversation about their concerns with the survey. We designed and implemented focus groups to review survey items. We worked to refine details of our implementation, and we attempted to build broader understanding of the survey's technical underpinnings. These actions allowed us to address several of the concerns raised by school and district personnel before the results of our external evaluation became available.

During the same period, principal and superintendent associations stepped forward to amend the legislation mandating the administration of the survey. These associations were successful in passing a law that would allow school districts the option of selecting an alternative to the state-supported survey. This solution will not allow full comparability of data between school districts. However, it is a solution that all stakeholders are working together to implement and one that will allow all districts to benefit from the project's primary purpose: data for school improvement.

As of this writing, the work to ensure Illinois' survey of learning conditions generates data that school and district leaders trust is still ongoing. Nonetheless, this case study demonstrates that there is much to be gained when stakeholders who disagree engage in continuous and sometimes difficult dialogue. Through this dialogue, solutions were generated that would not have been possible had the state simply moved forward with its initial reporting plan.

Implications for Professional Practice

In this article, I have outlined a variety of ethical perspectives on the public reporting of school performance data. To achieve professional success and deliver project results, education data professionals must learn to navigate an environment where these perspectives co-exist and sometimes collide. Grounded in the analysis presented in this article and my professional experience, the following tips are intended to assist education data professionals in navigating this complex issue.

1. The history of public reporting of education data is long and complex. Education data professionals, despite their best intentions, often do not have the luxury of working in an environment where stakeholders have a positive opinion about data, public reporting or accountability. Data professionals who ignore this history likely do so to their own detriment.
2. The *Forum Guide to Data Ethics* (2010) is a useful professional ethics resource for education data professionals. From a deontological perspective, the Forum Guide provides a framework for right and wrong based on the guidance of leaders in the field. Although this guidance is helpful, it is important to realize that aligning one's decision making with this guide will not necessarily lead to ethical decisions with which all stakeholders can agree.
3. Many in the United States place a high value on government transparency and accountability. This value may express itself through both deontological and utilitarian forms. In most situations, there will likely be some stakeholders who believe data should be made transparent based on this value system. In some cases this belief will be absolute and without regard to consequences.
4. Ethical decision making about public data reporting with an eye toward maximizing benefits for stakeholders can be effective. Cost-benefit analysis is a helpful tool for this analysis, but education data professionals also need to consider the relationship between utilitarianism and distributive justice. They also must be aware that different stakeholders may value various costs and benefits differently.
5. No Child Left Behind accountability has been largely ineffective and has left scars on our education system, our students and our educators. Examples of these scars are described in the work of Diane Ravitch, Jennifer McMurrer and Jeanne Theoharis. Education data professionals can be most effective when they develop an understanding of this situation and its impact on the education data field.
6. Given the variety of ethical perspectives on the public reporting of data, education data professionals would be well served to make their decisions informed by continuous and respectful conversation with a variety of stakeholders. Avoiding disagreement is likely not possible in this work, but working effectively through these disagreements can often be achieved through ongoing dialogue. These conversations may at times be difficult. Identifying the values and ethical framework underlying a particular stakeholder's perspective and analyzing the ethical basis for one's own beliefs may make these conversations easier.

Bibliography

Bentham, J. (1961). An introduction to the principles of morals and legislation. In *The Utilitarians*. Garden City, NY: Dolphin Books, Doubleday. (Original work published 1789)

Blair, F. (1914). *The one-room and village schools in Illinois, Circular No. 65*. Springfield, IL: Illinois Department of Public Instruction. Retrieved from http://books.google.com/books?id=ZLagAAAAMAAJ

Brito, J. (2010). All your data are belong to us: Liberating government data. In D. Lathrop & L. Ruma (Eds.), *Open government: Collaboration, transparency, and participation in practice*. Sebastapol, CA: O'Reilly Media, Inc.

Coleman, J. (1967). Equality of educational opportunity study. Washington, DC: U.S. Department of Health, Education & Welfare Office of Education. Retrieved from http://files.eric.ed.gov/fulltext/ED015157.pdf

Editorial: You can't be trusted [Editorial]. (2013, Oct 10). *Chicago Tribune*. Retrieved from https://login.ezproxy1.lib.depaul.edu/login?url=http://search.proquest.com/docview/1440648042?accountid=10477

Ellis, R. (1998). *Just results: Ethical foundations for policy analysis*. Washington, DC: Georgetown University Press.

Freedom of Information Act, 5 U.S.C. § 552 (1966).

Freeman, S. (2001). Deontology. In L. Becker & C. Becker (Eds.), *Encyclopedia of ethics*. Retrieved from http://search.credoreference.com/content/entry/routethics/deontology/0

Hursthouse, R. (2012). Virtue ethics. In *Stanford encyclopedia of philosophy*. Retrieved from http://stanford.library.usyd.edu.au/entries/ethics-virtue/

Illinois School Report Card Act, 105 IL C.S. § 5(10–17a) (2012).

Illinois State Board of Education. (2013). State Board of Education releases new school and district report cards showing student and school growth in new streamlined format [Press release]. Retrieved from http://www.isbe.net/news/2013/oct31.htm

Kant, I. (2012). *Groundwork of the metaphysics of morals*. Cambridge: Cambridge University Press. (Original work published 1785).

Karp, S. (2004). NCLB's selection vision of equality: Some gaps count more than others. In D. Meier & G. Wood (Eds.), *Many children left behind*. Boston: Beacon Press.

Klostermann, B., White, B., Lichtenberger, E., & Holt, J. (2014). Use of the Illinois 5Essentials Survey data (IERC 2014-2). Edwardsville, IL: Illinois Education Research Council at Southern Illinois University Edwardsville.

Lyons, D. (2001). Utilitarianism. In L. Becker & C. Becker (Eds.), *Encyclopedia of ethics*. Retrieved from http://search.credoreference.com/content/entry/routethics/utilitarianism/0

Madison, J. (1999). Letter to William T. Barry, August 4, 1822. In *James Madison: Writings*. New York: Literary Classics of the United States. (Original work published 1822)

McMurrer, J. (2007). *NCLB year 5: Choices, changes, and challenges: Curriculum and instruction in the NCLB era*. Washington, DC: Center for Education Policy. Retrieved from http://www.cep-dc.org/displayDocument.cfm?DocumentID=312

Mikulecky, M., & Christie, K. (2014). *Rating states, grading schools: What parents and experts say states should consider to make school accountability systems meaningful*. Denver, CO: Education Commission of the States.

Mill, J. (1961). Utilitarianism. In *the utilitarians*. Garden City, NY: Dolphin Books Doubleday & Company, Inc. (Original work published 1863)

Moore, G. (1907). *Ethics*. New York: Henry Holt and Company. Retrieved from https://archive.org/details/mooreethics008304mbp

National Forum on Education Statistics. (2010). *Forum guide to data ethics (NFES 2010-801)*. Washington, DC: National Center for Education Statistics.

No Child Left Behind Act, 20 U.S.C. § 6311 (2001).

Obama, B. (2009). *Memorandum for the heads of executive departments and agencies regarding transparency and open government*. Washington, DC: The White House. Retrieved from http://www.whitehouse.gov/the-press-office/transparency-and-open-government

Orzag, P. (2009). *Memorandum for the heads of executive departments and agencies regarding Open Government Directive*. Washington, DC: Executive Office of the President, Office of Management and Budget. Retrieved from http://www.whitehouse.gov/sites/default/files/omb/assets/memoranda_2010/m10-06.pdf

Piotrowski, S. (2007). *Government transparency: In the path of administrative reform*. Albany, NY: State University of New York Press.

Pritchard, H. (1949). Does moral philosophy rest on a mistake?. In *Moral obligation: Essays and lectures*. Oxford: Clarendon Press. (Original work published 1912)

Quinn, P. (2012). *Executive order 12-03: Establishing an open operating standard for Illinois: Using information technology to promote transparency, effectiveness and savings*. Springfield, IL: Office of the Governor. Retrieved from http://www2.illinois.gov/Government/ExecOrders/Documents/2012/execorder2012-03.pdf

Ravitch, D. (2002). *Testing and accountability, historically considered*. In Evers, W. & Walberg, H. Eds., *School accountability*. Stanford, CA: Hoover Institution Press.

Ravitch, D. (2012, Oct 15). *Two visions for Chicago's schools: A speech at the City Club of Chicago* [Video file]. Retrieved from http://cityclubvideo.wordpress.com/2012/10/15/diane-ravitch/#more-622

Rawls, J. (1971). *A theory of justice*. Boston: The Belknap Press of Harvard University Press.

Reporters Committee for the Freedom of the Press. (n.d.) Mission statement. Retrieved from http://www.rcfp.org/about/mission.

Reporters Committee for Freedom of the Press. (2011). *Open government guide*. Retrieved from http://www.rcfp.org/open-government-guide

Ross, W. (1930). *The right and the good*. Oxford: Oxford University Press.

Sidgwick, H. (2001). Utilitarianism. In *the methods of ethics*. Retrieved from http://www.earlymoderntexts.com/pdfs/sidgwick1874.pdf. (Original work published 1874)

Slote, M. (2001). Consequentialism. In L. Becker & C. Becker (Eds.), *Encyclopedia of ethics*. Retrieved from http://search.credoreference.com/content/entry/routethics/consequentialism/0.

Smart, J. (1973). An outline of a system of utilitarian ethics. In Smart, J. & Williams B. (Eds.), *Utilitarianism: For & against*. Cambridge: Cambridge University Press.

Steans, R. (2013, Oct 31). Illinois introduces new State Report Card [Web log post]. Retrieved from http://www.advanceillinois.org/from-the-desk-of-robin-steans-pages-346.php

Theoharis, J. (2009). "I hate it when people treat me like I'm a fxxx-up": phony theories, segregated schools, and the culture of aspiration among African American and Latino teenagers. In G. Alonso, N. Anderson, C. Su, & J. Theoharis (Eds.), *Our schools suck: Students talk back to a segregated nation on the failures of urban education*. New York: New York University Press.

U.S. Department of Education, The National Commission on Excellence in Education. (1983). *A nation at risk: The imperative for educational reform.* Retrieved from http://www2.ed.gov/pubs/NatAtRisk/index.html.

Weber, M. (1946). Bureaucracy. In H. Gerth & W. Mills (Trans.), *From Max Weber: Essays in sociology.* New York: Oxford University Press.

CASE STUDY

Dakota has been a water policy analyst for years and now works for an environmental agency. Although she is now responsible for analyzing other environmental policies, she still cares deeply about water policy, having grown up in a rural area that had significant water quality problems. Her boss has asked her to look through the current portfolio of proposed policies and provide a recommendation about which policy the agency should prioritize. The director of the agency has been prioritizing energy reduction policies lately, so she knows that if she picks a policy concerning the installation of solar panels it will likely receive political support and be successful, which in turn could create a favorable impression for her department. However, there is a water policy proposal, which is less likely to be successful than the solar panel proposal, given that it requires rerouting waterways, but which could have a bigger overall impact, given that it will improve water availability for many rural areas. She knows that her boss will follow her recommendation and that the way she presents the policy will make a big difference in the outcome (i.e., she can make the water policy seem more or less feasible). What should she do? What role, if any, should her personal values play in policy recommendations?

EXTENDED CASE STUDIES

Ethics of U.S. Government Action and Inaction

Is Louisiana Being Treated Like a Colony of the United States?

By John T. Lambert Jr.

ABSTRACT

The entire story of Louisiana in the post-Hurricane Katrina era is not yet written, as the facts and events and ethical issues are still unfolding. At first, it may seem to some that this article is premature, because the whole story of New Orleans and the post-Katrina recovery is years away. Certainly new findings by engineers, economists and investigators are to emerge in coming years which may support or refute some of the conclusions that are considered to be at the forefront of contemporary discussion about who or what lies at fault for the tragedy at New Orleans in 2005.

In this article, three key events are identified which lay outside of the control and influence of the people of New Orleans; these events started New Orleans on an economic death-spiral. These events were the result of direct actions of the U.S. Government. While the breaking-point for New Orleans may be Hurricane Katrina, New Orleans has suffered an ever-increasing burden that the United States Government, by its actions, put upon the city. These three include the Cuba Embargo, Louisiana's share of offshore oil and gas revenues, and U.S. Government-controlled failures associated with Hurricane Katrina.

John T. Lambert Jr., "Ethics of U.S. Government Action and Inaction: Is Louisiana Being Treated like a Colony of the United States?," *Journal of Legal, Ethical and Regulatory Issues*, vol. 11, no. 1, pp. 65-74.

INTRODUCTION

In the wake of Hurricane Katrina, for many reasons, some in Louisiana wonder if they are somehow something less than a full partner in the United States; in what it is to be part of the United States. A year after the hurricane flooded 80% of the City of New Orleans, despite the U.S. Government approving billions of dollars of aid, the money has by and large not made it to the people. Apathy, Katrina-fatigue, and detachment from the crisis have caused some in the country to turn their collective noses up in the air and ignore the ongoing cries for assistance. Moreover, the politically-connected, no-bid contracts that surfaced in the news seem ripe with at least the air of abuse of some of the funds that have made it to Louisiana. Given the failure of the money to trickle-down to the citizens, they wonder what the U.S. Government's response would have been, had a disaster of the magnitude of Hurricane Katrina befallen Washington D.C., San Francisco, CA, or Boston, MA.

Why should the U.S. Government bear the lion's share of the costs for the Katrina damages? News reports of engineering tests conducted on failed levees *clearly* show the hand of the U.S. Government was in the levees that failed. They hear that the specifications, the design, the mistakes, *were all activities that were totally controlled by the U.S. Army Corps of Engineers.* They ask, from their FEMA travel trailers, from their tents, from their moldy, damaged and crumbling homes, if they are being treated fairly.

The ethical question: *Is Louisiana being treated like a partner, equal to the other 49 states of the United States, or is it being treated as nothing more than a third-world colony; a colony that has served its purpose and is now being abandoned?*

Several key events started New Orleans on an economic death-spiral. These events were outside of the control and influence of the people of New Orleans; they were events spurred by direct actions of the U.S. Government. The breaking-point for New Orleans may be Hurricane Katrina, due to an ever-increasing burden that the Federal Government, by its actions, put upon the city.

- First, we review the Cuba Embargo and its impact upon New Orleans.
- Second, we review Louisiana's share of offshore oil and gas revenues.
- Third, we look at the U.S. Government's failures associated with Hurricane Katrina.
- Finally, we explore the ethical treatment of Louisiana as a state.

The Cuba Embargo

New Orleans has had long and historic ties to Cuba. In his online history of the Archdiocese of New Orleans, Nolan (2001) wrote, "Louisiana became a Spanish colony in the 1760s. Church jurisdiction was transferred to the Diocese of Santiago de Cuba and later Havana." (Para. 1). In

1771 Louisiana became part of the Diocese of Santiago de Cuba. In 1785, Cirilo de Barcelona was consecrated Auxiliary Bishop of Santiago de Cuba with his residence in New Orleans, with his responsibility, Louisiana and the Floridas. In 1787, the Diocese of San Cristobal of Havana is established; Louisiana and the Floridas become part of the new diocese." (Para. 8)

Louisiana's Governor Kathleen Blanco is attempting to reestablish some of the historic trade relationships with Cuba. Varney (2005) summarized the trade, social and economic ties that are part of our shared histories. "At the beginning of the 19th century," Varney wrote, "trade, primarily in coffee, sugar and slaves, meant heavy travel between Cuba and Louisiana. There were periodic exoduses from one place or another, part of a churning of populations between Haiti, Cuba and New Orleans," citing a statement by Ariana Hall, "the executive director of CubaNola, an arts organization that seeks to expand cultural ties between the island and the city" (Para. 4).

The Port of New Orleans enjoyed prominence in previous years as either the no. 1 or no. 2 port in the United States, competing for that honor with the Port of New York. "Ever since the end of World War II, commerce through the Port of New Orleans has steadily increased," per the *New Orleans Port Record* (1960, p.4). New Orleans competed well with most U.S. ports, and the Gulf and South Atlantic ports especially. The Port of New Orleans' ties to Latin American trade were of tremendous importance. "In calendar 1960, the three traditional and leading export commodities of Latin America—coffee, sugar and bananas continued their dominant role, and together accounted for ...80% of the total value of Latin American imports to the Port of New Orleans. These also "represented 45% of the total value of all imports at the Port of New Orleans." (Toledano, 1962, p. 11)

The June 1961 (p. 5) issue of the New Orleans Port Record, featured the address of Carlos Todd to a recent Mississippi Valley World Trade Conference. Todd, a native of Cuba. was the former political editor of the *Times of Havana*. He described the events away from New Orleans that changed the dynamic of its Port and the posture of the U.S. in Latin America. His prophetic warnings included perceptions by Latin Americans of U.S. policies toward challenges in the hemisphere.

Policies from Washington D.C., and the Cuba Embargo changed the Port of New Orleans. Trade flourished between Louisiana and Cuba until the Cuban Revolution in 1959. Robins & Trujillo (1999) of Tulane University's Cuban Studies Institute wrote:

> Prior to the revolution in 1959, Cuba had close trading ties with the U.S. Trade was very important to Cuba's economy, accounting for 57 percent of the GNP. The U.S. was Cuba's principal trading partner. In 1958, approximately one third of all goods passing through the Port of New Orleans were destined for Cuba. In 1958, Cuba was Louisiana's number one trading partner in imports and number seven (7) in exports. Imports amounted to 1,232,000 tons consisting of: sugar (988,000); molasses (234,000); vegetable fiber (2,000); fruit (900); and pigment paints and varnishes (900). Exports amounted to 269,000 tons consisting of: flour (51,000); chemicals

> (36,000); grain (35,000); vegetables (27,000); animal feed (22,000); and lumber (20,000). As Louisiana's largest single trading partner, over 6,000 Louisianians were employed in Cuba-related commerce. During this time, in the service sector, approximately 85% of Cuba's business was done with the U.S., most notably in the areas of banking and insurance. Likewise, 85% of foreign tourists visiting Cuba were United States citizens. (Paragraph 8)

Past issues of the New Orleans Port Record, a monthly journal of the *Port of New Orleans*, provide insight to its operations. Examination of past issues illustrates changes were taking place timed to the problems with Cuba. In the June 1961 issue (p. 64), the Monthly Report, Port of New Orleans showed that from May 1960 to May 1961, Total Cargo was down 23%; Inbound cargo was down 23% and outbound was down 25%. The schedule of sailings from the Port of New Orleans, January 15 through February 28, 1961, (New Orleans Port Record, March 1961, p. 58) showed a ship of the Cubamar Line sailing every Friday. The February 15 through March 31, 1961 schedule of sailings (New Orleans Port Record, April 1961, p. 58) and those thereafter do not show that listing again.

It appears that the loss of Louisiana's no. 1 trading partner, and the loss of the no. 3 destination of the Port of New Orleans, created a ripple effect. Table 1, featuring data from the U.S. Census Bureau, shows population trends of the State of Louisiana, and the parishes of East Baton Rouge, Jefferson, and Orleans. From 1900–2000, the State of Louisiana and East Baton Rouge show continuous growth. From 1900–1960, all four indicators showed growth. However, after 1960, Orleans Parish showed continuous losses in population per decade, while neighboring Jefferson Parish showed only one decade of loss, but an overall gain in population for the period.

Prior to U.S. government policy changes toward Latin America in the 1960's and the Cuba Embargo, the Port of New Orleans was set for continued growth and expansion. The Mississippi River-Gulf Outlet (MRGO), known the Mister Go in New Orleans, opened on Thursday, July 25 1963. It was touted as New Orleans' second "Gateway to the Sea" and was seen as a "shorter route between the Gulf of Mexico and the heart of the nation's busiest port," (New Orleans Port Record, August 1963, p. 4).

The Cuba embargo since its inception proved to be a mixed-bag of success and failure. It has shown to be an inconsistent policy. Tyree (1997, p. A17) "... we're doing business like gangbusters with Communist China, which still has the same party and system of government in power that it had in the ... 1950's," while not doing business with our Communist neighbor 90 miles to the south.

Until the Cuba embargo by the U.S. government, New Orleans enjoyed an ongoing commercial and cultural tie to Cuba. This Cuba-New Orleans relationship was important not only to the city itself but to the entire state of Louisiana. Thus, an ethical issue*: If U.S. foreign policies in Latin America in general, and toward Cuba in particular, are at the root of the depopulation and economic downturn of New Orleans, is there an ethical responsibility on the part of the United States to repair the damage? Is this part of a trend of inequitable treatment of New Orleans and the state of Louisiana?*

Table 1 Population of Counties by Decennial Census: 1900 to 2000

	STATE OF LOUISIANA	LOUISIANA GAIN OR LOSS*	PARISH OF EAST BATON ROUGE	EAST B.R. GAIN OR LOSS*	PARISH OF JEFFERSON	JEFFERSON GAIN OR LOSS*	PARISH OF ORLEANS	ORLEANS GAIN OR LOSS*
1900	1,381,625	n/a	31,153	n/a	15,321	n/a	287,104	n/a
1910	1,656,388	274,763	34,580	3,427	18,247	2,926	339,075	51,971
1920	1,798,509	142,121	44,513	9,933	21,563	3,316	387,219	48,144
1930	2,101,593	303,084	68,208	23,695	40,032	18,469	458,762	71,543
1940	2,363,880	262,287	88,415	30,207	50,427	10,395	494,537	35,775
1950	2,683,516	319,636	158,236	69,821	103,873	53,446	570,445	75,908
1960	3,257,022	576,506	230,058	71,822	208,769	104,896	627,525	57,080
1970	3,641,306	384,284	285,167	55,109	337,568	128,799	593,471	<34,054>
1980	4,205,900	564,594	366,191	81,024	454,592	117,024	557,515	<35,956>
1990	4,219,973	14,073	380,105	13,914	448,306	<6,2986>	496,938	<60,577>
2000	4,468,976	249,003	412,852	32,747	455,466	7,160	484,674	<12,264>

1900–1990 data from: "Population of Counties by Decennial Census: 1900 to 1990", located: http://www.census.gov/population/cencounts/la190090.txt
2002 data from: U.S. Census Bureau State & County Quickfacts, located: http://quickfacts.census.gov/qfd/states
* Losses indicated with "< >"

Louisiana's Share of Offshore Oil and Gas Revenues

On August 13, 2005, Scott Angelle, Secretary of the Louisiana Department of Natural Resources testified before the U.S. House of Representatives' Committee on Resources. In his testimony, he said:

> Louisiana has a long and distinguished history of oil and gas production, both on and offshore. Currently, approximately 34% of the nation's natural gas supply and almost 30% of the nation's crude oil supply is either produced in Louisiana, produced offshore Louisiana, or moves through the state and its coastal wetlands ... Together with the infrastructure in the rest of the state, this production is connected to nearly 50% of the total refining capacity in the United States.
>
> The offshore area beyond 3 miles from Louisiana's coast is federal territory. Other than in a 3-mile transition zone, the federal government receives all of the mineral revenue from production in the Outer Continental Shelf (OCS).

Based upon 2004 data, OCS production off Louisiana's coast constitutes 91% of oil and 75% of natural gas production from all U.S. OCS areas combined. Louisiana OCS territory has produced 88.8% of the 14.9 billion barrels of crude and condensate and 82.3% of the 150 trillion cubic feet of natural gas ever extracted from all federal OCS territories since the beginning of time.

Little did anyone know on August 13, 2005 that merely a couple of weeks later, Hurricane Katrina (August 29, 2006) would be the worst natural disaster to hit the Gulf Coast and the state of Louisiana. Tidal surges, now had unfettered access to populated areas, because of the disappearance of hundreds of square miles of coastal marshes and barrier islands. Much of this disappearance stems from saltwater intrusion of fresh-water marshes thanks to canals dug to serve the oil and gas industry. Hurricane Katrina flooded vast areas of south Louisiana, including in particular the City of New Orleans and the parishes of St. Bernard, Plaquemines, Jefferson and St. Tammany.

On September 7, 2005, Scott Angelle was again in Washington, D.C., appearing before the U.S. House of Representatives Committee on Energy and Commerce hearing on Hurricane Katrina's effect on gasoline supply and prices. He raised the issues of the disparity when landlocked states like Wyoming, New Mexico and Colorado host drilling on federal lands onshore, they receive 50% of the revenues in direct payments, thus receiving revenues to support the drilling infrastructure. In contrast, coastal states provide the infrastructure for OCS drilling on federal lands, but they receive little compensation to fund their support. Angelle testified, "...for example in 2001, of the $7.5 BILLION in revenues produced in the federal OCS area, only a fraction of one percent came back to those coastal states." He further testified that, "Production off Louisiana shores alone contributes an average of $5 BILLION dollars a year to the federal treasury, its second largest source of revenue."

Louisiana and other Gulf Coast states bear the cost for infrastructure but do not receive the same revenue sharing as other states hosting drilling on federal lands. Thus, an ethical issue: *If Louisiana bears the costs for hosting the oil and gas industry on federal lands, should it receive the same revenue share as other states which provide this hosting—but on federal lands of a different composition? Is this part of a trend of inequitable treatment of New Orleans and the state of Louisiana?*

U.S. Government Failures Associated with Hurricane Katrina

U.S. Army Corps. of Engineers

This information is still being determined and discussed. In short, levee systems designed and supervised by the federal government, along with federal wetlands policies left Louisiana and especially the City of New Orleans vulnerable. Bodies floated in the streets. Homes and businesses flooded. A year after the hurricane, much of New Orleans looks like it did after the storm waters receded.

The failure of the United States Army Corps of Engineers to properly design and build levees which were in their care and custody caused the loss of thousands of lives, and billions of dollars in damage. Warrick & Grunewald (2005), at a point eight weeks after Katrina stuck New Orleans identified that the three major levee breeches looked, "Less like acts of God and more like failures of engineering that could have been anticipated and very likely prevented" (p. A01). Stromberg (2006) identifies the (U.S. Army) Corps as having supervised the design and construction of the failed levee system in the 1960's (p.2). Vartabedian (2006) describes an unheeded report from the 1980's that the US Army Corps. of Engineers in the 1980's conducted tests and knew at that time that levees in New Orleans would fail, citing a study by the National Science Foundation that pointed to an unheeded study by the Corps. of their own work. In the tests by the Corps., a sample wall tilted and opened a gap when put under hurricane-type forces, much like the failures of the actual levees in New Orleans (p.4). According to U.S. Congressman Bill Jefferson, "The Army Corps of Engineers has acknowledged that they failed the people of New Orleans and the Gulf Coast who trusted that the levees the corps built would keep us safe. Unfortunately, the designs were flawed, leaving us vulnerable to the high winds and high tides of Hurricane Katrina," (Alpert, 2006 p. 9). Congressman Jefferson has filed a bill titled, "Federal Engineering Accountability Act of 2006, which would waive immunity from lawsuits enjoyed by the U. S. Army Corps of Engineers since 1928 (p.9). The United States Senate passed a bill requiring independent oversight of the U.S. Army Corps. of Engineers in the aftermath of the failures of the New Orleans area levees during Katrina (Alpert 2006 p.1) In addition to potential litigation against the U.S. Government if the barriers to litigation are lifted, contractors are concerned about their own exposure to lawsuits. Landers (2006) states, "many public officials and government agencies enjoy sovereign immunity," but expressed concerns of contractors who,"might be held liable for work it conducts at the behest of government entities" (p. 2). *If Louisiana was told to rely upon Federal levees, and if evidence shows that the Corps. knew years in advance that the levees would fail, is there an ethical responsibility of the U.S. Government to make those entities which experienced losses whole again? Is this part of a trend of inequitable treatment of New Orleans and the state of Louisiana?*

Federal Aid

Despite bearing the brunt of houses damaged, Mississippi is getting more money for housing from the Federal government than Louisiana. Post-Katrina Federal grant money for housing shows a huge disparity: Louisiana has received $6.2 Billion with 204,737 homes with major or severe damage while Mississippi has received $5.3 billion with 61,386 homes with similar damage (Russell, 2006, p. 1). These concerns about the distribution of Federal funds have been attributed to the relative political strengths of the states receiving aid, but also reflects a growing nation-wide sentiment that Louisiana's politicians have handled their responsibilities poorly. Indeed, large amounts of Federal Aid seems wasted. Nevertheless, a disparity of aid and treatment does exist. *Is it fair that the distribution of Federal disaster relief funds flows disproportionately between and among states? Is this part of a trend of inequitable treatment of New Orleans and the state of Louisiana?*

Conclusion

This paper presents several reasons to ask if New Orleans and the State of Louisiana have been treated equitably. The impact to Louisiana of the Cuban Embargo, Louisiana's disproportionate share of oil and gas revenues hosted on Federal lands (that happen to be OCS lands), and the failed levees and wetlands policies have us ask: Is Louisiana being treated as an equal state to the other 49 states in the Union, or is Louisiana in fact or in essence a colony—a resource to enrich the Federal treasury? If a disaster of the scale of Hurricane Katrina had hit Texas or Massachusetts or New York, given the failures of Federal systems and levees and the massive losses of life and property, would the Federal response have been different?

The disproportionate hardships imposed upon Louisiana by the United States via the Cuban Embargo when the Port of New Orleans lost a major shipping destination; the expectation of Louisiana to bear the burden of hosting offshore oil exploration efforts without sharing in the royalties from those efforts, and most recently, the catastrophe of the levee failures and the aid after Hurricane Katrina all indicate that Louisiana is not receiving ethical, fair treatment by the U.S. government. The census figures illustrate that New Orleans has not kept pace in population with the rest of Louisiana, with its neighboring Jefferson Parish, nor with its rival in size, Baton Rouge. The downward spiral is traced to the era of the Cuba Embargo, which started the process. Katrina in 2005 may be the *coup de gras.*

REFERENCES

1900–1990 data from: "Population of Counties by Decennial Census: 1900 to 1990", retrieved March 5, 2006 from: http://www.census.gov/population/cencounts/la190090.txt

2002 data from: U.S. Census Bureau State & County Quickfacts, Retrieved March 5, 2006 from: http://quickfacts.census.gov/qfd/states

Alpert, Bruce (2006, July 20) *The Times Picayune*; Senate OKs slap at corps in bill aimed at aiding La. Retrieved September 17, 2006 from http://biere.louisiana.edu:2097/universe/document?_m=80b5ba6cc580...

Alpert, Bruce (2006, September 15) *The Times Picayune*; Jefferson bill OKs suits against corps; Long-shot bid waives immunity on levees. Retrieved September 17, 2006 from http://biere.louisiana.edu:2097/universe/document?_m=80b5ba6cc580...

Austin, D.B. Carriker, T. McGuire, J. Pratt, T. Priest and A. G. Pulsipher, 2004. History of the offshore oil and gas industry in southern Louisiana; Interim Report; Volume 1: Papers on the evolving offshore industry, U.S. Dept. of the Interior, Minerals Management Service, Gulf of Mexico OCS Region, New Orleans, LA. OCS Study MMS 2004-049. 98 pp.

Comments to U.S. House of Representatives, Committee on Energy and Commerce, (2005, September 7) Hearing on Hurricane Katrina's Effect on Gas Supply and Prices

Landers, Jay (2006, Jan),. Civil Engineering Vol. 76 Issue 1, p10–11, 2p. *Senators Debate Limiting Liability for Government Contractors*. Retrieved on September 17, 2006, from http://library.louisiana.edu/cgibin/proxy?http://biere.louisiana.edu:2075/login.aspx?direct=true&db=aph&AN=21033476&site=ehost-live

Louisiana Energy Facts Annual 2005 Louisiana Department of Natural Resources, Technology Assessment Division

New Orleans Port Record, (1960, December) The Wharf-Tollage Situation. p. 4

New Orleans Port Record (1961, March) Schedule of Sailings, p. 58

New Orleans Port Record (1961, April) Schedule of Sailings, p. 58

New Orleans Port Record (1961, June) MVWT Speaker warns of Communism, p. 6

New Orleans Port Record (1961, June) Monthly Report, Port of New Orleans, p. 64

New Orleans Port Record, (1963, August) Another Gateway to the Sea...Mississippi River-Gulf Outlet is Opened. p. 4

Nolan, Charles E. (2001) A history of the Archdiocese of New Orleans; A Spanish Interlude. Retrieved March 6, 2006 from http://www.archdiocese-no.org/history/spanish.htm

Robins, Nicholas A., and Trujillo, Maria F. (1999, March 22), A Public Interest Report: Exploring the Potential Economic Impact on New Orleans and Louisiana of Normalized Trade Relations Between the United States and Cuba. Retrieved March 5, 2006 from http://cuba.tulane.edu/impact/#_Toc446133192

Stromberg, Meghan, (2006, Jan.) Planning. Vol. 72, Issue 1, p. 40–41. *Little good news on levees and wetlands*. Retrieved on September 17, 2006 from http://biere.louisiana.edu:2204/ehost/detail?vid=3&hid=108&sid=05d...

Russell, Gordon (2006, March 11) *The Times Picayune*. Louisiana damage tops the list; State will use data to make case for aid, p. 1

Testimony Before the Committee on Resources, United States House of Representatives (2005, August 13) Mr. Scott A. Angelle, Secretary, Department of Natural Resources, State of Louisiana; Hearing on the Benefits of Offshore Oil and Natural Gas Development

The New Orleans Times Picayune, March 11, 2006

Toledano, Jacques (1962, January) *New Orleans Port Record*; Port of New Orleans, Crossroad of U.S.-Latin American Trade.p. 11

Tyree, Benjamin (1997, December 4) *The Washington Times*; Coming to terms with the outcast, p. A17

Varney, James (2005, March 6) *The Times Picayune*; Louisiana, Cuba share deep roots; Their roots run 'firm and deep'. Retrieved March 5, 2006 from: http://www.nola.com/news/tp/capital/index.ssf?/base/news-2/1110094018202240.xml

Vartabedian, Ralph (2006, May 3) *Los Angeles Times*; The Nation; Study sees design issue in failures of levees. Retrieved September 17, 2006, from: http://biere.louisiana.edu:2097/universe/document?_m=5f0609131325a...

Warrick, Joby & Grunwald, Michael (2005, October 24) *Washington Post*; Investigators link levee failures to design flaws. Retrieved September 17, 2006, from http://www.washingtonpost.com

Fire or Be Fired

By John L. Pape and James M. Banovetz

Editor's Introduction

Public administrators typically must confront more complicated ethical dilemmas than their private sector counterparts because they must deal with all the ethical concerns confronting the private sector and, in addition, with the ethical expectations associated with what Woodrow Wilson called their "sacred trust," their obligation under democratic principles to be responsive to the interests, well-being, and preferences of the public at large.

This case demonstrates the level of complexity that can confront public administrators—in this case, a local government administrator. It describes an actual case in which several of the most severe kinds of ethical dilemmas occur simultaneously. At its root, it presents a challenge found in both private and public sectors and at all levels of organizational responsibility: what to do when your boss, in this case the city council, wants you to violate your personal ethical principles. That challenge is particularly severe when, as in this case, the action sought would not only violate the administrator's personal ethics, but his (the ICMA) professional code of ethics as well.

This case also demonstrates the clash between expediency and principle. In this case, the path of least resistance, and certainly the path to the outcome that is almost inevitable, is strewn with serious ethical problems. The manager's bosses—the city council—are demanding that the police chief be terminated despite the fact that there is no legitimate evidence that the chief has done anything to justify his dismissal. The expedient course of action would sacrifice the chief. The manager is left to ponder the extent to which he is ethically obligated to protect his innocent subordinate, keeping in mind the effect of his decision upon the life and well-being of that subordinate.

Either of these issues might afflict a decision maker in the private sector as well. But this case also demonstrates the added ethical complications involved in transacting the public's business. Josh Peters, the administrator in this case, must also deal with the ethical obligations imposed by the nation's system of constitutional democracy. He must measure the impact of his actions on his obligation to serve the best interests of the city's residents. He must consider both the consequences of his actions on his efforts to improve the quality of police services and the need to choose between responsiveness to a very vocal group of voters, on the one hand, and responsiveness to the general public interest, on the other hand.

Peters, the local government administrator, must decide, in short, how to apply the obligations imposed upon him by the tenets of democratic theory and Wilson's "sacred trust."

Case 21 Fire or Be Fired

Background

Adams, a southwestern city of approximately 17,000 people, has been afflicted with multiple, sometimes contradictory, forces of change. Economically, it has been feeling the effects of several years of economic downturn resulting from the decline of its once-prosperous oil industry. More recently, a local Native American tribe, in an effort to help improve the quality of life for its members, launched a number of new business ventures in the fields of health, transportation, and foreign trade. In an unrelated development, the city also recently became the home of a major new regional health center. The city has thus felt the effects of the serious decline of its major industry as well as the impact of a changing local economy.

As might be expected, these economic changes have been accompanied by changes in the city's politics. The five-member city council, once a relatively cohesive body, found itself increasingly divided as the "old guard" political structure struggled to retain its dominance over emerging political interests linked more closely to the city's new economic interests. Of particular significance, and certainly not unnoticed by the old guard, was the support for the new political forces coming from the city's Native American community.

As if these changes were not enough for the city's government, Adams's recent years of economic difficulty had left a backlog of escalating service needs, deteriorating infrastructure, and declining city services. Such problems are difficult to confront in the best of circumstances. Now, the difficulty of resolving them was exacerbated by political changes within the council. New and unfamiliar divisions among the city's elected leaders left the council unable to develop a clear direction or vision of how to address the community's rapidly increasing service needs. After less than three years on the job, Adams's most recent city manager had resigned out of frustration over the situation.

Moving quickly to recruit a new city manager, the city council named Josh Peters, a city manager from a neighboring state, to fill the post. Although the council vote to hire Peters was unanimous, it was readily apparent from the outset that Peters would have difficulty getting the council's unanimous support for any effort he might propose to address the city's problems.

On his first day on the job, Peters met individually with the department heads. In the meeting with Chief of Police William Maloney, Peters learned that Maloney was planning to retire within a few months. He was also informed that the local police union fully expected that the new chief would be appointed from among the ranks of the department, all of whom were union members. Former police chiefs in Adams had always been promoted from within the department. Hiring an outside chief had simply never been done, at least not in anyone's memory.

Although only 10 percent of the state's workforce was unionized, organized labor had traditionally exerted a great deal of influence on state and local elected officials. As in most of the state's cities, the police and fire departments in Adams were unionized while all other municipal employees were not. The police and fire unions had developed a strong relationship with the old guard council members, which was reflected in the fact that police officers and firefighters had been the only city employees granted a pay raise in recent years.

The new city manager had a strong background in law enforcement and had even served as a chief of police before moving into city management, yet the local police union hierarchy viewed his presence with concern. Peters had made it clear that he would align himself with neither political faction on the city council and would make independent decisions based on community needs. From the outset, he made it clear that Chief Maloney's successor would be recruited through a national search, with the best candidate being hired. Candidates from within the department would be evaluated by the same standard as all others. This move was immediately branded as an attempt at "union busting" by the union's leaders.

Four of the five council members privately commended Peters for his approach, but only the two who were members of the newly emerging faction on the council would publicly support him. The one council member who remained silent on the police chief issue was Mayor Bill Brown, a veteran council member. (Under the city charter, the mayor's position was not elected by the people but was filled each year for a one-year term by a vote of the council. By tradition, the largely ceremonial mayoral post was "rotated" among the council members.) Brown had been chief of the Adams fire department at the time of his retirement from the city. While an Adams firefighter, Brown had been an active member of the local firefighters' union, and he had continued to be a strong proponent of union-supported issues during his council tenure.

The Case

With the retirement of Chief Maloney, the recruitment of a new chief began in earnest. Assistant Chief Fred McKenna, a veteran of more than twenty-five years with the Adams police department, was named as interim chief of police. McKenna had disavowed any interest in being appointed chief, but he had been willing to delay his own retirement to serve as interim chief.

Under the city charter, the city manager had exclusive authority over all personnel decisions and city council members were expressly prohibited from involving themselves in personnel issues. Although Peters frequently consulted with council members about the recruitment and selection process, keeping all members equally informed, he made it clear that he was committed to selecting the best-qualified applicant for the post, whether that be an internal or external applicant.

It was apparent to Peters, however, that it would be difficult for the three internal candidates who applied to be competitive in a field of well-qualified applicants. The combination of underfunded training budgets and an indifferent approach to personnel development under a succession of police chiefs had resulted in, at best, semiqualified internal candidates. Further complicating the process, but making Peters even more resolved to find the most qualified applicant, were his serious concerns about the professional standards of the Adams police department. In recent years, the department had been plagued by problems with missing evidence, shoddy investigative work, allegations of widespread abuse, and several highly questionable incidents involving the use of deadly force.

Applications were solicited nationwide through such resources as the International City/County Management Association (ICMA) and the International Association of Chiefs of Police. More than seventy applications were received. Ultimately, Peters selected six candidates, including all three of the internal candidates, as finalists for the post.

Prior to the recruitment process, Peters had indicated to the council his intention to use an assessment center, facilitated by a professional firm, to evaluate the finalists. Since the assessment center was an unbudgeted item, a supplemental appropriation by the council was needed to fund the effort. Informally, four of the council members indicated their support for the assessment center process; only Mayor Brown was noncommittal.

It was at this point that the union first covertly attempted to influence the selection process in an effort to ensure the selection of an internal candidate. When the appropriation was put on the council's agenda, the union solicited a number of citizens to appear at the council meeting to voice their opposition to an outside firm assessing the candidates' qualifications. Before the council meeting, union representatives privately approached old guard council members to register their objections. While they did not explicitly oppose the recruitment process itself, they strongly protested as wasteful the expenditure needed for the assessment center. The local newspaper, which had been traditionally aligned with the old guard political faction, also blasted the proposal. Although the supplemental appropriation was ultimately approved, the city council reduced the amount to a point well below the lowest quote obtained. Lacking sufficient funding, the assessment center approach had to be abandoned.

The city manager then personally undertook a rigorous review and assessment of each finalist's qualifications and record. After a month of interviews and diligent evaluations, Peters announced his selection: John Wilson, a veteran police commander who had retired from a large metropolitan police force and was currently serving as chief of police in a small city in a neighboring state. Having never served in a police department in which the officers were organized into a union, Wilson himself was not a member of the police union.

The public announcement was received enthusiastically by the newer members of the city council. The old guard council members, the police union, and the local newspaper greeted the announcement with a lukewarm, "wait-and- see" attitude. Mayor Brown did not publicly comment on the selection; he was the only council member who did not attend the public announcement.

Chief Wilson's first few months on the job were relatively quiet, with no significant reaction by the police union. Shortly thereafter, however, disturbing rumors about his personal behavior began to circulate through the community. The rumors were initially vague. It was said that Chief Wilson had a drinking problem. One version had him driving home in an intoxicated condition after an evening at a local private club. Another suggested that he had been forced to retire from the large metropolitan force after twenty-five years of service because of alcohol abuse. These rumors eventually reached Peters.

Peters dismissed the early rumors primarily because he had strong evidence to the contrary. Having personally checked Wilson's background, Peters knew that Wilson had no history of alcohol abuse and that his retirement had been strictly voluntary. He was also aware that Wilson was not a member of the private club where he allegedly was seen in an intoxicated condition. In fact, Peters had been with both Wilson and the fire chief at the time of the supposed indiscretion.

The gossip had also reached the ears of the council members, and Peters quickly reassured them that the allegations had no merit. The old guard members were unconvinced, but the newer members voiced a high degree of comfort that the rumors were, in fact, baseless.

Over the next few weeks, the rumors intensified to a point where Peters reevaluated his previous background review of Chief Wilson. He again found that Wilson's reputation was unblemished in his previous employments and that there was no evidence to support any of the allegations.

Shortly after completing the review, Peters received a visit from Mayor Brown. In a closed-door session, Brown demanded that Peters dismiss Chief Wilson in light of the rumors. Peters explained that his review did not substantiate any of the allegations and, in fact, suggested the contrary. Nevertheless, the mayor held firm to his demand.

Brown pointed out that Peters could dismiss the chief without cause since Wilson was still in his probationary period. Peters conceded that he could do that, but he argued that it would be unethical in his estimation to dismiss any employee based on unsubstantiated, anonymous gossip. To support his contention, Peters cited tenet 11 of the ICMA Code of Ethics, which states the matter very clearly:

> Handle all matters of personnel on the basis of merit so that fairness and impartiality govern a member's decisions pertaining to appointments, pay adjustments, promotions, and discipline.

Peters explained that to dismiss Wilson as the mayor demanded would be clearly unethical, and that he, as city manager, would not violate his profession's code of ethics. Brown ended the meeting by heatedly informing the city manager that if he did not dismiss the police chief, it would cost both Peters and Wilson their jobs.

Not long after the meeting between Brown and Peters, the police union issued a press release announcing that it had taken a near-unanimous vote of "no confidence" in Wilson. Accompanying the announcement was a list of "substantiated" allegations of misconduct against the chief. Among them were that he purchased alcoholic beverages while driving a city vehicle, that he allowed his wife to drive a city vehicle, and that he was disrespectful to his officers. Also among the allegations were the previously debunked stories about Wilson's supposed intoxication.

The media, particularly the pro-union local newspaper, pounced on the story. Mayor Brown attempted to call an "emergency" council meeting to have the council formally investigate the allegations. Only after the city attorney informed him that the union's press release did not meet the legal requirements for an emergency meeting did Brown retract the call.

At the next regularly scheduled council meeting, Brown and another old guard council member placed an item on the agenda authorizing the city council to investigate the allegations. At that meeting, Peters read a prepared statement asserting that the allegations were a personnel matter and that, as city manager, he had the sole authority to handle personnel issues. He also called for the union, as well as any other party having any evidence of impropriety on the part of Chief Wilson, to provide the evidence to his office for investigation. Peters's firm stand clearly placed him in open opposition to both the old guard faction of the city council and the police union. Although he realized that this move would clearly damage his relationship with the old guard council members, Peters again turned to the ICMA Code of Ethics, tenet 10, for guidance:

> Resist any encroachment on professional responsibilities, believing the member should be free to carry out official policies without interference, and handle each problem without discrimination on the basis of principle and justice.

After clearly stating that they wanted the city council, not the city manager, to investigate Chief Wilson, the police union grudgingly turned their "evidence" over to Peters. The evidence consisted of several pieces of videotape, a statement from a police officer's wife, and statements from union activists and leaders that Wilson did not treat his officers with "professional dignity."

The statements were, essentially, a list of grievances about Wilson's management style. Wilson was attempting to bring about a greater degree of professional discipline in such areas as the use of force, interaction with citizens, and internal professionalism. Examples of the complaints were that the chief had reprimanded the current union president for using vulgar language to a citizen and had implemented a more stringent system for reporting the use of force. Additionally, he had forced two investigators, both of whom were union leaders, to divest their financial interest in a topless bar in a neighboring jurisdiction. In Peters's estimation, none of the complaints was valid. In fact, Wilson was appropriately addressing problems within the department.

The statement from the officer's wife indicated that she witnessed Wilson's wife driving the chief's city vehicle. Upon investigation, it was determined that Wilson and his family were out of town at the time the alleged infraction occurred and that the city vehicle was parked at the police station during that time.

The videotapes proved equally inconclusive. One tape, obtained by union leaders from a convenience store, clearly showed Wilson purchasing a six-pack of beer along with other grocery items. However, it did not show the chief drinking the beer or operating a city vehicle. The other tape, obviously taken from the rear of another vehicle following Wilson's city car, did show Mrs. Wilson accompanying the chief. It was subsequently determined that the chief and his wife were en route to an official function at the time, and city policy allowed for a spouse or guest to accompany the chief under such circumstances.

In short, none of the "evidence" showed anything beyond the fact that Wilson was attempting to correct unprofessional activities among certain police officers, and that the disgruntled officers had responded by covertly obtaining or making videotapes of the chief in an effort to discredit him. The investigation, which the city attorney conducted independently at the direction of the city manager, did not sustain misconduct on the part of the chief of police. Using the same standard that would be applied to allegations lodged against any city employee, Peters ruled that no cause existed to discipline or remove Wilson.

In announcing his findings, Peters made it clear that he would not take action against Chief Wilson, or any city employee, without justifiable cause. The union, local newspaper, and old guard council members immediately branded the investigation a whitewash, and calls for the removal of both Peters and Wilson were made. Within a week, Mayor Brown scheduled an executive session to consider terminating Peters's contract.

After lengthy deliberations in which Peters was not allowed to be present, the city council convened in public session to vote on terminating his contract. The two old guard council members, including Mayor Brown, voted to terminate the contract while the two newer members voted to retain Peters; the fifth member abstained. Without a majority voting to dismiss him, Peters kept his job. Under charter provisions, the abstaining member, a long-tenured member who had developed a strong relationship with Peters, was not required to state publicly his reason for not voting.

Over the ensuing days, pressure from the police union and old guard council members intensified. The union publicly called on the entire council to reconsider their positions "for the good of the community." One council member who voted to support the city manager and chief of police was told that her business would be picketed and boycotted by the police union and its supporters. The other supportive council member was publicly cursed and threatened with political retaliation by a union officer. The confrontation, which occurred in the lobby of city hall, was recorded by a radio news reporter. Yet after the abusive threat was repeatedly aired on news reports, the union not only supported its officer's action, but openly reaffirmed the threat of political retaliation against the council member.

Throughout this period, the council member who had abstained from voting was the object of the most intense union pressure. From repeated threats of political reprisal to the warning that his son's legal practice would be boycotted, the abstaining member was receiving numerous calls and visits from union members and pro-union citizens demanding he change his position and vote to terminate the city manager's contract.

Clearly, the position of both the city manager and the chief of police had been severely eroded by the unrelenting and hostile activity of the police union. What had begun as a whispering campaign to discredit and remove Wilson had turned into controversy that clearly threatened to undermine two of Adams's highest-ranking city officials.

The Decision Problem

The decision problem that Peters faced in this matter hinged on two pivotal events. The first was when Mayor Brown demanded that he dismiss Chief Wilson without cause. The second was when Peters resisted Brown's attempt to usurp the city manager's authority over what was clearly a personnel matter under the Adams city charter.

Without question, Peters could have terminated Wilson's employment during Wilson's probationary period without cause or explanation, thus ending the controversy with only minimal damage to the city manager's position. However, Peters also knew that reform in the police department was an action item whose time had come. What he could not know for sure was whether yielding to the union on the removal of Wilson would buy him support for other changes in the future or whether this victory would only encourage the union to fight other needed reforms.

Then, too, when the mayor attempted to have the city council investigate the chief of police, Peters could have chosen to stand silent and allow the council to intrude on his personnel authority. Again, he could not be sure whether this course of action would have solidified his support on the council or only encouraged the old guard to attempt further encroachments on his authority.

In either case, Peters could have taken the path of least resistance and caved in to the political pressures being exerted on him. Had he not asserted his principles, he could have removed himself from jeopardy by sacrificing Wilson to the political influence of the police union. The temptation to follow this course was strong, especially since it was becoming increasingly clear that Wilson would be fired anyway; if Peters did not relent and fire him, Peters's successor as city manager surely would.

Peters believed, however, that to fire Wilson would clearly violate the professional code of ethics to which he, Peters, subscribed. Yet he also realized that adhering to strong professional principles and his professional code of ethics might well cost him his job. Even worse, with council members experiencing badly divisive pressures that would make it even harder for them to work as a unit in the future, and with Wilson certain to be fired in any event, there seemed to be no certain benefit for Peters to gain by "falling on his sword" and sacrificing his own job. Furthermore, getting himself fired would most likely mean the end of the effort to bring needed reform to the police department. In short, adherence to ethics in this case might not even be in the short-term best interest of the community.

As Peters reflected on his options, he could identify several possible courses of action. He could

1. Consent to the mayor's demand and fire Wilson. This would relieve the intense political pressure on the council, enable him to keep his job, and, in all likelihood, even gain him the council's support for his effort to professionalize and reform the police department. But to do this, he would have to violate his ethical code.
2. Permit the council, even now, to undertake the investigation. This would undermine his authority as manager, force him to violate his professional code of ethics, and probably result in Wilson's dismissal for cause. The latter consequence would be most unfair to Wilson.
3. Call for an investigation of the chief by an independent outside agency, such as a state or federal law enforcement agency. The city attorney, however, advised him that this option was not open; such agencies could be asked to investigate matters only when a crime was alleged to occur and no such allegation had been made against Wilson.
4. Appeal the matter over the heads of the council and the union by going directly to the public. Given the newspaper's overt support of the union, however, this path appeared doomed to failure and it would, in any event, pose still more ethical problems. To go over the council's head would require that he act in a manner that could not be expected to "merit the respect and confidence of the elected officials" (tenet 3 of the code).
5. Hold firm to his present position, secure in his knowledge that he was abiding by his code of ethics despite firm evidence that such a path would result in the loss of his job, the dismissal of Chief Wilson, and, almost certainly, the failure of his efforts to professionalize the performance of the police department.

No matter which of the options he chose, the outcome would be a victory for the old guard and a discouraging defeat for the good government aspirations of the council's newer members. Peters had to decide what he was going to do.

Discussion Questions

1. If you were in Peters's position, what factors would you have considered in deciding on your course of action? How would you weigh each one?
2. Would you have taken the same position as Peters? Why or why not?
3. Were the ethical grounds for Peters's decisions valid? Why or why not? Would Peters have been justified in dismissing the chief of police based on the allegations filed by the police union? What ramifications might such a decision have had on Peters's ability to manage the city?
4. Is adherence to a professional code of ethics important enough to sacrifice one's job? Why or why not?
5. Under what circumstances should ethical considerations be set aside in order to achieve the best outcome for the community?
6. Leaving aside the question of ethics, what course of action do you think would have brought about the best outcome for the city?